Creating Solidarity
Across
Diverse Communities

Creating Solidarity Across Diverse Communities

International Perspectives in Education

EDITED BY

Christine E. Sleeter
Encarnación Soriano

Teachers College
Columbia University
New York and London

Published by Teachers College Press, 1234 Amsterdam Avenue, New York, NY
10027

Copyright © 2012 by Teachers College, Columbia University

Library of Congress Cataloging-in-Publication Data

Creating solidarity across diverse communities : international perspectives in
    education / edited by Christine E. Sleeter, Encarnacion Soriano.
        p. cm.
    Includes bibliographical references and index.
    ISBN 978-0-8077-5337-8 (pbk. : alk. paper)
        1. Multicultural education—Cross-cultural studies. 2. Community and
    school—Cross-cultural studies. I. Sleeter, Christine E., 1948– II. Soriano,
    Encarnacion.
    LC1099.C743   2012
    370.117—dc23   2012004817

ISBN 978-0-8077-5337-8 (paperback)

Printed on acid-free paper
Manufactured in the United States of America

19 18 17 16 15 14 13 12   8 7 6 5 4 3 2 1

Contents

Acknowledgments   **vii**

Introduction   **1**
    Christine E. Sleeter & Encarnación Soriano

PART I: SOLIDARITY AS SOCIAL UNITY

**1. Enacting Solidarity to Address Peer-to-Peer
    Aggression in Schools: Case Studies from Chile**   **23**
    Verónica López, Carmen Montecinos, José Ignacio Rodríguez,
    Andrés Calderón, & Juan Francisco Contreras

**2. Devalued Solidarity:
    A Problem of Education and Identity**   **45**
    José Luis Ramos

**3. Multiculturalism and Education in France and
    Its Former Colonized States and Territories: Prospects
    for Intercultural Solidarity Within a Secular Model**   **62**
    Isabelle Aliaga & Martine Dreyfus

4. Spanish Students Abroad: An Intercultural Education   **79**
    Maria Antonia Casanova

PART II: SOLIDARITY AS BUILDING ALLIES IN CONTEXTS OF STRUGGLE

**5. Multicultural Coexistence in Schools in Spain:
    New Challenges and New Ways of Organizing
    Education Through Solidarity**   **93**
    Encarnación Soriano

6. **Oral Histories in the Classroom:**
   Home and Community Pedagogies   **114**

   Judith Flores Carmona & Dolores Delgado Bernal

7. **Community Collaboration in School Improvement:**
   A Case Study of a California Middle School   **131**

   Gina Elizabeth DeShera

8. **Build Me a Bridge: Steps to Solidarity**
   Between a School and Its Community   **148**

   Gilberto Arriaza & Alice Wagner

9. **Challenges to the Development of Solidarity:**
   Working Across Intersections of Power and
   Privilege in New Zealand   **163**

   Anne Hynds

10. **Building Solidarity Between the Tribal Community**
    and the School in India: The Case of Srujan   **180**

    Mahendra Kumar Mishra

11. **Building Solidarity for Education in Complex Societies:**
    What Have We Learned?   **198**

    Christine E. Sleeter

About the Contributors   **209**

Index   **215**

Acknowledgments

This book grew out of a symposium at the 2009 annual meeting of the American Educational Research Association. That symposium featured a cross-language and cross-national dialogue about challenges and possibilities of building collaboration across racial, ethnic, and language differences in education settings. The dialogue among participants was fruitful enough to spawn the idea for this book.

As editors, we wish to thank the chapter authors for their excellent work. They not only contributed chapters, but pushed us to think about how their work connected. That thinking led us to realize the central importance of the concept of solidarity that was embedded in their various projects.

Our editor at Teachers College Press, Brian Ellerbeck, not only gave us enthusiastic support, but also very helpful ideas for developing coherence across chapters, particularly given the diverse national contexts, traditions of scholarship, and languages in which they were initially written. Wendy Schwartz at Teachers College Press gave tremendous help with her insightful and detailed feedback on the chapters; they are much tighter and clearer as a result of her work. We also appreciate the comments of anonymous reviewers of the book's prospectus, who affirmed the value of the project we had undertaken while offering helpful suggestions.

Several chapters were written initially in Spanish. We appreciate the work of translators, and particularly Rafael Martinez-Oña Lopez, who not only translated two chapters and parts of another, but helped bridge English and Spanish throughout the process of editing and producing this book.

Creating Solidarity
Across
Diverse Communities

Introduction

Christine E. Sleeter & Encarnación Soriano

Around the world, it is common to view ethnic, racial, linguistic, and social class differences as creating intractable problems that defy solutions. News headlines frequently present "diversity" as a problem, or call attention to anxieties that accompany growing diversity. For example, news stories that appeared on March 31, 2010, included the following:

- In Argentina, an article, "En un año, 22% más de inmigrantes [In one year, 22% more immigrants]," discussed challenges posed by the shifting demographic composition of the city of Córdoba, most of the immigrants coming from Peru and Bolivia (Redacción Lavoz, 2011).
- In Bolivia, a short news article, "Migración y educación [Migration and education]," expressed concern that "la migración ha llegado a afectar fuertemente el ámbito educativo. Casi el 50% de los estudiantes están vinculados a la migración internacional. [Migration has come to strongly affect the education environment. Almost 50% of the students are linked to international migration]" (Noticias, 2011).
- In Italy, a news item, "Mueren 12 inmigrantes tunecinos de camino a la isla italiana de Lampedusa [12 Tunisian immigrants die on the way to the Italian island of Lampedusa]," described immigrants who died in the wake of conflict in this African country. In 3 months, 21,725 immigrants from Africa disembarked on the Italian coast (Reuters/Tunez, 2011).
- In Spain, with the severe economic crisis leaving 4,910,000 unemployed out of a total population of 46 million, we read this news: "CIU (partido político que gobierna en Cataluña) propone financiar el retorno a su país de inmigrantes en paro [CIU (the political party governing Cataluña) proposes financing unemployed immigrants to return to their country]" (online). According to these nationalists, immigration is one of the most important challenges municipalities are facing; they emphasize

1

that in 10 years, 1.5 million immigrants have arrived in Cataluña. In addition, they point out that no society has unlimited capacity to absorb and integrate people from outside (Europa Press/Barcelona, 2011).

- In Spain, an article, "HRW denuncia que el Gobierno de Kenia repatría a somalíes a zonas de combate [The NGO Human Rights Watch denounces the government of Kenya for repatriating Somalis in combat zones]" discussed conflicts over humane treatment of refugees (Europa Press, 2011).

- In North Carolina, United States, an article, "Wake School Board Denies [racial] Bias," examined a controversial move by the county school board to end desegregation of schools on the basis of family income, which had replaced its previous policy of desegregating on the basis of race. While school board members said that desegregation was not working, critics expressed concern that the district will end up creating "extremely high-poverty, racially segregated schools" (Hui & Goldsmith, 2011, online).

- In the state of Minnesota, an article, "Diversity grows across south metro area since last census," pointed out that the most recent census data indicate "nearly 1 in 7 residents of Scott and Dakota counties is a nonwhite." A gathering of families had drawn more than 100 Somali parents, who were "all anxious to learn more about their local school district and ways to help their children succeed" (Humphrey, 2011, online).

- In the United Kingdom, an article, "Will a New 'Free' Primary School in Bradford Widen Ethnic Rifts in the City?," discussed controversy surrounding a new school championed mainly by Muslim parents who were concerned about underachievement of in local primary schools. While the parents believed this new school would meet their children's needs better, local non-Muslims worried that it would disrupt social cohesion in the community (The Independent Schools, 2011).

These examples highlight what seems to be the crux of an enormous difficulty: building working relationships across diverse and often unequally positioned communities—relationships that can enable people from different backgrounds to address problems and needs in ways that are mutually beneficial. In his introduction to an examination of building transcommunal social movements, Childs (2003) stated that, "A major problem of the twenty-first century will be the crisis of diverse, often competing, social/cultural identities among people uprooted by corrosively powerful global economic combines" (p. 7). Numerous commentators have discussed the fast pace of globalization, and its wide-ranging impacts on peoples around the world. These impacts include increased contact among people (both electronically and face-to-face), rapid spread of cultures (spurred by the growing availability of electronic media), displacements of peoples and mass migrations due to economic and political shifts, and increased incorporation of diverse peoples into a global economic system, or super-national political systems such as the European Union. Childs pointed out that diversity itself is not the problem; being affiliated with a community normally gives people a sense of strength and wholeness. The problem, rather, is how diversity is dealt with. Demonstrations of a lack of respectful interaction in diverse settings, imposition of power over others, and incorporation of peoples into highly unequal power hierarchies both create and reflect problems. Childs challenges us to develop respectful relationships of solidarity that will enable us to confront issues associated with difference.

This book brings together research studies that examine barriers to building relationships of solidarity between schools and marginalized communities, and possibilities for transcending those barriers, in diverse national contexts: the United States, New Zealand, Spain, France, Chile, Mexico, and India. Chapters throughout the book examine attempts to dispel negative myths about diverse populations in particular contexts, and to build relationships based on communication, respect, and mutuality. While some chapters report more success than others, we hope that readers gain a deeper sense of the challenges involved in working toward solidarity across differences, as well as strategies or tools that can help. In this introduction, we review how the concept of solidarity is used within education research, then widen our scope to review the concept's use outside of education. We conclude by providing a brief overview of the chapters.

CONSIDERING THE CONCEPT OF SOLIDARITY IN EDUCATION RESEARCH

Although the word *solidarity* is used with some frequency in both research and practice, too often what it means and how it develops are not examined very closely, particularly in education. Dobbie and Richards-Schuster (2008) note that "Building solidarity is perhaps the most crucial yet under-theorized process in organizing people for social change—an essential yet elusive component of any successful movement" (p. 138). Wilde (2007) observes further that the ideology of individualism clashes with an ideology of solidarity, and that the welfare state has neutralized solidarity. Both of these conditions are directing people away from consideration of how solidarity works.

In education research, although the concept of solidarity is often evoked in conjunction with other related concepts, such as social justice and equity, solidarity frequently goes undefined. For example, Katsarou, Picower, and Stovall (2010) present case examples of urban teacher preparation programs Chicago and New York, elaborating on how they seek to develop teachers' orientation toward social justice and relationships of solidarity between teachers and their students' communities. Implicitly, the authors conceptualize solidarity as meaning that teachers empathize with and care deeply about their students, and therefore work with students' communities within "the broader political project of identifying and eliminating oppression" (p. 3). Although the authors do not directly say this, we can infer that they conceptualize solidarity as meaning that teachers identify with the political goals of poor, urban communities, seeing themselves as engaged in a common struggle alongside the communities by virtue of their shared deep commitment to the community's children.

As in this example, it is common in education research to imply what solidarity means, and less common to unpack its meaning. The authors of just a handful of education studies explain more directly what they mean by solidarity.

Solidarity as Building Community

One conception of solidarity is building community among children or youth, especially in school settings. Richie, Tobin, Roth, and Carambo (2007) studied the emergence of solidarity among classroom members in a predominantly African American urban school, conceptualizing solidarity as meaning seeing others as "one of us" rather than as "one of them." They examined interaction patterns within the school to determine how faculty created distributed leadership among students and built trust, and how these conditions enabled co-construction of curriculum through dialogue. Based on the view that children's imagery contributes to affective education, Gil, Jover, and Reyero (2006) conducted a study from perspectives of toy advertisements and memories of moments of play. When the images depict other children, they produce responses, either of acceptance or rejection, of emotional identification. So the authors use these images, arguing that feelings of solidarity happen to favor educational situations where private feelings are pooled together communally, through means of communication.

Empathy Across Differences in Culture and Power

Some education researchers conceptualize solidarity as empathy that includes a shared sense of struggle among people across differences in culture and power. Nieto (2006) focuses on empathy between teachers and urban students. Drawing from her research with teachers of culturally and linguistically diverse students who "make a difference" in their students' lives (p. 461), she argues that the teachers shared a sense of solidarity with their students. Nieto explains: "For teachers who think deeply about their work, solidarity and empathy mean having genuine respect for their students' identities—including their language and culture—as well as high expectations and great admiration for them" (p. 466). This sense of solidarity then leads teachers to question mainstream knowledge and interpretations of their students, placing their students' well-being above conventional practices that do not support them.

One might also examine how empathy can be built among one's students and marginalized members of society. Epstein and Oyler (2008) present a case study of how a 1st-grade teacher worked to build solidarity between her students and people in the community who have been marginalized—child laborers being the example discussed in the case study. The authors argue that service learning as a form of pedagogy often teaches charity work rather than social change based on relationships of solidarity. To develop such relationships, this teacher engaged her 1st-graders directly with marginalized people, whom they interviewed about their own experiences. The authors posit that the students will continue to pay attention to the voices of marginalized people as they grow up, enabling them to become citizens who are able to develop relationships of solidarity to work for social justice.

Civic Virtue for Participatory Citizenship

Some scholars in education conceptualize solidarity as a civic virtue in which youth learn to regard all of humanity as sharing common concerns. Using this conceptualization, Santora (2003) discusses how she teaches her students to become participatory citizens in a diverse society. She views solidarity as reciprocal understanding and trust that transcends particular interests. She stresses that students not only need to know about social issues, but also need to learn to see those outside their social circle as people and learn to see themselves in relationship with others, which requires getting in touch with themselves as well as connecting with the personal stories of others. To this end, she uses autobiographical literature in conjunction with history and analysis of power and discrimination.

In Argentina, UNICEF is developing a project entitled "UNICEF goes to school to build a culture of peace and solidarity" that highlights the importance of developing skills in school to achieve integration. Although not explicit, solidarity is understood as a strategy to achieve a democratic and just society, where integration of children and adolescents takes place

(Acevedo, Duro, & Grau, 2002). Also in Argentina, Tapia (2001) discusses service learning in the school as a form for teaching, positing that through service learning, young people might develop civic virtues of solidarity, justice, and cooperation.

Identification with One's Own Marginalized Community

While the above articles discuss development of empathy and solidarity across sociocultural differences, solidarity can also mean identification with one's own ethnic community in the context of being marginalized. Hall, Özerk, Zulfiqar, and Tan (2002) discuss the development of solidarity among members of immigrant communities. The authors present case studies of four supplementary schools in the United Kingdom and Norway. Since mainstream schools do not maintain children's mother tongue (especially with the ascendance of political conservatives who oppose mother tongue education of immigrants), many immigrant communities have established supplementary schools for that purpose. The authors found that although the schools differed in many respects, all four reinforced a sense of group solidarity, meaning belonging to a community that supports its members. While the authors suggest that community interests took priority over individual interests, they also note that many participants regarded these as "one and the same" (p. 411).

Baraúna (2011) describes a project in theater of the oppressed (which uses drama to work out challenges to oppression in everyday life) that has been launched at a Brazilian university to help young people develop their artistic and intellectual potential. Through experience on stage, they gain a better understanding of the oppression and violence they face every day, and search for effective measures to solve these situations of exclusion and pain. Solidarity is understood as one of the measures that help to solve these kinds of social situations.

The studies above tend to focus on the need for developing solidarity, and the work of social justice educators that is directed toward that need, much more than on how students or teachers experience other people's efforts to engage them in relations of solidarity. The study by Richie, Tobin, Roth, and Carambo (2007) gives us the most detailed portrait of day-to-day development of trust through interaction, so that we can see from the perspectives of people who are developing relationships of solidarity how that process works, and what its challenges are. In other words, if we take the development of solidarity as a worthy goal, how does that development occur? To explore that question, we turn to studies outside education.

CONSIDERING THE CONCEPT OF SOLIDARITY
IN OTHER DISCIPLINES

When we turn to disciplines outside of education, particularly sociology, philosophy, and feminist studies, there, too, we find articles that use the concept of solidarity without defining it (e.g., Churchill, 2010; see also Fendler, 2006). But we also find a broader array of conceptions of solidarity, and a bit more empirical study of how solidarity develops and works. To organize an examination of these conceptions, we draw on the work of Wilde (2007), who wrote: "The paradox at the heart of solidarity has long been evident. On the one hand it has connotations of unity and universality, emphasizing responsibility for others and the feeling of togetherness. On the other hand it exhibits itself most forcefully in antagonism to other groups, often in ways which eschew the possibility of compromise." (p. 173). Below, we discuss, first, conceptions of solidarity that emphasize societal unity, and then those that emphasize a context of antagonism.

Societal Unity

A body of thought rooted largely in philosophy and ethics examines how social cohesion and an ethical stance that values humanity might be built. While much of this work addresses the challenge of building social cohesion in large complex societies, some of it explores communalism in small rural societies.

Many small, poor, and/or indigenous communities hold communitarian values in which solidarity among members is normal. Zibechi (2009) makes this point writing about rural communities in Latin America, and Pérez (2006) reflects it in a study conducted in a rural, agricultural community in the north of Spain. The children go to the fields to help from the time they are very young, learning values, norms, and patterns of conduct through modeling. The most helpful values that they learn are industry, effort toward economic progress, loyalty, and solidarity. It seems that in such rural communities, solidarity among everyone is fundamental to survival.

Dean's (1995) differentiation between three forms of social solidarity provides a useful analytic bridge between communitarianism in small societies and the challenge of building solidarity in mass societies. Affectional solidarity is based on bonds of love, friendship, and familiarity, such as those that characterize the family or village. Conventional solidarity is based on sharing common interests, traditions, struggles, or work. Dean argues that both forms of solidarity bind individuals to a group and provide norms of behavior that are expected for group members. She views the assumption of shared norms as problematic, however, when they silence diverse perspectives within a group or devalue the individuality of group members. She proposes a third conception—reflective solidarity—under which "we" does not depend on there being an opposing "they," but rather intentional communication among those who share a "we" relationship. Dean proposes that mutual expectations would be negotiated in an ongoing fashion rather than being established once and for all. Reflective solidarity demands that people take responsibility for relationships with each other, continually working through differences in order to create a dynamic sense of "we."

For large, complex mass societies in which face-to-face contact is limited, building solidarity is a challenge. For Zubero (1996), the doctrine of liberalism only strengthens individualism, making it difficult to conceptualize acting in solidarity. Similarly, Buxarrais (2005) asks how solidarity might develop in an individualistic society in which other values are accepted only as prerequisites to reaching individual goals, in contrast with the deeper solidarity found in communitarian societies, where goals are achieved collectively, and solidarity is by necessity a part of everyday relationships. Juul (2010) proposes developing "a just distribution of possibilities for recognition" (p. 266), in which the competing demands of diverse members who struggle to have their own needs recognized are coordinated fairly and justly. Dean's conception of reflective solidarity is useful for considering the importance of dialogue for creating a sense of "we" that acknowledges and works through, rather than minimizes, diversity.

There has been some exploration into the question of whether diversity within a society impedes solidarity. Using tools of philosophical analysis, Derpman (2009) explores the relationship between solidarity and cosmopolitanism. He maintains that solidarity implies moral obligation to a delimited, specific community, while cosmopolitanism implies moral obligation toward all of humanity. Although these seem to be competing values, based on an analysis of the European Union, he argues that they are not mutually exclusive, but can be built in conjunction with one another. Janmatt and Braun (2009) tested that idea. Using a conception of solidarity as meaning empathy toward fellow citizens, compassion toward those in need, and willingness to support meeting the needs of society's members (even reducing income disparity), they conducted a large-scale survey of national values within the European Union. They did not find a correlation between racial/ethnic diversity and social solidarity; the common belief that the more diverse a society becomes, the less compassion people will have for others, did not hold up. Based on an analysis of Poland's experience with the Solidarity trade union, Korab-Karpowicz (2010) would agree. She argues that a diverse society can still support broad-based human rights—that people can develop solidarity around life-supporting needs such as "food, shelter, family, and security," and also "liberty and respect" (p. 309).

However, Janmatt and Braun (2009) found some correlation between economic prosperity and compassion for fellow citizens—the better off citizens were, the more compassionate they were, and the more likely they were to regard others as fellow citizens. But Camps (1996) reflects on the proportionate relationship that seems to exist between the greater abundance and wealth of a society, and the lower degree of solidarity among its members. She offers Germany and Sweden as examples of countries in where citizens have arrived at their maximum level of individualism. Justice in these countries does not appear to result from real civic cooperation, but rather from a social policy taken and accepted, and above all, conditions of considerable wealth. In other words, social wealth enables citizens to support policies that are compassionate, even while citizens themselves uphold an ethic of individualism.

Camps (1996, 2000) believes that to nurture sensitivity toward nature and animals is relatively easy, but sensitivity toward suffering and those who suffer is much more complicated. Currently, we face a crisis in values under neoliberalism in which individual success is more attractive than solidarity. For that reason, Camps maintains that education should develop civic habits and routines that demonstrate deference and respect among people—young people should learn to practice and preach solidarity, promoting it in public life.

Unity in the Face of Marginalization

Solidarity as unity among members of an oppressed group, in a context of marginalization and struggle, is perhaps a more common meaning of the concept. Solidarity has certainly been conceptualized this way in relationship to struggles and revolutions around class, race, and colonialism; indeed, as Wilde (2007) noted, solidarity is most likely to develop in the context of struggle.

More's (2009) discussion of Black solidarity in South Africa provides a useful framework. More uses Sartre's distinctions among seriality (a social collective of individuals passively united by something such as waiting for a bus), group (a collective consciously united toward a common end), group-in-fusion (individuals in the process of becoming aware of sharing a fate), and pledge group (when individuals firmly bind themselves to the group as a process of institutionalizing it). He then shows that arguments against Black solidarity tend to equate group-in-fusion with pledge group, viewing solidarity as creating divisions that were not already there. Arguments against it also assume that individualism, which is written into constitutions, actually names how things work. What is needed to combat racism, however, which people experience as collectives, is work that shifts Black people from seriality (membership in a group that has no group consciousness) to group-in-fusion.

Hoston's (2009) study of the relationship between racial context (the proportion of Black and White in a given context) and Black solidarity has some relevance here. Like More, Hoston views solidarity as "the belief that individual Blacks share a common fate with a larger Black group and that the welfare of the larger group coincides with the welfare of the individual" (p. 721). With awareness of the group itself, and how one's fate is connected with that of the group as a whole, comes awareness of "the need for collective group action" (p. 722). Hoston found higher levels of solidarity among Blacks who live in a majority-White context than among those who live in a predominantly Black context. Both Hoston and More emphasize the significance of marginalized communities shifting from seeing themselves as individuals to seeing themselves as members of a group that shares a common struggle.

Kruidenier (2009) applies this understanding of solidarity to an analysis of French manifestos such as "Manifeste pour une littérature monde." In the case of such manifestos, the signatories questioned who counts as legitimate speakers of French, declaring a community, such as Québec, as a legitimate alternative to one that cements speakers of French with the nation of France. Kruidenier suggests that such manifestos offer marginalized people a way of relocating themselves at the levels of emotion and identity, and suggest actions the collective might take to challenge their marginalization.

Solidarity in the face of marginalization, which is essential to collective struggle, is not without problems. Fendler (2006) points out that community too often is conceptualized as homogeneous, thereby excluding members who do not fit the way the community is defined. This problem, which is taken up below, has been tackled most directly by feminists of color and postcolonial feminists, who have found themselves marginalized by White women and men of color.

Building Allies in the Context of Struggle

In contexts of political struggle, we can consider building two related forms of allies: those who share marginalization on the basis of one form of difference (such as gender) but not another (such as race), and those who do not share marginalization but choose to work alongside a marginalized group anyway.

Feminists have done considerable work building solidarity across lines of race, class, and nation. For example, Mohanty (2003) discusses ways in which she has "been preoccupied with the limits as well as the possibilities of constructing feminist solidarities across national, racial, sexual, and class divides" (p. 140). She points out that, "as a South Asian anticapitalist feminist" (p. 140), she is engaged in struggles on numerous fronts, working for solidarity across race and gender among workers, across class and race among women, and across national borders among Third World women workers. She argues that women workers can form solidarity on the basis of shared common interests, but what is shared needs to be made explicit. Similarly, Deslandes (2009) probes gender and sexual harassment within global social justice movements to illustrate how people with different social identities (for example, White women, women of color, and men of color) interpret common problems differently, such as sexual violence. She suggests that dialogue is essential to building alliances of solidarity that do not occlude oppressive relationships within the alliance.

Based on interviews with activist women, Cole and Luna (2010) take up the same problem. They maintain that personal experience, social location, social identity, and political identity are not the same; while one might be born into the first three, political identities "are constructed through political work" (p. 95). The question then becomes what kind of work builds and sustains political solidarity among people whose life experiences, social locations, and social identities differ. Cole and Luna found empathy and dialogue to be central. Empathy develops in various ways, such as through childhood experiences or sharing common problems with people in different social locations. Dialogue is necessary for confronting multiple subidentities that can fracture an alliance, and power differences between allies from unequal social locations. Those who enter an alliance with unequal power not only face histories of oppressor/oppressed relations, but may also have different goals that ultimately move them in different directions. The interviewees stressed that, "Rather than attempting to create false unity to achieve goals, engaging conflicting views while ultimately focusing on shared commitment allows activists to take on difficult questions while moving the coalition forward" (p. 95).

Childs's (2003) work in transcommunal solidarity grapples with similar issues. He views transcommunality as "coordinated heterogeneity" across lines of identity (p. 21). Childs differentiates between "conversion politics"—attempts to build an alliance that subscribes to a single set of beliefs, and transcommunal politics, which is based on mutual respect of diverse perspectives among allies. Based on his work with community groups, he argues that dialogue is central to the development of an ethics of respect and mutual trust that accepts differences. He argues further that through dialogue, people can learn to use their differences in perspective and experience as multiple points from which to examine common concerns. Similarly, Dobbie and Richards-Schuster (2008) show how differences can serve as building blocks for solidarity. Based on their study of youth organizing, they propose a framework for building solidarity that includes five components: 1) including new voices at the leadership table and providing opportunities for new leaders to develop new skills, given their historic exclusion from leadership roles; 2) negotiation and bridge-building across differences; 3) providing education about structural, systemic oppression to help people move beyond a focus on cultural differences; 4) providing spaces for informal social interaction; and 5) working on common issues through coalitions.

Building alliances of solidarity across groups that share marginalization is difficult. Building alliances between marginalized communities and people who do not share marginalization is even more difficult. One line of investigation into this challenge examines global organizing efforts, asking how allies are cultivated from outside a nation where a struggle is occurring, such as the South African anti-apartheid movement (Thörn, 2009); the boycott, disinvestment, and sanctions campaign against Israel (Bakan & Abu-Luban, 2009); and Latin American uprisings (Gould, 2009). Movements such as these benefited from the work of outside allies, particularly university students. Factors that seem to build solidarity—at least for the duration of a particular campaign—include framing an issue around ethical concerns that will galvanize potential allies, and as much as possible involving allies in related on-the-ground work, such as union struggles.

Of more relevance to the issues many chapters in this book take up is the question of how members of privileged groups (such as White teachers) might become allies with marginalized communities. In these chapters, one sees that to live solidarity means much more than having a superficial understanding that is reduced to looking away from poverty, injustice, discrimination, the distance between social classes, and the problems of society itself. Solidarity, as Yarce (2011) says, means to build with others a society in which quality of life is a possible opportunity for everyone (including students, immigrant families, and socioeconomically disadvantaged natives or marginalized social groups). Solidarity is a commitment that unites us with everyone: I have rights to expect of others, and others to expect of me. Collaboration is an act of solidarity itself. It overcomes the egotistical individualism that puts one's own welfare ahead of everyone else's.

Based on interviews with White allies within racial justice movements, Warren (2010) concludes that ultimately, "Whites can come to embrace the political project of racial justice as they see its centrality to their own values, transforming democracy toward the kind of society in which they want to live and raise their children" (p. 231). How one gets to that position, however, is the challenge. Warren found that White allies were initially driven by moral concerns about racial injustice, and prompted to action by direct experience with racism that provoked a deep emotional response and highlighted the gap between people's vision of how society should be and how it actually works. Allies learned to care deeply about racism through personal relationships with people of color. Warren stresses that allies share a sense of fate with those with whom they are working; in that regard, the term *ally* becomes a misnomer because it suggests that one is engaged in working on other people's issues rather than one's own; the White people he studied had come to see racism not just as someone else's struggle, but also as their own. Similarly, in a discussion of Hawaiian sovereignty movement, Kraemer (2007) notes that privileged allies bring marks of privilege with them. But allies from privileged social locations also bring resources that can be useful. She stresses that privilege needs to be confronted and acknowledged, and then the focus needs to be turned toward confronting systems of oppression that imprison everyone. Resources that allies bring can be very usefully mobilized to challenge larger oppressive systems.

OVERVIEW OF THIS BOOK

The chapters in this book are organized into two parts. The first part, which includes four chapters, conceptualizes solidarity as building social unity, although the contexts discussed in the chapters vary considerably. In Chapter 1, Verónica López, Carmen Montecinos, José Ignacio Rodríguez, Andrés Calderón, and Juan Francisco Contreras explore the relationship between student behavior and school climate of solidarity in schools in Chile. Conceptualizing solidarity as building community among children and youth, the authors present two studies that examine how peer aggression was addressed by schools' leadership teams. The studies found that schools that mainly punish children who display aggression reported higher levels of peer aggression than schools implementing practices grounded in solidarity, which in this chapter implies belief in the educability of all students, and the consequent willingness to provide students from different social backgrounds with opportunities to learn to live together.

In Chapter 2, José Luis Ramos explores differences between how indigenous and nonindigenous teachers in Mexico view the meaning of solidarity. Drawing from his research, he shows that for the indigenous teachers, solidarity is an important factor within their culture and ethnic identity; for the nonindigenous teachers, it does not have the same relevance. Indigenous bilingual teachers value solidarity as a condition and expression of the common good, while nonindigenous teachers see the term as indicating tenacity and pride. These opposing understandings hinder dialogue.

In Chapter 3, Isabelle Aliaga and Martine Dreyfus question the viability of the French republican model of solidarity, which has never affirmed different languages and cultures. French republican solidarity refers to identification with the French state, regardless of one's own cultural or linguistic background. After reviewing the historic relationship among linguistic diversity, language policy, and republicanism in France and its colonies, the authors describe two informal research studies that investigated the relationship between language use in linguistically diverse classrooms and how young immigrant children respond to school and view their own identity. The authors demonstrate that when children from immigrant backgrounds study only French, they gradually perceive that their own identity is unwelcome, which may explain the violence that African immigrant teenagers enact against French social institutions. The authors suggest that this violence may have its roots in a social model of solidarity that rejects them as soon as they are born, requiring them to be different from who they are.

In Chapter 4, Maria Antonia Casanova discusses how the government of Spain has built a system of schools abroad that serve the purpose of building solidarity among Spanish emigrants and their descendants, and the country of Spain. In the cases of exiles who historically needed to leave Spain to survive and their descendants, the voluntary service offered can be considered a joint commitment of the Spanish people through its government with its quasi-exiled population. In the cases of those who voluntarily left Spain due to job mobility or other interests, such solidarity is extended in order to preserve the culture and language of origin while students are also acquiring other languages and working with other curriculum requirements. Both cases illustrate active government policy to maintain cultural and linguistic solidarity among its people abroad.

The second part of this book includes seven chapters that examine challenges and possibilities in building allies across sociocultural and ethnic/racial differences, including in contexts of tension and struggle. In Chapter 5, Encarnación Soriano reflects on the implications of 20 years of research on the concerns of teachers in the south of Spain, who have immigrant students in their classrooms. She conceptualizes solidarity as seeing others with the heart, and in response, being willing to act in ways that support needs of others and confront injustices. The challenge she presents is that most teachers continue to see immigrant students in their classrooms as problems they do not know how to work with. At the same time, she sees optimism in the teachers who, even if they lack theoretical and practical knowledge for teaching immigrant students, sense the racism and discrimination that immigrants experience and are willing to engage with the students and their communities.

In Chapter 6, Judith Flores Carmona and Dolores Delgado Bernal examine an oral history project implemented in an elementary school in Utah that serves low-income students, most of whom are of Mexican descent. The authors critique notions of solidarity that mean charity, arguing that really hearing and sharing struggles, pain, and dreams builds an interdependent solidarity based on the idea that we are one. Their chapter asks what happens when the histories, stories, and knowledge of students of color, immigrant students, and other marginalized students are brought into the school curriculum through a project based in oral history.

In Chapter 7, Gina Elizabeth DeShera shows how building solidarity between a school and a historically marginalized community is complicated by existing power structures. She reports a study of an attempt to build solidarity between teachers and administrators in a middle school in California, and the Latino Spanish-speaking parent community the school serves. She shows how school parent councils that are required by law were able to function as platforms for generating genuine community input and building solidarity among the parents. However, these parent councils were often ignored or co-opted by the school's leadership, which was mainly White and monolingual English-speaking, especially when they presented concerns or perspectives that disrupted how the school leadership framed problems.

Addressing a similar problem, in Chapter 8, Gilberto Arriaza and Alice Wagner conceptualize solidarity as purposeful actions to eliminate social distance and to redress the tensions it has generated. Based on a case study of an ethnically and linguistically diverse school in California, they argue that solidarity can be sustained only when explicit treatment of race, social class, and gender takes center stage. The study began with an attempt to engage the mostly White teaching staff in home visits, probing why so few teachers participated, and it examines initiatives the Mexican American principal launched to close social distance among adults in the children's lives, having the greatest success in building solidarity among parents of diverse backgrounds. The authors attempt to make visible issues of race, social class, and gender that loomed in the background, present but unaddressed.

In Chapter 9, Anne Hynds explores possibilities of building solidarity among teachers in colonized societies, looking specifically at relationships between Māori and New Zealand European teachers in Aotearoa, New Zealand. Based on a case study of teachers, she argues that solidarity can develop when people collectively own the problem of power, privilege, and difference, and work through conflicts in the context of a dialogical "third space" where competing knowledges and discourses can be brought into conversation with each other. In her case study, the moral imperative for engaging in such difficult work remained sufficiently elusive that communication broke down; Hynds clarifies what would be a compelling moral imperative that might keep people at the table.

In Chapter 10, Mahendra Kumar Mishra discusses Srujan, a program he directed in tribal villages in rural India. He explains that while solidarity among villagers is a normal value, the formal education of teachers leads them to disregard the traditional knowledge of villages in which they teach, producing distance between teachers and the children they teach. Srujan was designed to bridge that distance by engaging the teachers in activities investigating local community knowledge. The author describes the resulting transformations in relationships among teachers, community elders, parents, and children, and how those transformations affected teaching.

In Chapter 11, Christine Sleeter synthesizes what we can learn about solidarity from the chapters considered as a whole. Rather than being a new concept, solidarity has long been part of the human social fabric when one takes into account relationships of mutual support and communalism that characterize many small traditional societies. However, the processes and challenges of building social solidarity are very complicated in mass, complex societies that are characterized not only by cultural and linguistic differences, but also by significant inequities and struggles for power. This chapter considers problems inherent in attempts to impose a particular version of national solidarity, as well as possibilities for social transformation when marginalized groups are able to leverage their own solidarity along with supportive legal frameworks and visionary leadership.

Differences in culture, religion, language, and identity will not disappear. Indeed, humans derive psychological and spiritual strength through personal and familial affiliations that support one's sense of self. The challenge is learning to make and remake social institutions so that they support rather than threaten or weaken communities. Chapters in this book offer an attempt to analyze how schools, and specifically the work of teachers, might address local conflicts that have, in many cases, long and complex roots, using the concept of solidarity as a tool. The chapters do not offer a panacea; they do, however, offer many insights.

REFERENCES

Acevedo, A. M., Duro, E., & Grau, I. M. (2002). *Unicef va a la escuela para construir una cultura de paz y de solidaridad* [Unicef goes to school to build a culture of peace and solidarity]. Buenos Aires: Argentina.

Bakan, A. B., & Abu-Luban, Y. (2009). Palestinian resistance and international solidarity: The BDS campaign. *Race and Class 51*(1), 29–54.

Baraúna, T. (2011). Vida en el arte: Diálogos entre teatro, violencia y adolescencia [Dialogues between theater, violence, and adolescence]. *Cuadernos de Pedagogía, 411*, 66–69.

Buxarrais, M. R. (2005). Educar para la solidaridad [To educate for solidarity]. Retrieved from www.campus-oei.org/valores/boletin8.htm.

Camps, V. (1996). *Virtudes públicas* [Public virtues]. Madrid: Espasa Calpe.

Camps, V. (2000). *Valores de la educación* [Values of educaton]. Madrid: Anaya.

Childs, J. B. (2003). Transcommunality: From the politics of conversion to the ethics of respect. Philadelphia: Temple University Press.

Churchill, D. S. (2010). SUPA, Selma, and Stevenson: The politics of solidarity in mid-1960 Toronto. *Journal of Canadian Studies 44*(2), 32–69.

Cole, E. G., & Luna, Z. T. (2010). Making coalitions work: Solidarity across difference in U.S. feminism. *Feminist Studies 36*(1), 71–98.

Dean, J. (1995). Reflective solidarity. *Constellations 2*(1), 114–140.

Derpman, S. (2009). Solidarity and cosmopolitanism. *Ethical Theory and Moral Practice 12*, 303–315.

Deslandes, A. (2009). Giving way at the intersection: Anticolonial feminist ethics of solidarity in the global justice movement. *Australian Feminist Studies 24*(62), 421–437.

Dobbie, D., & Richards-Schuster, K. (2008). Building solidarity through difference: A practice model for critical multicultural organizing. *Journal of Community Practice 16*(3), 317–337.

Epstein, S. E., & Oyler, C. (2008). "An inescapable network of mutuality": Building relationships of solidarity in a first grade classroom. *Equity & Excellence in Education 41*(4), 405–416.

Europa Press. (2011). La ONG Human Rights Watch denuncia que el gobierno de Kenia repatría a somalíes a zonas en pleno combate [The NGO Human Rights Watch denounces that the government of Kenya repatriated Somalis to combat zones]. *EPSocial.* Retrieved from www.europapress.es/epsocial/ong-y-asociaciones/noticia-human-rights-watch-denuncia-gobierno-kenia-repatria-somalies-zonas-pleno-combate-20110331143911.html

Europa Press/Barcelona. (2011). CIU propone financiar el retorno a su país de inmigrantes en paro. *Journal El Mundo.* Retrieved from www.elmundo.es/elmundo/2011/03/31/barcelona/1301579956.html

Fendler, L. (2006). Others and the problem of community. *Curriculum Inquiry 36*(3), 303–326.

Gil, F., Jover, G., & Reyero, D. (2006). La educación de la sensibilidad solidaria desde la reconstrucción de la memoria lúdica [Education of a sense of solidarity from the reconstruction of the playful memory]. *Teoría de la Educación, 18,* 153–174.

Gould, J. L. (2009). Solidarity under siege: The Latin American left, 1968. *American Historical Review, 114*(2), 349–375.

Hall, K. A., Özerk, K., Zulfiqar, M., & Tan, J. E. C. (2002). "This is our school": provision, purpose and pedagogy of supplementary schooling in Leeds and Oslo. *British Educational Research Journal, 28*(3), 399–418.

Hoston, W. T. (2009). Black solidarity and racial context. *Journal of Black Studies 39*(5), 719–731.

Hui, T. K., & Goldsmith, T. (2011). Wake school board denies bias. *News Observer.* Retrieved from www.newsobserver.com/2011/03/30/1091052/wake-school-board-denies-bias.html

Humphrey, K. (2011). Diversity grows across south metro area since last census. *Star-Tribune.com.* Retrieved from www.startribune.com/local/south/118681194.html

The Independent Schools. (2001). Will a new "free" primary school in Bradford widen ethnic rifts in the city? *Independent.co.uk*. Retrieved from www.independent.co.uk/news/education/schools/will-a-new-free-primary-school-in-bradford-widen-ethnic-rifts-in-the-city-2257709.html

Janmatt, J. G., & Braun, R. (2009). Diversity and postmaterialism as rival perspectives in accounting for social solidarity. *International Journal of Comparative Sociology 50*(1), 39–68.

Juul, S. (2010). Solidarity and social cohesion in late modernity: A question of recognition, justice and judgment in situation. *European Journal of Social Theory 13*(2), 253–269.

Katsarou, E., Picower, B., & Stovall, D. (2010). Acts of solidarity: Developing urban social justice educators in the struggle for quality public education. *Teacher Education Quarterly 37*(3), 137–153.

Korab-Karpowicz, W. J. (2010). Inclusive values and the righteousness of life: The foundations of global solidarity. *Ethic Theory Moral Practice 13*, 305–313.

Kraemer, K. R. (2007). Solidarity in action: exploring the work of allies in social movements. *Peace and Change 32*(1), 20–38.

Kruidenier, J. F. (2009). Francophone manifestos: On solidarity in the French-speaking world. *International Journal of Francophone Studies 12*(2&3), 271–287.

Mohanty, C. T. (2003). *Feminism without borders: Decolonizing theory, practicing solidarity*. Durham, NC: Duke University Press.

More, M. P. (2009). Black solidarity: A philosophical defense. *Theoria: A Journal of Social and Political Theory, 56*(120), 20–43.

Nieto, S. (2006). Solidarity, courage and heart: what teacher educators can learn from a new generation of teachers. *Intercultural Education, 17*(5), 457–473.

Noticias. (2011). *Iglesia.net*. Retrieved from www.iglesiaviva.net/novedades/1-ultimas-noticias/7084-tema-migracion-y-educacion-.html

Pérez, P. M. (2006). Valores y pautas de crianza familiar en los Montes del Pas [Values and family upbringing in the Monts du Pas]. *Teoría de la Educación*, 18, 115–136.

Redacción Lavoz. (2011). En un año, 22% más de inmigrantes. La voz ciudadanos [In one year, 22% more immigrants. The voice of citizens]. Retrieved from www.lavoz.com.ar/ciudadanos/ano-22-mas-inmigrantes

Reuters/Tunez. (2011). Mueren 12 inmigrantes tunecinos de camino a la isla italiana de Lampedusa [12 Tunisian immigrants die on the way to the Italian island of Lampudesa]. *Journal El Mundo*. Retrieved from www.elmundo.es/elmundo/2011/03/31/Internacional/1301540789.html

Richie, S. M., Tobin, K., Roth, W., & Carambo, C. (2007). Transforming an academy through enactment of collective curriculum leadership. *Journal of Curriculum Studies 39*(2), 151–175.

Santora, E. D. (2003). Social studies, solidarity, and a sense of self. *The Social Studies, 94*(6), 251–256.

Tapia, M. N. (2001). *La solidaridad como pedagogía. El aprendizaje-servicio en la escuela* [Solidarity as pedagogy: Service learning in the school]. Buenos Aires: Editorial Ciudad Nueva.

Thörn, H. (2009). The meaning(s) of solidarity: narratives of anti-apartheid activism. *Journal of Southern African Studies 35*(2), 417–436.

Warren, M. R. (2010). *Fire in the heart: How white activist embrace racial justice.* New York: Oxford University Press.

Wilde, L. (2007). The concept of solidarity: Emerging from the theoretical shadows? *British Journal of Sociology of Education 9*, 171–181.

Yarce, J. (2011). *Comunidad y comunicación, participación y solidaridad* [Community and communication, participation and solidarity]. Bogotá, Colombia: Instituto Latinoamericano de Liderazgo Desarrollo Humano y Organizacional. Retrieved from www.liderazgo.org.co/documentos/2010/comunidad_y_solidaridad.pdf

Zibechi, R. (2009). Time to reactivate networks of solidarity. *Socialism and Democracy 23*(2), 110–112.

Zubero, I. (1996). Construyendo una sociedad solidaria: Una propuesta para el análisis y la acción [Building a caring society: A proposal for the analysis of action]. *Cuadernos de Trabajo Social, 9*, 303–327.

Part I

Solidarity as Social Unity

1

Enacting Solidarity to Address Peer-to-Peer Aggression in Schools

Case Studies from Chile

Verónica López, Carmen Montecinos, José Ignacio Rodríguez,
Andrés Calderón, & Juan Francisco Contreras

> So, in the end, where do we take them? Where are we supposed to take
> them? I mean, if the paid private school definitely cannot handle him [the
> student], [then] it sends him to a private-subsidized school, and later he is
> sent to a municipal school, [and then] municipal schools keep transferring
> [him] from one building to another, what do we do next?
> —Radio journalist referring to the practice of expelling
> aggressive children from schools (Toro, 2010)

Peer-to-peer aggression in the schools is an increasing concern for Chilean
society. Whereas public opinion and teachers often locate the roots of the
problem in students' morals and family background, in this chapter we associate the problem with school policies and practices. In two studies examining how peer aggression was addressed by schools' leadership teams, we
found that schools punishing children who assaulted peers reported higher
levels of peer aggression compared with schools that implemented management practices grounded in solidarity. By solidarity, we mean a belief in
the educability of all students, thus providing students from different social
backgrounds, with diverse levels of ability and behavioral dispositions,
opportunities to learn together to live together.[1] The main thesis we advance
is that peer-to-peer aggression is one form of student violence that can be
reduced by reducing institutional violence that is engendered by school policies that promote exclusion and social segregation. Given the high level

of social segregation that characterizes Chile's educational system,[2] school leadership teams that are guided by an ethic of solidarity not only impact peer-to-peer aggression; they also work against furthering social exclusion that operates through educational exclusion.

SEEKING QUALITY WITHOUT EQUITY: EXCLUSION AS EDUCATIONAL PRACTICE IN CHILE

Before presenting data describing contrasting approaches implemented by Chilean schools to address issues of school violence, we briefly discuss some key policies that account for the educational trajectory Toro (2010) described for students who exhibit aggressive behaviors in school. These policies and their negative effects on schools as social institutions that must further equity and social cohesion can provide a perspective on Chile's educational system which, in turn, highlights the importance of incorporating solidarity as a core organizing value of school leadership and policies.

In the 1980s, Chile began the implementation of a market-driven model for the provision of educational services. The General Education Law (*Ley General de Educación*, or LEGE) created two types of publicly funded schools: those owned and administered by the municipalities (municipal schools) and those owned and administered by the private sector. Each type of school receives an attendance-based, per pupil state subsidy. Today, students from lower socioeconomic backgrounds are concentrated in municipal schools; those from the low-middle and middle class are concentrated in private-subsidized schools, and upper-class students most often attend private-paid schools (Bellei, 2008; García-Huidobro, 2007). Belfield and Levin (2002) have argued that an educational system that is segregated may be inequitable, and that polarizing students undermines the public school system and produces schools that enter "spirals of decline"(p. 47) that are observed in a vast number of Chile's municipal schools. Over the last decade, enrollment in municipal schools has shown a steady decline, from 58% in 1990 to 42% by 2009 (Ministerio de Educación, 2011a). On the national assessment of educational quality, over the last 20 years, average scores in municipal schools are below the averages attained by private subsidized and private-paid schools (Sistema de Medición de la Calidad de la Educación, 2009). This differential performance has also been observed on international achievement tests (e.g., Program for International Student [PISA], 2006).

According to LEGE, with few exceptions, municipal schools must serve all students who seek enrollment. Private schools that receive public funding can use selective admissions processes and cancel the registration of students who fail to meet the school's academic or behavioral standards. This stipulation introduced a perverse effect as many families opted to send their children to private-subsidized schools, believing that selection leads to a better education, ensuring that their children will socialize with children who are similar in terms of intellectual and sociocultural characteristics. Schneider, Elacqua, and Buckley (2006) studied the school selection behavior of parents in a large urban area in Chile and found that a key factor in parental decisions, particularly in the middle and upper socioeconomic groups, was the social class composition of the student body. On the other hand, Montecinos, Sisto, and Ahumada (2010) noted how low-income parents also wanted to exert their right to school choice, but were precluded by the low-quality education their pupils were receiving at their municipal neighborhood schools. Given that they were underprepared, the better-performing schools did not accept them, or if they were accepted, they could not keep up with the academic standards. This speaks of the social exclusion that geographically operates through educational seclusion, leaving whole communities without quality schooling opportunities (Torche, 2005; Valenzuela, 2008). Policy and parental behaviors have colluded to generate a systemic mechanism of segregation that is taken for granted and becomes almost invisible and naturalized (Atria, 2010).

The voucher system in Chile gives the subsidy to the school and not to the parents. Instead of parents choosing schools, in Chile school selection mostly operates the other way around (Redondo, Almonacid, Inzunza, Mena, & de la Fuente, 2007). This has resulted in schools actively—but not overtly—seeking those students who are cheapest to teach, and "suggesting" to students who are more expensive to teach—such as students with special learning needs and students with behavior problems—to "look for some other schools" (Contreras, Bustos, & Sepúlveda, 2007). The following excerpt from an interview conducted by the first author of this chapter (López, Carrasco, Ayala, Morales, López, & Karmy, 2011) in the context of an ethnographic study examining discursive practices around school violence illustrates the phenomenon as understood by a municipal school principal:

Let's see. We have reached the conclusion that the Chilean educational system is, I don't know how to express the exact word, perhaps discriminated or divided into different groups. We are told *you* municipal schools will only have students who have problems, be it learning difficulties, or behavioral problems, emotional problems, those types of things. That is, as the system is currently constructed, that seems to be our final destiny. I have received calls from the ministry telling me, "Look, sir, you must enroll this boy from private-subsidized school X." (I will not provide names.) "He has problems over there, and parents are complaining. That boy cannot stay there, he has become a child who assaults his peers and he is generating problems and you have to enroll him." I answered "and why do *I* have to receive him?" If it is in order to have a boy with those characteristics, I have 20, and therefore we can exchange. You send me that child and I will send you one of mine. That seems fair. Why does a private-subsided school which is also financed by the state not have to do that [serve all students who seek enrollment]? I ask myself, why?

This excerpt clearly exemplifies how LEGE operates through practices that exclude certain students from an opportunity to learn and study according to their "parents' choice," the foundation of the market-driven model. It also exemplifies how segregation occurs by slowly excluding students from attending certain types of schools, concentrating hard-to-teach students in schools that by law must accept all who seek access.

The paradox is that concomitant with an expansion of compulsory education from ages 8 to 12 and an expansion in total coverage from 91% in 1990 to 99% in 2001 for elementary grades (grades 1–8), we can observe an intensification of various forms of segregation. The first criterion is social class, and within social class, students are sorted again based on achievement and behavior. To reverse this situation, a law was passed in 2007 to generate a subsidy formula tied to the socioeconomic status of the student—the voucher value is now significantly higher for students whose families of origin are socially vulnerable. This will, supposedly, create an incentive for private providers to enroll students from lower-income backgrounds. The logic of a consumer-oriented economy, notes Bauman (2005), places an emphasis on the "disposal of things, rather than on their appropriation" (p. 308). As aptly articulated by the principal quoted, when schools operate to serve private interests, students become commodities that can be traded. As a consequence, education as an institution that provides the social foundations of solidarity is undermined. Bauman (2005) writes:

> Individual exposure to the vagaries of commodities and labor markets inspires and promotes divisions, not unity; it puts a premium on competitive attitudes and degrades collaboration and teamwork to the rank of temporary stratagems that need to be suspended or terminated the moment their benefits have been exploited in full and used up. (p. 304)

Through the policies and practices described earlier, Chile has created a system by which municipal education receives the largest proportion of hard-to-teach students. This, in turn, has created a climate of learned helplessness in many schools, opting for the referring spiral to address problems they believe are beyond their control and professional capacities. Hard-to-teach students are referred to specialists, who in turn refer them to further specialists, and so on. The referral process leaves these students without opportunities to participate and engage in classroom activities with peers. At the same time, schools miss opportunities to act on bullying and other forms of school violence through educative interventions.

SCHOOL CLIMATE-RELATED PRACTICES IN SCHOOLS WITH PEER-TO-PEER AGGRESSION

Parés (2006) proposed different levels of intervention to address peer-to-peer aggression. She distinguished among interventions that can be ordered on an exclusion–inclusion continuum. Each level describes alternative roles for those involved in the situation: victims, aggressors, and spectators. At the exclusion end of this continuum, we find measures that are reactive, that reject students who act in aggressive ways and focus on controlling their behavior. For aggressors, these actions include control and threats that clearly communicate zero tolerance and the consequences of continuing with those types of behaviors. For victims, this would entail protective measures such as providing adult supervision so that the student is never alone as well as legal protective measures. For spectators, the measures involve stimulating them to denounce the acts either publicly or privately.

At the inclusive end of this continuum, interventions with the perpetrators of aggression entail actions that will break up the group that is responsible for aggression and including those students in alternative groups, such as sports, study groups, and so on. With victims, interventions aim at elevating their status within the group by enhancing these students' "public image" through leadership assignments within the classroom. For spectators, interventions aim at teaching them how to behave in ways that make all classmates feel included, particularly those who have been victimized. Students are taught how to engage in solidarity by taking care of each other. In what follows, we illustrate specific practices associated with both ends of this continuum through an analysis of data produced in two studies that examined management practices developed to address *convivencia* (getting along together), and in particular, peer-to-peer aggression in the school (Calderón & Contreras, 2011; Rodríguez, 2010).

Differences Between Schools with Low and High Levels of Peer-to-Peer Aggression

Rodríguez's (2010) study sought to describe and compare *convivencia* management practices in five schools concentrating a high proportion of 7th- and 8th-grade students who scored very high (over 75th percentile) and those of three schools with a high proportion of students with very low scores (below the 25th percentile) on three peer aggression measures ($n = 444$)[3]. In each school, the school principal, the inspector general, a teacher, and a student were asked to respond to a questionnaire that purported to examine how these schools managed issues related to *convivencia* ($n = 40$).[4] This was operationalized in the following three dimensions:

1. Developing, communicating, and administering policies (norms and regulations) specifically designed to promote healthy interpersonal relationships and to address issues of aggression and violence.
2. Level of autonomy to develop school policies and to implement violence prevention programs (versus passively accepting policies and programs developed by external institutions).
3. School practices and activities designed to promote social cohesion in a trusting environment where all community members are welcomed and feel safe in school (e.g., information sharing practices, socialization activities to bring community members together).

Table 1.1 summarizes the main research findings. These data showed important management practices that *differentiated* schools with low and high levels of peer aggression and victimization. Although in both types of schools expulsion from school was the last measure used to manage students' violent behaviors, these two types of schools differed in the primary and secondary interventions implemented. Schools with low levels of peer aggression tended toward actions aimed at promoting student participation in decision-making processes involving issues pertaining peer-to-peer aggression. Students were asked to be actively involved in bullying and school violence prevention. Adults took proactive measures aimed at intervening and/or preventing school violence and provided for the inclusion of aggressors and victims within the regular classroom. Opportunities were created for community-building and the development of emotional bonds among all members of the school community.

In schools with high levels of peer aggression, questionnaire respondents described the implementation of actions that did not promote social cohesion among the various school actors. School behavioral norms and regulations were handed out but not discussed in the classroom. Students did not participate in the elaboration of these norms and regulations, and parents were not seen as allies.

Table 1.1: Management Practices of Schools with Low and High Levels of Peer-to-Peer Aggression

School policies and practices	Schools with low levels of peer aggression and victimization	Schools with high levels of peer aggression and victimization
Developing, communicating, and administering policies	Policies related to school climate are discussed with students. The school informs to the community climate-related policies through the "*Convivencia* Handbook" and other official documents relating to the discipline code, conduct and policies for dealing with disruptive students, and consequences for transgressions. In addition, a number of activities are implemented within classrooms to engage students in a discussion of the social norms that need to be followed to create a positive climate.	Documents that define policies related to school climate are handed to the school community. The school informs to the community climate-related policies through the "*Convivencia* Handbook" and other official documents relating to the discipline code, conduct and policies for dealing with disruptive students, and consequences for transgressions.
Level of autonomy to manage school climate	Autonomous and proactive management. In addition to selectively using resources and programs endorsed by the ministry to address school violence, the school develops local initiatives. For example, an internal anti-bullying campaign and inviting specialists to develop internal capacities to address social conflicts.	Passive management. There is no evidence that schools have proactively developed initiatives to solve social conflicts within the community. These issues are believed to be addressed by adopting programs or initiatives that external agencies ask the school to implement. Teachers report that climate- related issues have not been a topic for professional development.

(continued)

29

Table 1.1. (continued)

School policies and practices	Schools with low levels of peer aggression and victimization	Schools with high levels of peer aggression and victimization
School practices and activities designed to promote community-building	Student involvement is promoted. Through surveys, focus groups, and assessments, the school requests students' opinions when deciding on issues related to school climate.	Student involvement is not sought out. There are no formal or informal mechanisms to consider students' opinions when deciding on issues related to school climate.
	Inclusion as the main intervention. Measures that seek to help integrate the victim and the aggressor within the classroom activities are favored over measures that exclude, punish, or isolate the aggressors. Addressing behavioral problems is coupled with plans to support the academic behavior of low-performing students. The use of suspension and expulsion is infrequent; they are used as the last option.	Exclusion as the main intervention. To address instances of peer-to-peer aggression, various forms of punishment are the most common actions. These students are labeled, isolated, and referred to "specialists." By entering a "referring spiral," students are prevented from participating in regular classroom activities. Students report that low-performing students do not receive additional academic support. The use of measures such as suspension or expulsion is the last option.
	Promotion of social activities to bring school members together. The school exhibits a culture that values positive school climate, promoting community-building. School events go beyond socializing as they promote emotional bonding among community members. This enables trusting relationships, fluid communication, and stronger support systems.	Low levels of social activities to bring school members together. The school exhibits a culture that does not explicitly value a positive school climate. Social gathering within classes is promoted without the explicit intention of generating bonds among members.
	Parents are seen as close allies. Frequently, when a student assaults a peer, parents are brought into the conversations seeking to resolve the issues. According to administrators, when students are involved in an act of aggression, they first tell their parents.	Parents are not involved. When a student assaults a peer, most often, administrators call the student and hand down the punishment. According to administrators, when students are involved in an act of aggression, they first tell the principal.

Leadership for Promoting Social Inclusion in School Climate-Related Practices

To better understand how these inclusive and exclusionary practices were implemented, Calderón and Contreras (2011) used in-depth interviews with at least two members of the leadership teams of 12 schools (eight of which had participated in Rodríguez's study). Here, we report an analysis of interviews conducted at one of these schools with two of the three members of the leadership team: the principal and the inspector general. This school was the only municipal school that exhibited low levels of aggression and in the previous study was characterized as implementing inclusive practices. This K–12 school is classified by the ministry as enrolling students from families of medium-low socioeconomic status. The criteria for this tier are: Most parents' schooling ranges from 9 to 19 years; average monthly household income ranges from US\$300 to US\$460; and between 50% and 80% of students are in a condition of social vulnerability (Ministerio de Educación, 2011b). This was a comprehensive grades K–12 school that had experienced severe enrollment decline because of poor educational results and general social anomie. A new principal and leadership team were brought in 2 years prior to when data were collected and the school was exiting the "spiral of decline." Next, we analyzed how these two informants understood *convivencia* as built on practices that promoted community-building to support students' development for positive participation in life, not just in school.[5]

Convivencia is a result of consensus and participation. By law, each school must develop a *Convivencia* Rules and Procedures Handbook. Although the ministry guidelines stress the importance of writing the handbook through participatory and consensual processes, as shown in Table 1.1, that was not the case in schools with high levels of peer-to-peer aggression. In this municipal school, the leadership team had developed the handbook with formal participation by the different members of the school community.

> *Inspector:* Yes, yes [the inspector general gets up in search of something]. Here we have the *Convivencia* Rules and Procedures Handbook. I mean, here are a series of situations regarding *convivencia*, but all of us who act within the school are a part of *convivencia*. My responsibility is that each person is treated properly, that they perform their functions, if the teacher is expected to teach, that he is teaching, [those] who should be reading, students who come in late, call their parents.
> *Interviewer:* How was this handbook developed? The *Convivencia* Rules and Procedures?
> *Inspector:* It is being developed, it is more or less completed but it is a contribution by all stakeholders.

Not only were the rules developed in a participatory manner but their implementation did not rest in the hands of the administrators or teachers. The administration had created a "*Convivencia* Committee," involving different members of the school community. The mission of this committee was to participate in the design and implementation of school climate policies. This form of school governance, currently, is not mandatory in Chile. According to the principal:

> What happens is that we developed the *convivencia* rules and procedures; the leadership team validated the document, but then gave it to the Committee. The Committee has what you just said, the responsibility for managing those rules, engaging in actions that will install this procedures in the school, engaging in actions to see to *convivencia*. So the teachers from their point of view, youth from their point of view, and we negotiate at a democratic table how we are going to proceed with these rules and procedures.

This kind of community participation was a conscious and actively driven process. This implies that decisions were made to ensure *decision making with participation*. Decisions were thus *made*, not just received, by all who were affected by them. Nor were programs just received from external sources; the school also exercised autonomy in developing activities. As can be surmised from the previous excerpt, the leadership understood the challenges of this approach—"it's very hard to come to agreements"; confronting them generated a sense of pride and accomplishment.

A continuum of interventions for addressing behavioral problems and interpersonal conflicts that may lead to violence was defined. The first response was conflict resolution with the children involved, including other adults when violence had been observed. Bullying and other forms of aggression were defined and the roles for various actors in a case of bullying identified:

> *Interviewer:* How is the problem of school violence
>   approached in this school community?
> *Inspector General:* We have it here, first we examine the child's
>   situation on that day, we inform ourselves, we read any
>   prior records for that child, we then see in what context he
>   finds himself, we see if we can resolve it prior to initiating
>   a [formal] notification of the situation . . . , we try to work
>   out a peaceful resolution of the conflicts. If it is aggression
>   that is different, we inform the principal, we inform the
>   *Convivencia* Committee, we take measures, we evaluate the
>   situation. There is a whole procedure, particularly if it is

bullying, here we have everything concerning bullying . . . the procedural protocol in case of bullying. . . . As I was saying, a series of steps defined in the *Convivencia* Handbook, call the parents, inform parents, conduct a thorough study when there is bullying, the type of victim that is produced.

Convivencia is an opportunity to educate everyone. Having a handbook that made explicit the norms, conduct codes, and sanctions to promote *convivencia* was coupled with other interventions that went beyond managing students' behaviors. The aim was to develop citizens by developing a sense of responsibility for the community. Additionally, the link between behavioral disruptions and pedagogical practices was made explicit, prompting changes in the pedagogical conceptions of teachers. New instructional practices were being developed in order to make schooling more appealing to students.

Interviewer: How do you address *convivencia* in this school?
Principal: That is a complex question because when I arrived, there
was nothing, we found nothing and we developed the rules
of procedures governing *convivencia* issues. It has 12 points,
from the institutional principles, misconducts, typification of
sanctions, how you call that, tribunals, in quotes, where students
have the right to respond [to any charges] and more formative
types of sanctions. For example, if a child throws a stone, [as
a form of reparation, he then] picks up papers, engages in
a pedagogical task. What is the nature of these pedagogical
tasks? Help assess [other students'] homework . . . help younger
students . . . we are in the diaper stage, we are just beginning.
A second action is during the homeroom periods where we have
taken the juvenile course which is a state plan that has been
around for a while, that has modules from learning to know about
themselves, through, by 12th grade, developing a life plan, their
project. Through the assessment policy and rules of procedures
we have addressed those dispositions that are desirable in the
classroom, ... and we have also designed the participation
of the student association, it is complete, all stakeholders and
starting August, we have a leadership project and they [students]
coordinate it in their classroom with the educational assistants.
We have designed ten workshops. We have already implemented
two. From the definition of conflict through mediation, so they
develop communicative social skills, an understanding that conflict
is daily, it is inherent to the human condition, that conflict is not
just there, every day it is an opportunity to develop skills. And

with teachers we have a workshop . . . one, two, three workshops
on life skills development that are being implemented through
JUNAEB [Junta Nacional de Auxilio Escolar y Becas, which is
the state-funded national program for social protection within
the school]. Therefore, we have installed five or six programs
or dimensions to assist with our *convivencia* in the school.

The above quote shows the whole-school approach that the school principal and his team developed. They have approached the issue by addressing
several of the dimensions of school climate identified by Cohen, McCabe,
Michelli, and Pickeral (2009). As we can see, he and his team "took charge"
and, with participation from different members of the school community,
came up with actions aimed at different levels—classroom, school grounds,
cafeteria—and different actors: students, teachers, teacher assistants,
inspector general. Altogether, from their perspective these interventions had
proven to have an effect on reducing peer aggression and school violence.

Convivencia is to promote a sense of belonging. Separate in-depth
interviews with the inspector general and school principal showed that both
of them thought that one of the factors explaining the low levels of peer
aggression was the principal's leadership. At the time of the study, this was
the principal's second year in the school and, at least for him and the inspector, much had changed during the last 2 years:

Interviewer: What do you think is the main change affecting
     the problems the school had experienced in the past?
Inspector: Behavior, the behavior of kids has improved a lot.
     That does not mean we have, but it has improved a lot.
Interviewer: How did you achieve that?
Inspector: Through more supervision in the schoolyard, greater
     participation and presence of the educational assistants, myself,
     the work done at faculty meetings, all that, there has been work.
     There is no one thing one can say "I, I". No, one is just a part of.
     But yes, our principal, he has always been in front of all this.

The principal's leadership was administrative, as well as pedagogical.
The school principal noted that one of the elements behind the changes produced was "changing consciousness" about education, about school, and
about students.

Interviewer: You just told us that the school also
     developed a new perspective. What changed?
Principal: Work in consciousness-raising. This school was had
     an enrollment of 220 students, now we have 350 and the

facility is designed for 500. We had been suffering a whole
bunch of events, like personal violations . . . therefore first,
we have generated the conditions for trust, trust in that what
we are doing will not hurt others. I really value the student
association [and have] convinced the educational assistants of
this new perspective, I mean not to use force to impose this
new perspective and the use of transition but that these are
fully formative relationships. Additionally, it is not convenient
to develop *convivencia* rules that will not be compatible with
their performance once they leave the 12th grade but you need
to teach them, formatively, how these [rules] will operate.

Though the principal tended to stereotype children who grew up in
poverty by assuming that their environment fostered violent responses, he
did not see their background as an impediment. He strongly believed in
the educability of all students based on the relationships that adults in the
school developed with them. The principal reported that teachers had used
students' backgrounds as a means of judging their behavior but now they
sought to understand the children:

Interviewer: How do you address school violence in this school?
Principal: You see, a characteristic of our children is that
        they have an impoverished cultural level, the term is
        impoverished not deprived, it is impoverished.
Interviewer: What is the difference?
Principal: Very hard. Impoverished means that they have the skills,
        but not the tools. Deprived that they have been left without the
        use of those human faculties. Therefore as impoverished, they
        only understand solving their conflicts through aggression because
        they come from poor socioeconomic backgrounds. [The ones who
        are] weak have to struggle. At the end the stronger over the weak
        and their struggle is to hit someone, punch them or do whatever
        and they bring that to the school. These are cultural patterns
        that are transported into the school. And we are, we have taken
        some very complicated steps and we, the leadership team, were
        present during recess, at 1:30 we were in the schoolyard *making
        presence* and not punishing, trying to get students to understand
        that you can resolve conflicts without punching or kicking.
        Second, in the lunchroom there was a long line and things
        were broken, they punched each other, threw apples at each
        other, we have 300 chairs, 300 kids who eat here. We decided
        to have the whole lunch process in the dining room, we
        put a television, we started serving them well, on trays, we
        placed trash cans, everything was cleaned up, neatly ordered,

*therefore there was an environment that did not provoke
all that.* In addition, *we were there, watching.* Ah . . . from
there we started incorporating the *convivencia* rules.
This also happened in the classroom, teachers were not
punishing, rather they became more welcoming, understanding
they came from cultural poverty which is more conflictive and
they began to be welcoming. Today we do not have so many
kids out of the classrooms. In March [at the beginning of the
school year] half of the students were in the hallways because
teachers would send them out for throwing papers, teachers
kicked them out; they did not understand those things. We
changed our methods and *practices for how knowledge was
delivered to constructing knowledge* because it is very boring for
kids to listen to some guy talk for 45 minutes. Thus, changing
modes of action with respect to instructional practices, giving
them some responsibilities in the assessment rules so they
could co-assess and self-assess. This is what we have done.

A school culture of conviviencia embraces solidarity. During the interview, the school principal reflected on the possibilities of changing a school
culture that was previously infused with norms based on punishment and
negligence into one where students felt listened to, contained, and welcomed.
Creating a welcoming environment was deeply rooted in understanding and
building from cultural differences:

But the idea is that each child feels like his truth is listened to, that you
are empathic, that you provide him with the solutions, and everything,
that things are done for a reason, that when a social service is
needed, needs a psychologist, has a person, a professional who can
help uncover that part, the causes of the behavioral manifestation
of the child, be it the aggressor, be it the victim. (Principal)

The centrality of positive interpersonal relations was at the heart of
how *convivencia* was to be constructed by community members:

Principal: No, *convivencia* is a sociocultural issue, it has to do
with the ways they behave at home, at different places, within
different communities, because *convivir* (cohabitation) is
to be by someone it is not *to be with someone, convivir* is
a close relationship. What happens is that the school must
establish some learning activities so this living together is
fruitful and develops social skills. That is the first function of
education, a social function. That is where the problem lies.

Interviewer: Of the elements you just mentioned, which ones
    do you think contributed most to reducing violence,
    control of public spaces, more welcoming teachers?
Principal: I think not one by itself, there is no, no, no one variable
    that by itself will produce results. . . . I think you need to provide
    a mixture of welcoming with presence, a mixture of norms that
    will allow you to contact . . . allow you to improve *convivencia*
    but the central [piece] is the classroom, that is where the child
    feels welcome, and you teach in a way that generates interest in
    what they are learning. The teacher–student relationship, the
    educational assistants are central because they know the kids very
    well, they spend a lot of time with them. Therefore, welcoming
    and this new perspective held by teachers and educational
    assistants, not discounting the other measures, for sure.

Clearly, building a community of solidarity within the school is not an easy task and is a long-term process. One of the key elements that the school recognized and recommended had been involving students in actions of reparation of the damage provoked by peer aggression. Their social development as a member of a community was at stake:

Therefore, within the rules, instruments or actions that allow
for that [reparation] need to be in place. Evidently, if a kid
damages private property, such as a sweater, he has to restitute
the sweater, but in addition he must do something that benefits
the community as this benefit is a pedagogical action. If he
is a good student, he will go to the 4th, 1st or 2nd grade
to do three or four hours of assistantship. (Principal)

SOLIDARITY AS A CORE VALUE OF SCHOOL LEADERSHIP

Inasmuch as a school displays leadership for *convivencia* built around the idea of inclusion, the chance for a healthier school climate, which in turn serves as a protecting factor against peer aggression, is significant (Astor, Benbenishty, & Estrada, 2009). An inclusion-oriented school is one where the leadership and faculty assume responsibility for the behaviors students demonstrate in the schools. Instead of externalizing blame or blaming the students, changes are developed within the school to solve the problems encountered. The focus is placed on transforming the school culture such that improving *convivencia*—"living together"—becomes an opportunity to learn to *"be by someone."* An educative response to behavioral problems seeks to develop a sense of belonging, something that can hardly be developed if the school response to violence is merely punishment or expulsion. School leaders, as well as teachers, parents, and students, would attempt to see, and help others see, the similarities with respect to pain experienced by all those who are affected by violence.

The principal and inspector general from a municipal school that had curbed social anomie in the school through their words and actions exemplified three forms of solidarity described by Cheung and Ma (2011). Distributive solidarity refers to policies and practices that ensure all members of the community have equal access to resources and opportunities. In schools, this form of solidarity may be enacted through policies and practices that ensure that all students have equitable access to quality learning opportunities, thus alleviating social inequalities generated in the wider society. Distributive solidarity was evidenced in the commitment to the success of all students, changing instructional practices that failed to engage students' interest in learning and asking students to engage in community service to help the learning of younger children.

Inclusive solidarity refers to symbolic feelings of acceptance and friendliness that lead to social inclusion though the sharing of symbolic meanings, such as a shared identity. Cheung and Ma note that "social inclusion is conducive to a common identity . . . for resisting prejudice and discrimination" (p. 148). Inclusive solidarity was practiced by ensuring feelings of acceptance and friendliness that lead to social inclusion.

Finally, dialogic solidarity refers to developing mutual understanding through communication. It is this understanding that enables social order and fosters progress. Following Habermas's communicative action theory, Cheung and Ma (2011) posited that the assumption is that this dialogue takes place in social relations that are free from oppression and power differentials. In schools, this form of solidarity will be enacted through policies and practices that generate trust and openness among all parties to collectively solve problems that emerge from various forms of social interactions (Montecinos, Sisto, & Ahumada, 2010). Practices fostering the development of mutual understanding through communication (dialogic solidarity), were exemplified in the instauration of "tribunals" where students had opportunities to tell their side of the story, as well as in the Convivencia Committee, which included all stakeholders. Trust has been identified as a key aspect for school improvement (Bryk & Schneider (2003). As explained by Roth (2000),

> Trust itself can arise from a sense of solidarity which is only possible once we abandon traditional notions of hierarchy related to schooling and develop a sense of "we are in this together for the learning". That is, solidarity implies that we extend our sense of "we" to people whom we previously thought of as "they". (p. 243)

IMPLICATIONS FOR POLICY AND PROFESSIONAL DEVELOPMENT

Data from the two studies reported in this chapter suggest that when school leadership approaches the problem of peer-to-peer aggression through interventions that seek to include rather than punish students who assault peers, less peer aggression is reported. These are practices that promote students' participation in the school community and a sense of belonging and feeling welcomed (Orpinas, Horne, & Staniszewski, 2003; Parés, 2006). Although the methodological approach used in these studies does not allow us to establish a causal relationship, the data are sufficiently strong to suggest that there is a relationship between school-level practices of solidarity and levels of peer-to-peer aggression. The more evidence we provide that schools, through their climate and leadership practices, *do* and *can* make a difference, the more feelings of self-helplessness associated with working in stigmatized municipal schools can be addressed. These feelings were addressed in the municipal school we studied. Enrollment in this school has gone up, and is now more than 400 students.

Implications for Educational Policy

Probably due to the high visibility of bullying incidents presented by the mass media during the last few years, two Chilean senators have recently proposed a law on school violence. The proposal includes provisions such as mandatory reporting of acts of bullying to the police and sanctions to schools with high levels of reported acts of bullying—one sanction of which is providing financial compensation to parents. This proposal was drafted by a law firm specializing in criminology, and contained not only criminal-law terms, but most important, a logic of penalty that criminalizes students who engage in acts of violence. In October 2010, the Minister of Education announced that he wanted to give this law proposal maximum urgency in the Senate, so its implementation could start at the beginning of the school year in March 2011.

During November 2001, a congressman, Deputy Mr. Rodrigo González, invited researchers from the Observatory for School Violence to discuss this proposed law. A debate session, followed by a seminar,[6] was organized by the Chamber of Deputies, in which different research groups, one of which included the first author (López, 2010), presented their views and provided empirical evidence on the issue. These researchers also provided expert testimony before the Commission of Education of the Chamber of Deputies, after the above-mentioned proposal was passed by the Chamber of Deputies and sent to the Senate to be passed. The researchers participating in the Observatory helped draft an alternative law project for school *convivencia*, which involved primary (promotion) and secondary (prevention) interventions. In this alternative law, communication and school community participation were explicit and interventions for addressing acts of aggression were diverse. Following the seminar, the commission agreed to postpone its decision on the bill, but members were being pressured by the ministry. The bill was finally passed on September 8, 2011, and integrates the two projects in a rather hybrid way, proposing both actions for promoting school *convivencia*, as well as punishment for breaking rules of *convivencia* (Castro, 2010). This law is now being implemented. We provide this as an example of how research *can* be linked to educational policymaking and how researchers engage in solidarity with educators and students who may be affected by legislation.

Implications for Professional Development

With respect to professional development, the theoretical and empirical foundations for positive school climate need to be a part of teacher training, as well as of the preparation of school principal and other leadership positions. We have started to do this at our university and will continue to pursue this line of work. Leading for social inclusion involves educational policy and practice that recognize children who engage in aggressive behaviors as members of the community and involve them in solving the problems that generate and that are generated by violence. A first step involves consciousness-raising, so principals and school leadership teams deepen their understanding of themselves within a micro-political perspective and "make visible" the nature, character, and quality of their school climate, and how they contribute toward reproducing or changing this climate. The findings of the studies we reported stressed the importance of helping school professionals recognize and assume their role in contributing toward a "toxic" or "nutritive" climate (Arón & Milicic, 2000). Externalizing the causes of, and solutions to, school violence on students, families, and local communities limits their opportunities for change and furthers a sense of learned helplessness. A second phase entails the development of skills in order to help them redirect their practices, while at the same time reflecting on them as reflexive practitioners. We, as researchers, can help school management teams become action-researchers in order to improve their school climate and build stronger communities based on values of inclusion and solidarity.

NOTES

The preparation of this manuscript was partially funded by the Centre for Advanced Research in Education (PIA-CONICYT, Project CIE-05) and a grant from the Chilean National Fund for Scientific and Technological Development (Fondecyt 11080055).

1. In Chile, the concept used to address interpersonal relations and social conflict in schools is *convivencia*. A literal translation of the concept is "cohabitation" or "living together." The Ministry of Education defines policy and procedures related to convivencia as "the promotion and development among all members of the school community of the principles and elements that build a healthy cohabitation, with special emphasis in a preparation that favors the prevention of all types of violence or aggression" (Ministerio de Educacion de Chile, n.d., p. 1). In this chapter, we have used the concept of school climate as a translation for "convivencia," as both address similar issues. It is noteworthy, however, that in the U.S. literature, school climate tends to be defined more broadly than the norms related to interpersonal relationships or social conflicts (Cohen, McCabe, Michelli, & Pickeral, 2009).

2. An external evaluation of Chile's educational policies since 1990 conducted in 2003 by the Organisation for Economic Cooperation and Development (OECD) stated:

> The important point is not whether the value-added differs that much—it does not—but rather the fact that the educational system is consciously class structured. The rules of the game are different—and unjustly so—for municipal and private schools. Private schools can both select and expel. Municipal schools—with the exception of the few prestigious ones that are in high demand—are obliged to accept all students asking for access. Under these circumstances, results can be expected to differ in favour of private subsidised schools. (OECD, 2004, p. 255)

3. Aggression and Victimization Scales (Orpinas & Frankowski, 2001, adapted by López & Orpinas, 2010) and the INSEBULL [Instrumentos para la Evaluación del Bullying], a self-report and a peer-report scale (Avilés & Elices, 2007).

4. The principal or assistant principal was included because they lead the organization. The inspector is the staff person who has direct responsibility for students' out-of-classroom needs and behaviors, enforcing discipline codes and sanctions. Teachers were included because, through their daily interactions with students, they witness classroom incidents of aggression and also are enforcing discipline codes and sanctions. Students were included, as they tend to be the protagonists in the incidents of aggression and sanctions that were investigated in the study. By including all of these stakeholders, a 360-degree perspective on how the school managed situations of convivencia could be attained.

5. The interviews were conducted in Spanish. Transcript excerpts have been translated into English, with some editing when deemed necessary to increase clarity.

6. Seminario Violencia Escolar: Una Mirada desde la Investigación y los Actores Educativos [School Violence Seminar: Perspectives from Research and Educational Actors]. November 17, 2010, Library of Congress, Valparaíso, Chile.

REFERENCES

Arón, A. M., & Milicic, N. (2000). Climas sociales tóxicos y climas nutritivos para el desarrollo personal en el contexto escolar. [Toxic and nutritious social climates for personal development in the school context]. *Psykhé, 9,* 117–124.

Astor, R. A., Benbenishty, R., & Estrada, J. N. (2009). School violence and theoretically atypical schools: The principal's centrality in orchestrating safe schools. *American Educational Research Journal, 46*(2), 423–461.

Atria, F. (2010). ¿Qué educación es "pública"? [What education is "public"?] In C. Bellei, D. Contreras, & J. P. Valenzuela (Eds.), *Ecos de la revolución pingüina: Avances, debates y silencios en la reforma educacional [Echoes from the penguin revolution: Advances, debates and silences in the educational reform]*, (pp. 153–182). Santiago, Chile: Universidad de Chile–UNICEF.

Avilés, J. M., & Elices, J. A. (2007). *INSEBULL: Instrumentos para la evaluación del bullying [INSEBULL: Instruments for evaluating bullying]*. Madrid: Editorial CEPE.

Bauman, Z. (2005). Education in liquid modernity. *The Review of Education, Pedagogy, and Cultural Studies, 27,* 303–317.

Belfield, C. R., & Levin, H. M. (2002). *Educational privatization: Causes, consequences, and planning implications (Fundamentals of Educational Planning, No 74)*. Paris: UNESCO.

Bellei, C. (2008). The private-public school controversy: The case of Chile. In P. Peterson & R. Chakrabarti (Eds.), *School choice international: Exploring public-private partnerships* (pp. 165–192). Cambridge, MA: MIT Press.

Bryk, A. S., & Schneider, B. (2003). Trust in schools: A core resource for reform. *Educational Leadership, 60*(6), 40–44.

Calderón, A., & Contreras, J. F. (2011). Representaciones sociales del bullying en equipos directivos de establecimientos educacionales de la Quinta Región [Social representations of bullying among school leadership teams in schools in the Fifth Region]. Unpublished undergraduate thesis. Valparaíso: Pontificia Universidad Católica de Valparaíso, School of Psychology.

Castro, L. (2010). *Proyectos de ley sobre violencia escolar: Coincidencias y diferencias* [Law proposals on school violence: Coincidences and differences]. Unpublished document. Valparaíso, Chile: Biblioteca del Congreso Nacional.

Cheung, C., & Ma, K. M. (2011). Coupling social solidarity and social harmony in Hong Kong. *Social Indicators Research, 103*(1), 145–167.

Cohen, J., McCabe, E. M., Michelli, N. M., & Pickeral, T. (2009). School climate: Research, policy, practice, and teacher education. *Teachers College Record, 111*(1), 180–213.

Contreras, D., Bustos, S., & Sepúlveda, P. (2007). *When schools are the ones that choose: The effect of screening in Chile*. Santiago, Chile: Universidad de Chile.

García-Huidobro, J. E. (2007). Desigualdad educativa y segmentación del sistema escolar. Consideraciones a partir del caso chileno [Educational inequality and segmentation of the educational system. Considerations based on the Chilean case]. *Pensamiento Educativo, 40*(1), 65–86.

López, V. (2010, November 17). *La agresión entre escolares: Variables contextuales* [Aggression among students: contextual variables]. Paper presented at the Seminar Violencia Escolar: Una Mirada Desde la Investigación y los Actores Educativos [Seminar on School Violence: A View from Research and Educational Actors]. Valparaíso, Chile.

López, V., Carrasco, C., Ayala, A., Morales, M., López, J., & Karmy, M. (2011). Visibilizando la violencia escolar: Análisis de prácticas discursivas en una escuela municipal de la región de Valparaíso [Individualizing school violence: analysis of discursive practices in a public school in the region of Valparaíso]. *Psykhé, 20*(2), 75–91.

López, V., & Orpinas, P. (2010). Las escalas de agresión y victimización: Validación, prevalencia y características en estudiantes chilenos [The Aggression and Victimization Scales: Validation, prevalence and characteristics in Chilean students]. Manuscript submitted for publication.

Ministerio de Educacion de Chile. (n.d.). *Reglamento tipo de convivencia escolar* [Prototype for the School Convivencia Rules and Procedures Handbook]. Retrieved from http://www.mineduc.cl/biblio/documento/201009131508470. Reglamento%20Final%20(11%209)1-1.pdf

Ministerio de Educación de Chile. (2011a). Tasa de matrícula en escuelas municipales [Student enrollment rate in municipal schools]. Departamento de Estudios y Desarrollo, División de Planificación y Presupuestos, Ministerio de Educación. Retrieved from http://w3app.mineduc.cl/DedPublico/anuarios_estadisticos

Ministerio de Educación de Chile. (2011b). Ficha del establecimiento [School data record]. Sistema de Medición de Calidad de la Educación, Ministerio de Educación. Retrieved from http://www.simce.cl

Montecinos, C., Sisto, V., & Ahumada, L. (2010). The construction of parents and teachers as agents for the improvement of municipal schools in Chile. *Comparative Education, 46*(4), 487–508.

Organisation for Economic Co-operation and Development (OECD). (2004*). Reviews of national policies for education: Chile*. Paris, France: Author.

Orpinas, P., & Frankowski, R. (2001). The aggression scale: A self-report measure of aggressive behaviour for young adolescents. *Journal of Early Adolescence, 21*(1), 51–68.

Orpinas, P., Horne, A., & Staniszewski, D. (2003). School bullying: Changing the problem by changing the school. *School Psychology Review, 21*, 431–444.

Parés, M. (2006). Proyecto de intervención sobre bullying en la escuela [Project for an intervention on bulling in the school]. Retrieved from http://www.belt.es/expertos/HOME2_experto.asp?id=3412

Program for International Student Assessment (PISA). (2006). *Iberoamerica PISA 2006: Regional Report.* Retrieved from http://www.oecd.org/data oecd/37/42/45753892.pdf

Redondo, J. (Coord.), Almonacid, C., Inzunza , J., Mena, P., & de la Fuente, L. (2007). *El derecho a la educación en Chile* [The right to education in Chile]. Buenos Aires: Fundación Laboratorio de Políticas Públicas. E-Book. (Libros FLAPE; 8). Retrieved from http://www.foro-latino.org/flape/producciones/co leccion_Flape/08Chile_Derecho.pdf

Rodríguez, J. I. (2010). Incidencia de la infraestructura, el clima de aula y el sistema de organización en las conductas de intimidación y victimización de alumnos de 7°, 8° y 1° medio de la Región de Valparaíso [Incidence of the infrastructure, classroom environment and the system of organization on intimidation and victimization behaviors of 7th, 8th and 1st secondary (grades) in the Valparaiso Region]. Unpublished undergraduate thesis. Valparaíso: Pontificia Universidad Católica de Valparaíso, School of Psychology.

Roth, W. M. (2000). Learning environments research, lifeworld analysis, and solidarity in practice. *Learning Environments Research, 2,* 225–247.

Schneider, M., Elacqua, G., & Buckley, J. (2006). School choice in Chile: Is it class or the classroom? *Journal of Policy Analysis and Management, 25*(3), 577–601.

Sistema de Medición de Calidad de la Educación. (2009). *Informes de resultados para docentes y directivos SIMCE 2009* [Report of results for teachers and administrators SIMCE 2009]. Retrieved from http://www.simce.cl/index. php?id=241&no_cache=1

Torche, F. (2005). Privatization reform and inequality of educational opportunity: The case of Chile. *Sociology of Education, 78*(4), 316–343.

Toro, A. (2010, August 19). Interview on school bullying in Valparaíso, Chile. Valparaíso: Radio Valparaíso.

Valenzuela, J. (2008). *Segregación en el sistema escolar chileno: En la búsqueda de una educación de calidad en un contexto de extrema desigualdad* [*Segregation in the Chilean educational system: In search for quality education in the context of extreme inequality*]. Santiago, Chile: Universidad de Chile.

2

Devalued Solidarity

A Problem of Education and Identity

José Luis Ramos

In recent decades, modern societies have been experiencing significant changes due to wider and more frequent contact among individuals and communities with different cultural references. This situation has created many problems in social relationships between groups, as well as in the internal organization of each society. Personal contact between people who migrate and those who are part of the host society has led to the necessity of devising new policies to facilitate appropriate communication in each contact situation. Intercultural education aims to respond to this new need.

Education that seeks to help students from different cultural environments, and above all, to promote mutual understanding and the development of new social relationships, is based on a respectful dialogue. Dialogue based on an understanding of cultural diversity facilitates development of positive social relationships based on respect and solidarity, and the successful formation of new citizens. However, it is necessary to recognize the real and concrete situations that teachers experience in order to evaluate problems and possibilities for cultivating new, positive relationships.

Among the problems to review and investigate are those regarding cultural differences that individuals who come into personal contact experience. Individuals who consider themselves different from others assume that others behave under different cultural codes. However, it appears to me that, in doing so, they insist on addressing only the issue of cultural difference, even though individuals also hold distinct social positions that generate unequal relationships, including those of domination. Therefore, I regard it as important to investigate both references: cultural differences and social inequality (derived from political relationships between different groups). Now, with the intention of providing an example of the interdependence between these two conditions, in this chapter, I discuss the situation experienced by Mixtec indigenous teachers (who live in southern Mexico).

We can recognize social and political inequality at the symbolic and identity levels, wherein individuals not only establish their cultural differences and identities, but also value them differently. For example, the very word *indigenous* implies a negative image of the indigenous people, as opposed to a positive image of the *nonindigenous*, clearly expressing a dispute over the value of these different identifications. In this way, we see how the construction of identities represents a level of social and political conflict. Conflicts are not unique in identifications, but will also be present in cultural distinctions, the different and sometimes opposite senses individuals and groups that come in contact give to the social world. We can acknowledge the difficulty that is implied for intercultural dialogue when different meanings are given to specific aspects, such as the concept of solidarity. In this chapter, I explore specifically differences in how indigenous and nonindigenous teachers view the meaning of solidarity.

INTERCULTURAL EDUCATION IN NATIONAL CONTEXT

Reviewing the intercultural educational literature reveals the existence of a large number of studies whose goal is to propose and recommend multiple learning activities to address the problem of cultural differences,[1] trying to soften the process of cultural integration among students. In contrast, studies and essays are scarce that are relevant to the global context in which predominantly intercultural education systems are located. Thinking in intercultural education is not abundant regarding the impact of these levels of social and political construction of society. Therefore, I think it is important to have a collective text, such as this, which gives us a wider perspective on the phenomenon of intercultural education.

A first major difference among countries is in the very concept of intercultural education that is being developed, as well as in the designation of who should be its recipients. For example, in some cases, this kind of education began to be developed as part of a response to the phenomenon of large migration from so-called Third World countries to First World countries (see, for example, García, 2002). These educational programs are for people moving from Africa, Asia, Latin America, and Eastern Europe to Western Europe and the United States, where they are seeking a way out of the economic and/or political problems in their homelands. That is, education with an intercultural emphasis began to be thought of as serving the immigrant population from other countries.

Mexico has not been indifferent to the presence of literature with such an orientation, essays and writings coming mainly from Spain. But although there are people who have arrived from other places, in different historical moments, and because of very different reasons, they have not been the subject of special education policies of the kind that have happened with the indigenous population. In the 19th century, Chinese and Germans landed in Mexico, and the French, Americans, and Irish who had come earlier remained in the country. During the 20th century, Mennonites, Chinese, Jews, Gypsies, Turks, Lebanese, Japanese, and Spanish arrived as a result of world-wide armed conflicts (World War II and the Spanish Civil War). Subsequently, due to the military dictatorships in South America in the decades of the 1970s and 1980s, as well as civil wars in Central America in the 1980s and 1990s, Argentineans, Chileans, Uruguayans, Bolivians, Paraguayans, Salvadorans, Guatemalans, and Nicaraguans came to Mexico. And recently, retired Americans and Koreans also reached the country. Despite this influx of immigrants and political exiles, at the end of the 1970s, when the Mexican government publicly acknowledged that we are a multicultural country, that concept did not refer to this immigrant population, but rather to the indigenous and Black populations (which the Spaniards had brought from Africa in the 16th century).

Mexican authorities began to build new government offices to design and develop a public policy to deal with this condition of cultural plurality. One of these offices was the General Directorate of Indigenous Education (DGEI), charged with tackling bilingual and bicultural education for indigenous people. Their activities have been framed under the central goal of stressing the need for including in basic school education the language, culture, and identity of indigenous peoples. Textbooks were published in several native languages, bilingual teachers were trained, and schools were opened to implement this educational model. This educational experience will become a basis on which the government will be ushering in the most recent thinking about intercultural education (imported from Spain). Thus, when speaking in most education institutions about intercultural education, in fact most professionals are thinking and acting on indigenous education (bilingual and intercultural) as previously described. This precedent lies in the continued discussion of the kind of nation Mexico wants to become, as the political context that outlines potential projects and education programs for the culturally diverse Mexican population.[2]

Within the discussion of intercultural education, social and political experience forced consideration of the kind of society that is desired without stopping to recognize its historically defined bounds as a nation-state. And the responses that emerge will shape the future of the culturally diverse populations. It is legitimate to imagine pluralistic (multi-ethnic and/or multinational) and not just singular nation-states.

Mexican history, like that of other Latin American countries, demonstrates its aspiration to establish a culturally homogeneous nation from its inception (1821) until the late the 20th century. When New Spain acquired its political independence and began to set up the new Mexican nation, the state directed its role and labor toward the edification of a homogeneous nation, in the face of the existence of cultural diversity[3] as a condition of a modern and developed country. The new Mexican nation assumed from the outset that diversity is a problem, like a liability for national development. This idea was shared by diverse political groups that contended for power throughout the 19th and 20th centuries. No matter whether they were federal or central, conservative or liberal, from left or from right, there were no differences among them on this matter. All of them agreed that indigenous people should be assimilated, incorporated, integrated into the Mexican nation, through schooling as the key to reach this goal. They expected that through education, indigenous people might be able to learn the national language and culture, forgetting their own ethnic language and culture, in order to sustain a project of Hispanicization and acculturation. According to the homogenizing model, education policy, linked with policies in economics, agriculture, and so on,[4] was expected to create a "modern and developed nation."

On the other hand, it is important to recognize that in those historical moments in which there were military confrontations (national and international), the participation of indigenous people was continuous, with the hope of prospering at the end of each conflict. A highlight is their contribution to the 1910 Revolutionary Movement, primarily as Zapatistas. However, when the new policy was outlined in the 1917 constitution, the policy was settled once again under the homogenizing view. So, during several decades, national policies regarding the indigenous population were completely geared toward the integration of a nation through Hispanicization and acculturation. Nevertheless, during the latter part of the 1970s, due to efforts of some leaders of groups and movements (such as organizations of indigenous peoples, farmers, and indigenous teachers) along with some anthropologists, the persistence of the native people finally achieved the open and official recognition by Mexican authorities that Mexico is a multicultural country.[5]

Therefore, Mexico's education policy that responds to cultural diversity focuses on ensuring education for indigenous people, who exclusively represent this diversity. In the context of shaping a nation, Mexico first sought to make it a culturally homogeneous nation, but now admits the possibility of imagining a multicultural nation. This situation immediately places us in a very different position to consider an education policy for immigrants, who are willing and indeed need to integrate themselves into a new nation. Mexico is finally trying to recognize the presence of an internal cultural diversity, setting up at the same time a pluralistic nation with a recognized place for the indigenous population as part of the Mexican nation. Mexicans can stop worrying about an education policy for immigrants, who are willing to become part of a new nation. The challenge is to recognize the presence of an internal cultural diversity and, at the same time, the need to configure a pluralistic nation in which the indigenous population would really have a worthy place as part of the nation. And so the kind of education needed for a plural Mexican society must be understood and placed inside the project of the pluralistic nation.

The social and political configurations that set the view of pedagogy occur in the terrain of interethnic relationships between ethnic individuals and national education policies. The main concern emphasizes school experiences between indigenous people and the national culture. The indigenous student's school life occurs every day in relationship to the national school culture, the curriculum content, the teaching strategies, and the teachers who are responsible for guiding the education process. These educational experiences express the way to live interethnic relationships between the indigenous and nonindigenous (national) population. An important part of these relationships is recognition that the students' own social interactions and identifications determine who is an indigenous student in comparison with who is not.

IDENTITY AS SOCIAL REPRESENTATION

When speaking about culturally diverse students who come in contact within a school environment with the idea of establishing ties of solidarity as a precondition of intercultural education, we immediately realize that we are talking about people who are perceived as different from each other; hence, a first task is to recognize identities that are present. These identities reveal who people think they are, who they think they are not, with whom they think they identify, and from whom they differentiate themselves. To address this issue I will describe the situation of indigenous versus nonindigenous identities, showing as an example the situation of Mixtec indigenous teachers. But first, I will provide some theoretical and conceptual underpinnings about identity.

I propose as a beginning premise that the social identity of subjects is constructed, valued, complex, and historic. What appears at the level of ideas and emotion is cultural in its content. The social identity of individuals and groups is constructed by contrasting social relationships that occur between members of a collective, and others. It is not given in advance, nor is it essential, but people acknowledge that they share identity with someone else by establishing distinctive contrasts with others whom they consider different from themselves. Now, the interesting point about these identifications and distinctions is that they are valued, thus creating negative identities (to be stigmatized) and positive identities (worthy of prestige). So, each cultural element that serves as a sign of identification may have a positive or a negative value. This kind of conditional value reflects and expresses social confrontation existing at the level of identifications, in which one collective assumes a positive identity while claiming to devalue the identity of the other group. We witness a conflictive and evaluative contrast.

On the other hand, in the literature one frequently reads about appreciating identity as multiple, global, or complex, without authors providing more detailed descriptions that would enable readers to operationalize what they mean (Pujadas, 2000; Universidad Autónoma Metropolitana, 1991). I seek to correct this omission by recognizing the complexity of identity as a system of processes, forms, layers, and dimensions. Doing so allows me to conceive of identity as the synthesis of three processes: self-identification, alter-identification, and hetero-identification. The first process is what a person, subject A, places upon him/herself. The second depicts what subject A projects onto the other, subject B. The third process indicates what subject B signals in regard to subject A. This conceptual proposal enables me to address issues that have been neglected in previous work. For example, the majority of studies appreciate self-identification as a synonym for identity without considering the two other processes. An example is Laborador's (2001) study of Peruvian migrants in Spain. As for the second process (alter-identification), only a few studies have addressed it (Montes de Oca, 2005; Turrent & Villaseñor, 2005), but also without acknowledging the first process. The same applies to the third process.

It should be noted that it is also necessary to recognize two ways in which the process of alter-identification occurs. There is a direct way in which subject A points out how he/she perceives subject B. But there is also an indirect way in which subject A identifies as A in relationship to subject B, as completely opposite of B.

In terms of dimensions, the identifications correspond to the multiple social affiliations of people, such as gender, generation, economic activity, professional activity, age, nation, ethnicity, and so forth. I will show an example, only to unpack it, related to the ethno-political dimension of indigenous (and nonindigenous).[6]

Another question is the conceptual definition of identity, which also varies widely in accordance with the different authors who have addressed it. In the extant literature, we find identity defined as a feeling, a concept, an idea, an image or representation that a subject maintains of him/herself. These formulations are useful in understanding this social phenomenon, but somewhat problematic to apply efficiently in research (Pujadas, 2000). In order to address this problem, I took on the task of finding a more operational concept. It is Gilberto Giménez (2002, 2005) with whom I found a way of addressing identity as the very representation a subject has of him/herself. The key is that he is specifically talking about social representations.[7] Giménez pointed toward social representation theory, inaugurated by Serge Moscovici (1979), and later expanded by a group of his French followers (Abric, 2001; Flament, 2001; Jodelet & Guerrero, 2000). In applying this theoretical and conceptual orientation, I was able to deal with two main issues: development of a clear concept of identity and adherence to certain indications whose purpose is to develop an operational research methodology.

Thus, the conceptual definition I propose here is to accept identity as a social representation that subject A develops in contrast to subject B. Social representation is understood as a hierarchical structure of social thought that includes information, values, emotions, and prescriptions, all of which are important features that enable attending to the existence of valued, controversial, and hierarchical identities. And its hierarchical structure (divided into core and peripheral levels) allows me to recognize that all elements of identity do not have equal weight. The core elements are much deeper and correspond to the culture and history of the community, while the peripheral components are more contingent and superficial. Acknowledgment of the two levels of identity leads us to understand the role of the peripheral layer in hiding the deeper and more defining core level of identity. In the particular case of ethno-political identity of indigenous teachers, one will be able to see more clearly the analytical advantage of including these theoretical and conceptual considerations.

There are several functions performed by social representations (identity), among which is facilitating communication between individuals who share a common social representation. This condition facilitates the function of establishing identification between subjects themselves. But, as social representation is valued, the next step is to legitimate represented facts, giving rise to ideological explanations. For example, negative social representations emerge about a given social group, permitting movement toward devalued, stigmatized identities. In this way, what emerges is justification for engaging in degrading actions toward that group, making ideological that which originally was a cultural distinction.

Finally, in addition to clearly establishing the image of those indigenous teachers in contrast to nonindigenous teachers (through their social representation), I can acknowledge identity differences because of cultural content used in the development of social representations. In other words, another level of identification is reached by way of describing oneself and others. And it is at this level where, as we shall see below, bilingual teachers choose solidarity as a social and cultural element that identifies them as such.

THE ETHNO-POLITICAL INDIGENOUS IDENTITY

Confusion frequently occurs when one refers to indigenous as synonymous with a particular ethnic group, without establishing an analytical distinction. That is, when someone reads Nahuatl as a synonym for indigenous, the two being different but closely related social phenomena, it becomes difficult to appreciate them separately.

For this essay, I offer a conceptual distinction: When talking about *Mixtec*, I will be applying ethnic-cultural criteria, that is, I will be referring to a particular ethnic group. But when alluding to *indigenous*, I will be applying Bonfil's (1995) criterion, classifying *Mixtec* as a colonial category, a term that was of general application for the indigenous ethnic population at the time of the Europeans' arrival, and a term that blurs any indigenous group's specific ethnicity. So, when calling someone *indigenous*, we are talking of an individual who belongs to any of the existing ethnic groups (Nahuatl, Maya, Mixtec, and so on), without specifying or recognizing the ethnic group, but rather categorizing individuals as culturally different. Most important, they are people who are being recognized and treated as individuals and communities placed in a disadvantaged and dominated social position. Therefore, as noted above, the mere designation of one's identity as *indigenous* sets up a process of identification of negative value. I propose to call identity (following Bonfil) as ethno-political, to recognize these general cultural distinctions, but under a relationship of political disadvantage or domination.

Now, in regard to the specific case study of the Mixtec indigenous teachers, let's see how frequently this valued identification occurs. Or, perhaps, let's see if this situation has been improving in a way that permits attempting intercultural education. First, I will present the general identification of indigenous and nonindigenous, and some historical references, then move on to recognize the significance of solidarity as a special distinction of identity.

THE CASE OF MIXTEC INDIAN TEACHERS

One of the earliest requirements of the newly established 1978 General Directorate of Indigenous Education (DGEI) was hiring teachers who would operate the new bilingual and bicultural educational program. Among the requested requirements, it was emphasized that they must originate from indigenous communities, in order to permit hiring teachers who speak the language and have knowledge of their indigenous culture. And, in order to solve the problem of their demonstrated low level of education, they would be given a 3-month training course on administrative and education issues. Thus, many educators were hired from many different ethno-linguistic groups in different regions of the country.

The way to enter into teaching for Mixtec bilingual teachers was no exception. When I established contact with them late in the 1990s, they had already worked 20 years in the education program for the indigenous population. My own direct approach with the bilingual teachers who were studying for licensure in indigenous education allowed me to learn that their teaching practice was not designed to meet the objectives of the education program developed 2 decades earlier. Their work was not intended to give value to the language or the indigenous culture and identity; on the contrary, the teachers apparently kept the pre-1978 model of Hispanicization and acculturation of indigenous children.

A variety of legal, material, financial, educational, linguistic, social, and cultural reasons explained the situation I found, and led to my interest in inquiring about the role their ethnic identity and their personal influence was playing. That gave me the chance to formulate a research study. The study was based on the hypothesis that privileged the valorization of identity, that is, the presence of devalued indigenous identity was limiting the application of the indigenous educational program. The education authorities hiring native teachers took for granted that belonging to indigenous communities ensured that the program would operate effectively because they thought the teachers could clearly identify with the project objectives. However, they never considered the possibility that those teachers might adopt a negative identity that would prevent the realization of the bilingual education program.

After designing the project, the first activity was to request support for the study from the Mixtec indigenous teachers. This activity was focused on developing biographical evidence relating to their school careers, where various contacts with nonindigenous people and the identifications that were built from these social experiences could be recognized. Results of analyzing the teachers' testimonies gave evidence that they had been building a refusal of indigenous identity during their lives, as opposed to embracing a positive nonindigenous identity. Their self-identification as indigenous appeared to be a broad negative evaluation, in contrast to the strong positive evaluation of being nonindigenous (Ramos, 2001).

The results clearly confirmed the hypothesis with which I began the research, and which Gutierrez (2001) had proposed in his research. However, in the academic context, there were discordant voices. Research colleagues pointed out that the negative indigenous identity was declining, and we could even speak of a new, revalued positive indigenous identity. Those challenges pushed me to continue the research, trying to either confirm or modify the initial findings. I needed a research strategy that allowed me to discover what teachers were thinking, without relying on whether or not empathy existed between us. The choice was to work with social representations that allowed me to reach the teacher's unconscious social thought.

So, some years later, with this new theoretical and methodological tool (i.e., social representation), I again requested the collaboration of other indigenous teachers who were studying at the same headquarters at the Subsede de la Universidad Pedagógica Nacional (UPN) in Huajuapan, Mexico. There was also a significant change in the conception of the project; it became necessary to count on the hetero-identification process, which is why I included in the new research nonindigenous teachers who were also attending the same regional headquarters. The findings obtained with this second phase of research partially confirmed the earlier findings. While negative valuation of the indigenous remained alongside positive valuation of the nonindigenous, the most important discovery was that the two valuations occurred for both subjects, but on different levels. The indigenous was perceived positively, and the nonindigenous negatively. Thus, the structural hierarchy of social representations would offer me a viable heuristic resource to find an answer to the inconsistent results between my own research and that of my colleagues. It became evident that the positive identification of being indigenous appeared superficial, while the negative evaluation of the indigenous was deeply embedded. Now I will break down this scenario in detail.

Although the theoretical section of most articles about social representation indicates the existence of a hierarchical structure, in the findings section this existence is not clearly spelled out, a sufficient limitation to address. But above all, one must recognize that the picture obtained through a hierarchical structure is indeed completely different from that constructed from a list of identifiers. Therefore, I reasoned that the way to proceed was to compare operational core elements of each social representation with the five most frequent components. In addition, I include the established valuation for each point that was raised.

Let me begin with the identification (social representation) provided by indigenous teachers. I used 20 descriptors offered and valued by the Mixtec teachers. In the case of indigenous social representation, the resultant description portrays the indigenous as boring, creative, intelligent, humble, proud, kind, good, honest, respectful, persistent, responsible, honest, sincere, squat, industrious, lazy, brown, poor, supportive, and simple. And indeed I found important differences when using different strategies. When applying the five most common descriptors, the resulting self-image is more than favorable (four positive aspects for one negative). But when locating the deeper core elements, the identity value is modified significantly, resurfacing the presence of a negative evaluation of the indigenous.

Now, following the same analytical approach, for the hetero-identification that nonindigenous teachers established for the indigenous, the description is also more positive than negative (three positive for every two negative elements). Nonindigenous teachers describe the indigenous as boring, introverted, stubborn, courageous, humble, caring, honest, respectful, strong, dark, hardworking, intelligent, silly, sincere, literate, responsible, dirty, poor, marginalized, and simple.

This strategy leads us to contemplate the presence of a positive indigenous identity, but as we shall see in terms of social representation, it is also a superficial contingent identity (based on peripheral constituents). The result is important not only to clarify the possible dilemma regarding the apparent change in ratings, but most significantly, to show that the positive image is hiding the negative identity, which is stronger and more central because of its link with collective and cultural history.

Now I will show detailed images of the indigenous and the nonindigenous, highlighting the fact that solidarity[8] is regarded as a feature of indigenous identity.

To recognize the identification (representation) that bilingual teachers adopt, I use the 20 descriptors expressed in a hierarchical structural sense. Of the 20, 12 are rated positively and 8 negatively. The result suggests that the identification is tilted slightly toward the positive side. However, the theory of social representation indicates that they form a hierarchical structure. Therefore, the indigenous identification includes four core components (three of them negative); among them is the strongest element of social representation. Meanwhile, the only positive factor refers to recognizing oneself as supportive. We can appreciate an ethno-political indigenous identity that is contradictory, designating individuals that are simple, dark, and poor, and at the same time mutually supportive.

Although I will only refer more broadly to the ethno-political indigenous identity, the study also includes the ethnic-national and the economic-professional dimensions. Thus, for those who are nonindigenous, Mixtec, and teachers, the bilingual teachers will also use the same criterion of solidarity as a core representation, that is, being mutually supportive is a very present element inside the indigenous teachers' culture.[9] Later, I will indicate whether the meaning attached to it is the same for all identifications.

Now I am interested in exploring the social representations of nonindigenous teachers in order to recognize a tendency in the same direction as the bilingual teachers. Regarding the self-identification of the nonindigenous, it will be negative, as it includes four negative and one positive element, reflecting the hetero-identification made by bilingual teachers, in which they also propose a nonindigenous social representation with four negative aspects. This representation is striking and largely negative.[10]

With regard to hetero-self-awareness that nonindigenous teachers project onto indigenous identity, the number of negative elements increases to ten in relation to ten positive, so there is a balance in assessment. The scenario is modified considerably in focusing on the core issues that are largely negative, with four negative and one positive element; the resulting devaluation is greater than the one bilingual teachers had. It is important to notice also the ignorance they have in regard to solidarity as an element of identity when classifying indigenous identity. But, if it is used to establish a positive self-identification of being nonindigenous, with four positive elements and one negative, the image is completely opposite of what appears on the surface. Another difference is that indigenous teachers use the solidarity factor in several of their identifications, but nonindigenous teachers apply it only to peasants and no one else.

In summary, although for indigenous teachers, solidarity (being mutually supportive) is a core component in their identifications, for nonindigenous teachers, this turns out to be an unimportant factor. Interestingly enough, nonindigenous teachers ignore this factor in regard to the indigenous population when they apply it to themselves. This apparently contrary point may be explained by recognizing the meaning solidarity confers in either case.

MEANINGS OF SOLIDARITY IN IDENTITY

In order to understand the practices and social relationships that individuals establish, it is essential to understand the ideas, rules, and values they display with respect to the type and form of these practices and relationships. That premise allows me to investigate ideas that individuals and groups profess about solidarity. Diverse, even opposite, ideas result in environments, such as multicultural schools, where people bring different cultural references.

In the case I have been discussing, these cultural differences are present in the identifications that indigenous and nonindigenous teachers establish. Moreover, there is not only a different meaning for solidarity between these two types of teachers, but for bilingual teachers, it is an important identity distinction. To assume oneself as a Mixtec native means the conscious acceptance as a member of a solidarity community. While nonindigenous teachers also take up this concept to identify themselves, at the same time they give it a different meaning from the one the indigenous teachers give.

I indicated earlier that indigenous self-identification (by bilingual teachers) offers a mixed picture, with a tendency toward a negative identity because it includes three negative core components and only one positive—solidarity, an element that is also stressed due to its significance. On the one hand, the kindness and sincerity that indigenous teachers can offer is supported by their sense of solidarity.[11] The work involves not only an economic or processing activity, but most important, work in solidarity to generate a common good.

This positive component is also found in the Mixtec ethnic identification, which the bilingual teachers elaborate. It shows a generally positive identification (14 positive descriptors for 6 negative), which includes three core positive elements and one negative. Mixtec assume themselves as supportive, hardworking, and clever. Mixtec ethical traits of kindness and respect are based on solidarity.[12]

On the other hand, bilingual teachers in their professional identity (teaching) include the category of solidarity, along with being hardworking and responsible. Core elements are positive (three positive per one negative) of a generally positive social representation (12 positive and 8 negative items). The indigenous teacher is assumed to be a reflective, sociable, intelligent practitioner because of his/her profile of mutual support. Part of his/her ethical life meaning is based on displaying acts of solidarity toward others, that is, the common good is the basis for social life.

Now I draw attention to the meaning given to solidarity in the alter-identification that bilingual teachers have for nonindigenous teachers. It is noteworthy that indigenous teachers have developed a deep negative global picture of nonindigenous teachers (14 negative and 6 positive items); however, this negative picture contrasts with their assessment of core issues (4 positive and 2 negative elements). That is, they superficially perceive the nonindigenous teachers negatively, but at a deeper level, they identify them positively, as part of that picture, jointly recognizing their character of mutual support.

However, the meaning given to solidarity in nonindigenous teachers is different, even opposite, as pointed out the self-identification of a bilingual Mixtec teacher. While acknowledging the intelligence and tenacity of nonindigenous teachers through solidarity, they also see them as capable of enacting solidarity hypocritically and as being liars, that is, showing a false solidarity that is maintained by arrogant people. Furthermore, this solidarity is stamped with a political exercise of power that is not for the common good.

In turn, the nonindigenous teachers also offer their own representations. In their alter-identification of the indigenous (of the bilingual teachers), they perceive them globally with a contradictory identity (with ten positive and ten negative elements), although deep inside, the negative aspects (four) override the positive (one). The interesting thing is that they do not include solidarity in the core, locating it on the periphery of social representation. That is, they look at the indigenous as supportive, but with a simple kind of solidarity, of less importance.

In contrast, nonindigenous teachers, in their self-identification (of being nonindigenous), include solidarity as a core and positive element (along with being White and bold), with a greater presence than the negative components (proud and racist). They provide a slightly positive global representation (11 positive and 9 negative). Nonindigenous teachers perceived themselves as people with a tenacious solidarity, thanks to intelligence and honesty, which makes them proud, even though they are somehow introverted. As for their identification of Mixtec and teacher, for the nonindigenous teacher, solidarity is a peripheral element, having less value.

To summarize, we see the different meanings of solidarity due to cultural differences and sociopolitical positions occupied by people when they come into contact. We can even say, as in the example of Mixtec teachers, that solidarity may be a central element of their identity, but with a completely different significance. When recognizing this fact (thanks to the social sciences), possibilities are opened for having more accurate depictions of what happens in multicultural environments. That leads us to anticipate social and communication problems to be faced when designing strategies and activities that are oriented toward building respectful intercultural education and dialogue.

REFLECTIONS

As educators, we are constantly concerned about realizing our ideals regarding what we should be doing to promote the coexistence of pedagogical actors who bring different cultural references, intercultural education being an example intending to address multicultural school settings. However, we usually do not start by recognizing the real situation these actors live, a fact that results in designing again and again education programs that do not respond adequately to particular problems. It is therefore necessary to diagnose, learn about, and assess the school environment to identify key points that should be addressed. As an example, cultural differences and power relationships exist between people and communities within an education institution. And they serve as a framework within the sociohistorical context, for developing a shared sense of solidarity that will provide a basis for a desired respectful coexistence between different individuals.

The example given throughout this essay shows that the greatest difficulties can be understood in order to arrive at a respectful dialogue, as indigenous and nonindigenous teachers give strongly opposing meanings to solidarity. For the former, solidarity is an important factor within their culture and ethnic identity; for the later, it does not have the same relevance. Although both apply it as central to identifying indigenous/nonindigenous, how it is stressed radically changes its very meaning. Thus, solidarity for bilingual teachers is a condition and expression of the common good, but for nonindigenous teachers, the term indicates tenacity and pride. These are opposite meanings that hinder dialogue because they are not understood in the same way.

The continuing history of discrimination against the indigenous population makes education work difficult, and the significant bridge of solidarity cannot be directly and immediately addressed. However, it is easier to address other cultural aspects that can be shared in shorter periods, such as beginning pedagogy with the recognized trust that nonindigenous people place upon the indigenous, and on the industriousness that indigenous people recognize in the nonindigenous. The dyad of work–responsibility might be a starting point. A greater effort in educational policies in Mexico is needed and must not be forgotten in order to amply attend to the nonindigenous (national) population, because as we saw, continuing to devalue the indigenous delays progress toward an appropriate intercultural education.

NOTES

1. For example, by dividing the class into multiple groups, playing games, giving personalized attention, and so on (Alcudia, et al., 2002), a point that has not been adequately explored or promoted within schools. In addition, there are authors who propose perceiving cultural difference not as a problem, but rather as an advantage, but this, too, has not been not sufficiently explored or promoted within the schools. See *Inclusión y Diversidad* (IEEPO, 2003).

2. Even though intercultural education is conceived as promoting respect and equity in relationships between cultures in the education environment, when speaking of the foreign and national populations, significant weight leans toward the indigenous population. Although an important change exists with the creation of the General Coordination of Intercultural and Bilingual Education, intercultural education is promoted at a baccalaureate level and above, universities being an example (CGEIB, 2008).

3. I emphasize that the diversity referred only to native population.

4. There were miscegenation policies. The nation's doors were opened to admit White Europeans, in order to mingle with the indigenous population, thus raising the entrepreneurial spirit of the new emerging inhabitants. But during certain periods of the 19th century, there were also some ethnocide and genocide practices, mainly with indigenous groups in northern Mexico (Ramos et al., 1984).

5. Recognition is not sufficient to solve the economic, social, and political problems of the indigenous population. Context for understanding this is, in part, the reason for the Zapatistas uprising in early 1994.

6. In the research project, I work with three dimensions, including two contrasting identifications: a) ethno-politics: indigenous/non-Indian, b) ethnic-national: Mixtec/Mexican; and c) economic-professional: farmer/teacher.

7. This concept is clearly different from that of collective representations (Durkheim, 1995) or cultural representations (Mauss, 1971).

8. The Spanish word *sólida* does not translate directly into English. *Supportive* or *mutually supportive* serve as close but not exact translations.

9. With reference to Mexican peasants, this criterion does not appear among the nuclear factors, only between the peripheral components.

10. Also, the nonindigenous teachers consider solidarity among the most common constituents of the other identifications (indigenous, Mixtec, Mexican, teacher, and peasant).

11. The meaning of each aspect is given by its association with other elements, stressing more heavily the nuclear components. Another level of significance corresponds to the social context of individuals who construct representations, stressing their social and political position.

12. In Mixtec indigenous communities (as in other Oaxacan and national ethnics), people work collectively to carry out labor or activities of benefit for the population (roads, health clinics, wells, schools, and so forth). The Mixtec call this kind of activity *tequio*. There is a proper match between the meaning of solidarity and the advertised social practices.

REFERENCES

Abric, J. C. (2001). *Prácticas sociales y representaciones* [Social practices and representations]. México D. F., México: Ediciones Coyoacán.

Alcudia, R., del Carmen, M., Gavilán, P., Gimeno Sacristán, J., Giné, N., López Rodríguez, F., et al. (2002). *Atención a la diversidad* [Attention to diversity]. Barcelona, Spain: Editorial GRAÓ.

Bonfil, G. (1995). El concepto de indio en América: una categoría de la situación colonial; and El indio y la situación colonial: Contexto de la política indigenista en América Latina [The concept of Indian in America: A category of the colonial situation; and The Indian in the colonial situation: Context of Indian policy in Latin America]. In L. O. Güemes (Ed.), *Obras escogidas de Guillermo Bonfil*. México D. F., México: Instituto Nacional de Antropología e Historia & Instituto Nacional Indigenista.

Coordinación General de Educación Intercultural y Bilingüe (CGEIB). (2008). *Líneas de investigación en educación intercultural* [Lines of investigation in intercultural education]. México D.F., México: CGEIB.

Durkheim, E. (1995). *Las formas elementales de la vida religiosa* [The elementary forms of religious life]. México D. F., México: Ediciones Coyoacán.

Flament, C. (2001). *Prácticas sociales y representaciones* [Social practices and representations]. México: Ediciones Coyoacán.

García, F. J. (2002). Inmigración, educación e interculturalidas [Immigration, education, and interculturalism]. In H. Muñoz, A. Brand, F. J. García, & A. Granados (Eds.), *Rumbo a la Interculturalidad en educación*. México D. F., México: Universidad Autónoma Benito Juárez de Oaxaca/Universidad Autónoma Metropolitana Universidad Pedagógica Nacional Oaxaca.

Giménez, G. (2002). Paradigmas de identidad [Paradigms of identity]. In A. C. Amparán (Ed.), *Sociología de la identidad* (pp. 35–62). México D. F., México: Universidad Nacional Autónoma de México/Miguel Ángel Porrúa.

Giménez, G. (2005). *Teoría y análisis de la cultura* [Theory and analysis of culture], Vol. 1. México D. F., México: Consejo Nacional de la Cultura/Instituto Coahuilense de Cultura.

Gutiérrez, N. (2001). *Mitos nacionalistas e identidades étnicas: los intelectuales indígenas y el Estado mexicano* [National myths and ethnic identities: Indigenous intellectuals and the Mexican state]. México D. F., México: Consejo Nacional de la Cultura/Plaza y Valdés.

Instituto Estatal de Educación Pública de Oaxaca. (2003). *Inclusión y diversidad: Discusiones recientes sobre la educación indígena en México* [Inclusion and diversity: Recent discussions about indigenous education in Mexico]. México D. F., México: Author.

Jodelet, D., & Guerrero, A. (2000). *Develando la cultura. Estudios en representaciones sociales* [Uncovering culture: Studies in social representations]. México D. F., México: Universidad Nacional Autónoma de México.

Labrador, J. (2001). *Identidad e inmigración. Un estudio cualitativo con inmigrantes peruanos en Madrid* [Identity and immigration: A qualitative study with Peruvian immigrants in Madrid]. Madrid, Spain: Universidad Pontificia Comillas.

Mauss, M. (1971). *Institución y culto* [Institution and worship]. Barcelona, Spain: Barral Editores.

Montes de Oca, L. B. (2001). *Imaginario identitario en el discurso educativo oficial mexicano. La estereotipia sobre el "otro-indígena"* [Imaginary identity in Mexican official education discourse: The stereotype of the "other indigenous"]. México D. F., México: Escuela Nacional de Antopología e Historia (Tesis de Licenciatura de Etnología).

Moscovici, S. (1979). *El psicoanálisis, su imagen y su público* [Psychoanalysis, its image and its public]. Buenos Aires, Argentina: Huemul.

Pujadas, J. J. (2000). Minorías étnicas y nacionales frente al Estado y la globalización: Reflexiones desde el otro lado del Atlántico [Ethnic minorities in the face of the State and globalization: Reflections from the other side of the Atlantic]. In L. Reina (Ed.), *Los retos de la etnicidad en los Estados-nación del siglo XXI* (pp. 101–121). México D. F., México: Centro de Investigaciones y Estudios Superiores en Antropología Social/Instituto Nacional Indigenista /Miguel Ángel Porrúa.

Ramos, J. L. (2001). La identidad étnica: ¿recurso excluido de un desarrollo sustentable? [Ethnic identity: Excluded resources from a sustainable development?]. In V. Sieglin (Ed.), *Desarrollo sustentable, cultura e identidad* (pp. 213–245). México: Fondo Estatal para la Cultura y las Artes de Nuevo León.

Ramos, J. L., Chávez, J., Escobar, A., Sheridan, C., Tranquilio, R., & Rojas Rabiela, T. (Eds.). (1984). *El indio en la prensa nacional mexicana del siglo XIX: Catálogo de noticias* [The Indian in the national Mexican press of the 19th Century: News catalog], (Tomos I, II y III). México D. F., México: Centro de Investigaciones y Estudios Superiores en Antrolopología Social.

Turrent, J., & Villaseñor, M. C. (2005). *Los niños y los otros. Dos estudios de caso acerca del imaginario y la diferencia* [The children and the others: Two case studies of imagery and difference]. México D. F., México: Escuela Nacional de Antropología e Historia (Tesis de licenciatura en antropología social).

Universidad Autónoma Metropolitana. (1991). Identidad. *Revista Alteridades, 1*(2).

3

Multiculturalism and Education in France and Its Former Colonized States and Territories

Prospects for Intercultural Solidarity Within a Secular Model

Isabelle Aliaga & Martine Dreyfus

After almost 20 years of experience at the IUFM (Teacher Training Institute) of Montpellier[1] as initial and in-service trainers of primary and secondary teachers in French as the first language and Spanish as a foreign language, we would like to consider the position of the French education system toward multiculturalism by analyzing how language and culture are taught. In particular, first we examine the French model of secular[2] citizenship with its concept of solidarity, which is the fruit of specific historical events. Next, we examine resistance to the heterogeneous and multicultural aspects of society illustrated by the omnipotent role given to the French language and French culture, both in colonial schools and in those of the mother country. We then present results of research conducted in a class of children with migration backgrounds to illustrate the impact of language teaching on children's sense of self and regard for differences. Finally, we characterize the difficulties the French education system has to face today because of its "secular" model in a context of globalization and radicalization of certain cultures. We will argue that the French republican model of solidarity, which has never affirmed different languages and cultures, causes serious fundamental problems today and therefore must be re-examined.

AN EDUCATION SYSTEM THAT REINFORCES A PARTICULAR KIND OF SOLIDARITY

The French education system, more than anything else in the history of the French Republic, has consolidated the foundation of the state and solidarity among its citizens. Solidarity in this sense refers to identification with the French state, regardless of an individual's own cultural or linguistic background. Below, we examine how this system was constructed historically, and how language policy has undergirded this system.

Historical Elements

After the French Revolution of 1789, during the second year of the period called the Convention (1793), a founding text was voted for a compulsory, secular education, provided by the state and free of religious teaching. The new political system thus claimed to train and develop its citizens and to release them from the church[3]; in this way, they would adopt the essence of the Republic indefinitely. Later on, under Napoleon, education reinforced its position as a state monopoly, this being a characteristic of the French system, and it can be said that since the 19th century education has been used as a political device. On June 28, 1833, the law called "Law Guizot" introduced state primary education for the working classes, which meant that from the early date of 1848, two-thirds of the newly recruited soldiers could read, write, and count. The decisive stage in the development of education as a means of reinforcing national solidarity was during the 1880s. Jules Ferry, then minister of Public Instruction, made state primary education free (1881) and then founded compulsory, secular education for all (1882).

These laws were based on the idea that education would generate a diffusion of democratic principles of the French Republic and adherence among the people to these ideas. This ambitious project for the people was always a noble idea; however, it was transmitted in only one language, French. All the regional languages—of Brittany, Auvergne, the French Pays Basque, French Catalonia, and so on—like all the languages of the colonies (Arabic, Kabylian)[4] were considered "*patois*"[5] and finally prohibited because they were not considered the language of progress, of civilization.

Thus, if the French education system actually created a form of true economic and social solidarity by offering free access to schooling to any citizen, it inevitably did so by programming the disappearance of all the individual languages with historical origins.

And thus, both state education and the army, which have been the two most powerful systems to consolidate the French nation-state, are based on a type of solidarity that indicates a major contradiction, which is to be given a free education, an opportunity to climb the social ladder by the Republic, but at the same time citizens are expected to renounce any linguistic or cultural particularity. For 3 centuries, French has been imposed in all schools as the sole language of communication on the pretext that the great ideas of the Enlightenment, in the 18th century, could only be conceived in French.

French Monolingualism

Several theorists have argued for recognition of the contradiction embedded within the schooling policy between French monolingualism and "the language of France exercised in plural ways." This oxymoron is taken as a reference by Renee Balibar, in the introduction to a work entitled *France, Multilingual Country* (Vermes & Boutet, 1987, p. 9). It refers to the fact that, while France has but one official language, its diversity of speakers use French in quite a variety of ways. A few years later, a periodical intended for teachers, *Les Cahiers Pédagogiques,* published an issue whose title was "75 Languages in France, and What About in School?" (Rispail, 2004). In 2010, Hugues Lagrange, a sociologist at the National Center for Scientific Research, which is one of the main research institutions in the country, published a very controversial piece of work called *The Denial of Cultures* (Lagrange, 2010).

These few titles, selected among many publications on this topic, perfectly illustrate the specificity and paradox of France, since it is "the only nation in the world whose legislation has imposed (since 1794) the exclusive use of the national language in all public and private acts" (Balibar, in Vermes & Boutet, 1987, p. 9). At the same time, many languages and cultures are in contact with each other on French territory: local regional languages or "native" languages (Alsatian; Basque; Breton; Catalan; Corsican; Creole; Occitan [the former language of the southern half of France]; the language of the Moselle region; of Picardy; and languages of migrants [languages without a definite geographical delimitation] originating from territories near or far, that is, Arabic, Berber, Armenian, Chinese, Spanish, Italian, Riffin,[6] Romance languages, Peul, Vietnamese, and Wolof).

This linguistic policy resulted in preventing regional and immigration languages from being transmitted and from spreading throughout French society. According to 1999 census data that are quoted by the website of the Délégation générale à la langue française et aux langues de France (2011a), 26% of the adults living in France had regularly used a language other than French in their childhood: Alsatian (660,000 people), different southern languages (610,000), northern languages (580,000), and Breton (290,000); and each of these languages had been spoken occasionally by at least the same number of people.

However, the "languages of France," according to the official terminology, are hardly any longer transmitted through the family. They are particularly dependent today on being taught in schools or used in artistic and cultural fields (Délégation générale à la langue française et aux langues de France, 2011b). They are defined, in the current legislation, as languages that are traditionally spoken by French citizens on Republican territory, but which are not the official language of any state. According to this criterion, more than 75 different languages are spoken today. In metropolitan France, they are Romance languages, German, Celtic, and Basque languages. In the overseas territories, they are Creole, Amerindian, Polynesian, Bantu (from Mayotte), or Melanesian (from New Caledonia) languages. The number of speakers of each of these languages varies considerably: Arabic numbers 3 to 4 million speakers in France, *neku* or *arhâ* just a few dozen. Between the two, Berber and various Creole languages are spoken by nearly 2 million French people.

During the last 2 decades, the linguistic policy of France has gradually made way for "different" languages: Since 2001, the "High Council for the French Language"—later the "General Board for the French Language" (1984)—has changed its name to "General Commission for the French Language and Other Languages of France." But there is still an ambiguity as to the aims of this organization, which at the same time seeks to promote the use of French as a means of international communication and to show consideration for the different languages in France by developing plurilingualism: "The primacy of French on the national territory *contributes to the effort of social cohesion as well as to the promotion of cultural diversity in Europe and all over the world*" (emphasis added; Délégation générale à la langue française et aux langues de France, 2011a).

AN IDEOLOGY OPPOSED TO MULTICULTURALISM

Lack of solidarity among multiple cultures goes beyond the issue of the colonial linguistic politics of France. Moreover, the construction of values and principles of our society during its history make clear the reasons that prevent a simple relationship to human diversity in our country today. Below, we examine the situation in France today, then in the former colonized states and territories.

Metropolitan France

In spite of these new attempts at acknowledging different languages, and even if France has always been a country that has welcomed immigrants, at least until the 1990s, recognizing that individuals in society are heterogeneous and diverse has not been easy. Consequently, the multicultural model, which is so common in the Anglo-Saxon world, has never been generalized in France, and in a certain way meets great resistance. The concept of multiculturalism generally creates hostility among French intellectuals since it evokes the specter of individual and communitarian isolation that may lead to ghettos. In fact, the issue of cultural and linguistic diversity is often presented as having the potential to result in social breakdown, as being an obstacle to a social pact, a bit like assuming that being different necessarily means having different and irreconcilable values.

That is the reason why the "intercultural" concept has always been preferred to that of "multicultural"; thus, the term *intercultural* appeared in 1975 within the school framework (Abdallah-Pretceille, 1999, pp. 44–52) to be applied subsequently to the rest of society. The first research in this field was that of Louis Porcher and Martine Abdallah-Pretceille. As the latter stresses, the concept of interculturalism is almost exclusively centered on the problems of immigration. Comments about heterogeneity or differences arouse suspicion. Everything happens as if equality necessarily implies a shared identity between individuals. Talking about differences therefore inevitably provokes suspicions of racism and questions the Republican pact.

We use the concept of "interculturality," which describes, rather, the creation of dialectical links and contacts between linguistic systems; but at the same time, we prefer to ignore the diversity inherent in any human society as a danger for a social pact. Indeed, French terminology regarding politics as well as scientific research creates unease over this phenomenon. The term *multiculturalism* is avoided, giving way to *interculturalism* or *diversity*. This means that there is real resistance toward accepting pluralism as an essential component of human societies.

From a legal point of view, the French Republican tradition is based on a system of integration drawn from the model of a public sphere that is common to all and isolated from private differences (Semprini, 1997). This is one of the pillars of the above model. Traditionally, citizenship is conceived as an abstract political sphere in which all individuals are absolutely equal. In such a system, all individual differences of religion, language, or culture are thus relegated to an exclusively private sphere. Another pillar of this tradition is that French citizens are expected to follow a kind of "rationality," represented by the state, with its laws and bureaucratic norms. The immigrant is therefore "integrated" into the nation, provided he/she agrees to keep the public and the private spheres separate and submits to the laws and official norms of the country. In the French model, all differences are eliminated from the public sphere; they are relegated to the private in a certain way. It is a question of a social contract in which we are all equal but do not have the right to express individual differences publicly. This is what our society calls solidarity. Homogeneity is the standard, as opposed to heterogeneity.

We should wonder why this particular French model could have thrived in the past, in a rural France as it was at the end of the 19th century. The reason was probably that this system offered the working classes real social promotion, thanks to schooling; consequently, it has filled its role until recently. Farm workers stopped speaking Occitan or Breton in exchange for a free, compulsory state education carried out in the French language, which allowed their children to go to school and get some qualifications. This was made possible by the arrival of the railway in remote villages. Thus, the model was generalized, leading to the idea that a generation of agricultural workers would produce a generation of railway or post office civil servants, then schoolmasters, then teachers, and finally doctors; it was the famous social ladder, so favored by the Third Republic at the end of the 19th century with regard to its educational model. In this system there resided what could be regarded as a form of social solidarity.

The Former Colonized States and Territories

Most migrants come from old French colonies (in North and West Africa, and Asia). They bring with them to France their communities, their cultures, their languages, their patterns of language use, and a multilingualism made of French and vernacular languages. Studies of languages used in the family show that migrants stop speaking their languages at the end of three generations. Similarly, some of the first migrants who came to the colonial cities and afterward to France stop speaking their mother tongues or native languages in exchange for a state education in the French language. The Republican model was exported to the colonies, particularly to Central Africa, at the expense of multi- or "pluri-" cultural communities and multilingual ones.

French colonial policy was heavily influenced by the concept of "assimilation" and the colonial administrators seemed convinced of the universal and "civilizing" impact of French culture. At that time, there was a very influential stream of thought in France that developed the idea that "French peace" would aim at transcending the contradiction between "colonization" and "democracy" by transforming "subjects" into "citizens" who shared metropolitan values (cf. Coquery-Vidrovitch & Moniot, 1974). The institution of French as the language of universal civilization among colonized peoples was the extension of the political, cultural, and linguistic power of France. The institution of French as the official language in the colonies was carried out by imposing French as the language of instruction in primary school. The French authorities put a whole set of teaching devices in place to teach the children in the colonized states to read and write the ·French language, to the detriment of their national African languages (such as Arab, Berber, Diola, Haoussa, Mandingue, Wolof, and Fulani). School, the place where the French language could be taught and spread in all overseas French territories, ensured and guaranteed the standardization of the language across the colonies.

This policy was implemented by means of the education system and the diffusion of the French language, the choice of different types of schools and their location, along with the objectives and the contents of the curriculum. At the same time, many of the first colonizers were interested in local languages and cultures, thus developing the concept of "multiculturalism" à la française, applied to the colonized territories. A person who played an important part in the institution of the French language in the colonies was Georges Hardy. As the editor of the teachers' bulletin in French West Africa, he elaborated specific teaching methods to be used in teaching French to the native population. In 1913, Hardy set out the ways and the conditions in which schooling could promote assimilation and acculturation to the values of the French Republic while taking care to select: "those whose family has always honorably supported our task of spreading civilization" (cited in Leon, 1991, p. 21).

He took the pupils' source languages into account and did not underestimate their cultural importance, without giving them a precise role and status in the curriculum. However, he advocated their transcription into the Latin alphabet. The interest shown in the languages and cultures of the colonies was generally guided by the concern for a rudimentary knowledge of the way of life in those countries in order to understand the societies and hence develop the colonies better. The action of Andrew Davesne, inspector of primary school education in French West Africa from 1931 to 1936, completed the organization of schooling and teaching in the colonies. Davesne is particularly well known as the author of the series of textbooks called Mamadou and Bineta. They were modeled on the books used in primary schools to teach reading and writing in France at the time; this method of teaching French was reprinted right up to the year 1993. In a way, the series established the policy of cultural assimilation, the choice of French as the sole language used in teaching, and at the same time made an attempt, albeit succinct, to adapt to the cultures of the countries where French was taught. The characters in the textbooks and the topics of the reading lessons corresponded to real life in Africa, and often conveyed clichés or stereotypes originating from a foreign point of view.

At the time of their independence (1960–1965), the states of French-speaking Africa, even those that appeared to be the most "revolutionary and Marxist," massively chose French as their official language, for various reasons. The language of colonization was preserved because of the will to provide mass education in a short time and to achieve quick development. Another reason was related to the possible political risks that new linguistic choices would have entailed. All political, economic, educational, and scientific infrastructure inherited from colonization functioned in French; none of the African languages was able to take on the same role, because hardly any of them were either standardized or widely used (see in particular Chaudenson, 1998, 2000).

This education system is contradictory and ambivalent on more than one score. A certain number of ambivalences can still be found in the education system and schools in West Africa nowadays. First, there is political and social ambivalence: From the beginning, there was opposition to compulsory schooling from some traditional ruling classes, who were also opposed to colonial power and wary of its cultural and social consequences. Thus, the ruling classes, the influential politicians, and members of the clergy were generally hostile toward the French system and, in spite of the regulations of the colonial authorities, often sent other people's children, instead of their own, to school. To some extent, the colonial education system contributed to an upheaval of the traditional social classes by destroying the solidarity that already existed, particularly in societies based on a caste system. The local intermediaries, administrative assistants, and soldiers needed by the colonial authorities were often recruited among the lower classes. They gradually understood that the colonial education system gave them access to a new social status.

Second, there is ambivalence and contradictions with respect to the aims of the colonial education system, which targeted both children and adults in the villages (the teaching of oral French, primarily as a means of communication) and which would allow some of them (a minority) to continue on to high school. Very quickly, for various reasons, the gap widened (among other reasons, lack of teachers, lack of training, and lack of money) and the colonial system did not succeed in making the majority of the population literate.

Finally, there is methodological and pedagogical ambivalence: The first methods used in West Africa copied either a method used in France to teach French, which was cognitively and culturally unsuitable, or a method inspired by foreign language teaching (the "direct method" at the beginning of the 20th century) based on oral work, with a delay between the spoken and the written word. This methodology was hardly adapted to teaching all school subjects, however. African languages, present at the beginning of colonial teaching in an experiment carried out by Jean Dart at an experimental school in Saint-Louis (Senegal), were later abandoned. After World War II and during the early years of African independence, the debate concerning the right to teach native languages was revived with the UNESCO charter.

In most of the former French colonies in West Africa, French has the status of being the official language and the main language of instruction. Some countries, like Mali, have developed bilingual teaching programs in African languages and French in primary school. But in university and in secondary education, the language of instruction remains French. The choice of national languages as the languages of instruction, along with French, is potentially a source of tension because most communities wish to see their own language achieve this status, and many of them refuse the vehicular language—often the language of social relations or "lingua franca"—as the language of instruction for their children, sometimes preferring a language that they consider "neutral," such as French or English. In some countries, however, a consensus is being reached about a vehicular language capable of expressing the idea of the nation (which seems to be the case of Wolof in Senegal, although we must be very wary of this interpretation concerning linguistic attitudes and representations).

RESEARCH INTO LANGUAGE INSTRUCTION AND IMMIGRANT CHILDREN

If we come back to teaching practices in metropolitan France, it is clear that difficulties in working with culture and language are not uncommon during the training of teachers. Our professional workplace, the IUFM of Montpellier (Teacher Training Institute), is located in an area where roughly a quarter of the population is of Spanish origin, either because the parents or the grandparents emigrated due to the civil war or because of the economic situation in Spain during the 1950s and 1960s. This Spanish emigration, after Italian and Polish emigration at the beginning of the 20th century, is now fully installed into French society. People emigrating from Africa face some segregation and discrimination.

Despite the significant proportion of Spanish immigrants, less than 10% of classes at school use Spanish, compared with 90% that use English. In fact, teachers and parents seem to agree that you need to have a command of one language—i.e., French, to live in France—and of another—i.e., English, to travel—and that is all that matters. African languages are almost nonexistent in school.

In the course of our professional experience, in order to depart from monolingualism or French/English bilingualism, we try to investigate how communicative competence prevails over linguistic and cultural variations, asking to what extent communicative competence is innate in any child, and in what way the presence of multiculturalism in education is a much more important and relevant factor in cognitive development than monoculturalism or monolingualism, whatever the child's language. We supposed that this competence could be revealed through relevant "stimuli," in the term of Noam Chomsky (Piatelli-Palmarini, 1979). Then again, we know that all languages have constants—for instance, the type of vocabulary acquired by all children who are starting to talk (Kern, 2005). These elements have led us to postulate that human beings possess latent isomorphic structures for the learning of languages; hence, we set up a collaborative teacher training project between the IUFM of Montpellier and the Autonomous University of Barcelona. The project consisted of introducing two foreign languages, namely Spanish and Catalan, to the pupils at a nursery school in an immigrant area of West Montpellier where clashes occur among the population. The children, between 3 and 6 years old, were mostly from African immigrant groups. Our initial idea was that the linguistic capacities of these early learners within the framework of the global communicative approach would improve their acquisition of French.

From a psycholinguistic point of view, children younger than 6 years old have a greater linguistic and cultural adaptability than older children. Moreover, the idea that early bilingualism is very beneficial cognitively has been widely developed and "current knowledge on the regression of learning capacities . . . and on the advantages of early bilingualism . . . indicate that starting at an early age, i.e., at the first stage of infancy, is essential" (Petit, 2001, p. 81). In addition, if elements such as 1) becoming aware of standards and norms in a language, 2) mapping between objects and words, and 3) acquiring better articulation and interacting more socially produce a lexical explosion observed in 2-year-olds (Kern, 2005, p. 289), we could suppose that awareness of categories like the native tongue and foreign languages, building mental semantic networks, and social interaction would prepare these children for better mastery of plurilingualism and multiculturalism later on. We wondered: Might plurilingual instruction lay the foundation for the development of social solidarity in the context of cultural and language diversity?

A Plurilingual School Context

Some bilingual Erasmus students from the Autonomous University of Barcelona thus proposed a weekly lesson in Spanish or in Catalan using language-integrated activities. The activities were guided, filmed, and analyzed by a group of teacher trainers from both institutions. These oral activities included games, total physical response, and particularly storytelling. They associated various channels of communication and various subjects such as foreign languages, French, art, and design or drama. An interactive whiteboard was frequently used in order to support language with pictures. This was essential for children who could not yet write. The project made use of three Romance languages that are culturally and geographically present in the school's vicinity: French, Catalan, and Spanish. While launching the project, we came up against opposition from the establishment, which was to be expected, taking into account the regulations that govern the use of French in school and owing to the fact that our choice of languages did not include English.

Two successive evaluations were carried out between 2004 and 2007. Our objective was to compare the responses of pupils in the Test Group (TG) that was monolingual with those of the Plurilingual Group (PG), examining whether the pupils who had benefited from a multilingual approach (PG) had in any way modified their way of communicating.

Plurilingual Instruction Gets Better Results
Than Monolingual Instruction

For the first evaluation, most of the pupils from the TG—the monolingual group—were obviously disturbed by an activity that was far removed
from the norm—namely, an oral activity in another language. They did not
understand what was expected of them and the majority expressed rejection, lack of concentration, and lack of motivation through verbal and nonverbal signs. The multilingual group, however, welcomed with open arms
the Spanish student who was telling a story in Italian for the evaluation,
while immediately trying to communicate with her. This group easily understood the story in Italian and manifested a real interest in the activity. The
nonverbal signs of their participation, identified on video, were just as obvious as the marks of rejection shown by the children from the first group.
The PG children were very active in trying to understand the story. Looking
back, their understanding of the meaning was much more accurate than that
of the TG; further, a 5-year-old in the PG recognized the language as being
Italian, because it was a language spoken by his mother.

The second evaluation was carried out over the period from 2005 to
2007. The monolingual TG had 9 pupils, and the PG, which was a multilingual class of 12 pupils, had had lessons in Catalan and Spanish during the
year. At the end of the year, after having listened to short poems or songs
in Chinese, Spanish, and Catalan, each individual child was filmed in an
interview on their subjective and cognitive perceptions.

Once again, the pupils from the TG oscillated between indifference and
pronounced hostility. A child from a Berber family (of Northern African origin) identified Chinese as an "Arabic" language, that is to say, one that was
foreign to his culture. Three pupils to whom we suggested speaking Arabic
(the home language) forcefully affirmed that they did not speak any foreign
language. All we could obtain was a simple "hello" in Arabic from a girl
after asking her insistently. The constants for these children were that their
home language was not for them a "language" and probably not a viable,
shameless, or legitimate one. We could quote a long list of constants in the
TG with the repetition of nonverbal signs of:

- lack of attention, concentration, or interactivity
- inactivity
- a lack of comprehension strategies
- hostility toward the activity
- lack of curiosity about another language.

It is fitting to indicate that the hostility of the pupils from immigrant
backgrounds was stronger, because they were aware of not corresponding

to the cultural and linguistic standards of the school. They undoubtedly felt ashamed and vicitimzed by the experience, which they imagined was intended to reveal their differences. We could make the assumption that as the education system does not take the linguistic and cultural differences of these pupils into account, it probably creates a tacit form of prohibition of their difference, the prohibition of diversity. It may appear paradoxical that the system manages to convince them, without doing so explicitly, that they have no right to be what they are: Algerian, or Senegalese, or of any other nationality. Our observations, although limited, indicate serious psychological damage that must have an effect on the acquisition of the language used at school.

On the contrary, the results for the PG appeared to confirm those of the first evaluation. The footage clearly showed a much deeper understanding than for the Test Group, including comprehension strategies on the part of several children who tried to find similarities with French words they knew. None of the 12 was indifferent or inactive. All were able to sing nursery rhymes that they had learned in class in Catalan or Spanish without really being able to distinguish between the two languages. Only one of the 12 pupils was able to distinguish between the two languages, but he had already done 2 years of work in foreign languages with us and was almost 6 years old. Only three pupils of the PG were actually able to identify one or two words as either Catalan or Spanish, and this underdeveloped metalinguistic awareness was probably due to age and lack of maturity.

In regard to the attitudes observed in both groups, the perception of the languages learned in class was predominantly emotional and psychological; in fact, more than sentences or words, the pupils remembered the emotions associated with what they had learned ("Olivia was nice, and took care of animals/the song was nice/the voice in the song sounded like that of Maribel, their Spanish teacher"). As for the children from Algerian, Moroccan, Tunisian, or African families, the contrast with the Test Group was striking. They all readily agreed to talk about their foreign identity, and one of them even claimed that he understood his native language best when he was "over there" (in Africa). What was a taboo for the first group had become a bonus for the second. Consequently, the list of constants for the PG could include:

- nonverbal signs of attention, concentration, and interactivity
- difficulty in identifying and distinguishing between known languages (probably because of their age)
- a strong motivation to participate in the activity
- a rich interpretation of the language
- a definite improvement in global communication
- a strong assertion of mixed identity when it was present.

Valuing Students' Diversity

All things considered, the introduction of new languages into the class appeared to have improved the children's global communication. Their teachers admitted that there had been a definite improvement in French language work. We were not able to evaluate their improvement in French, but indeed, the teachers affirmed that communication, which was often difficult with children from African families, was facilitated by the contact with other languages.

For some teachers who have been involved in these schools in immigrant areas for years, this diversity is part and parcel of classroom practice, in spite of the official linguistic regulations. They make an empiric guess that evidence of solidarity with a pupil's identity is the key to his/her academic achievement. It must be said that teachers who do integrate diversity into their teaching are rare. This short experiment would obviously need further development to merit adequate scientific validity, but it nevertheless shows that in a certain way, without suspecting it, the establishment probably condemns to failure all the children who are taught that their identity is bound to be scorned or hidden in our society.

SOLIDARITY IN QUESTION

The research presented above calls to question our Republican model of equality and solidarity in schools. If we analyze the situation of the present-day immigrant populations in France, we can observe a strong tendency toward cultural isolation of communities and a deep dissension between the latter and French society. We see the beginnings of that dissension with the children who, experiencing monolingual teaching, are learning that they have no right here, in contrast to those who experience plurilingual teaching. No one has forgotten the dreadful, violent protest movements in certain areas of Paris in autumn 2005, which put young residents of the same districts in opposition to the police while they burned as many cars as public or commercial buildings. French public opinion was probably shocked the most by the fact that they burned schools; TV channels all over the world broadcast images of horror. Why?

There is no doubt that the notion of citizenship in France remains abstract and exclusively political; the heavy economic and sociocultural tension that is troubling French society today discredits the Republican model, considering the economic and cultural discrimination against groups such as Northern African immigrants, for example. A contract of alleged equality cannot be imposed on citizens when, every day, these communities are the object of blatant, continual socioeconomic and cultural discrimination. In fact, nowadays, many highly qualified graduates of North African origin trained in France prefer to look for work in countries around the Persian Gulf or in London rather than stay in France, where they know in advance that racial prejudice will delay their chances of employment and the advancement of their careers. The education system plays the cruel part of misleading youngsters by making them dream of a so-called equality, of a better future that will never happen because society has not yet managed to eliminate prejudice toward North African populations who not only bring other languages, but whose ethnic identity is physically visible. They suffer from a social handicap that will not improve as long as mentalities do not change.

The trouble over the Islamic headscarf since 1994 is a clear example of these problems. In 1994, the then Minister of Education banned wearing the headscarf on school premises by putting forward arguments that were clearly political and based on the concept of equality. A memorandum from the ministry at the time stressed that all forms of discrimination, whether sexual, cultural, or religious, were to stop at the school gate,[7] and even if the text did not mention the headscarf, it clearly insisted on the fact that the secular Republic could not allow any attempts at religious conversions. Many girls were thus excluded from school because of this symbol of identity. Indeed, among the immigrant population of North African origin, the social ladder that had functioned so well for the Italians, the Poles, the Spanish, or the Portuguese did not function. The headscarf, and its more radical version, the burka, has always posed two problems as to its legality. On the one hand, it is criticized because the idea of a woman hiding her identity is by nature incompatible with the rights of all citizens within the framework of human rights and the rights of the country. On the other hand, it is claimed that girls or women who wear it can be manipulated by foreign Islamist networks. Schoolgirls might have used the headscarf as a claim to identity in a country where identity must be private; but since then, in a global context of tension between the Arab world and the Western world, this kind of symbol of identity is perceived very negatively in France today from an emotional point of view. This is so true that current French laws against wearing the burka have led France to be seriously threatened by the Al-Qaeda terrorist movement.

We are obviously going through a period of multicultural conflict in which we have not been able to create solidarity among languages and cultures, solidarity that would give all people a place and that would prevent the quest for religious radical options, going beyond language and culture.

CONCLUSION

We have seen how French society, both at home and in its colonial territories, has created a form of solidarity that has never taken into account different languages and cultures. This fact causes serious fundamental problems today.

Monolingualism, with its deep historical and political roots, such as the heritage of the French Revolution or of the Third Republic, cannot be effective in a globalized world. As shown in our research, when children from immigrant backgrounds do not study any language other than French at an early age, as is almost always the case in our country, they gradually perceive that their own identity is unwelcome, perhaps even clandestine and taboo. This may explain their violence, including violence that they show toward the education system years later when they are teenagers. However, this violence is initiated not by them but by a social model that rejects them as soon as they are born, by refusing to acknowledge them and by requiring them to be different from what they are. This cannot be a viable form of solidarity in education today.

If, by working in a much more pragmatic way, it is possible to develop a didactics of modern languages based on multiculturalism, it is undoubtedly the most important challenge that we have to face: that of letting children from minorities feel that their difference is legitimate and of helping them to succeed in life by means of their education.

There may not be an ideal age to start learning languages, as has been believed, but perhaps children *should* learn how complex the world is at an early age in order to live with that complexity later on. Children must understand right from the start the indivisibility of the paradox "l'un et de ce qui est multiple"[8] (Morin, 2005, p. 21). If it were to be developed in education, it would really be possible to create "a new transnational citizenship" (Zarate, 2003, pp. 95–96). If the language of universality is neither French, nor any other language, if the dream of universal linguistic homogeneity has not been achieved, there may be foundations of communication common to all human beings that could prepare the way for a transnational citizenship, a new social contract. These principles would consider meaning rather than form, and would be based on common values independent of the 6,000 languages and cultures that exist in the world. Probably language is not the only way to a greater solidarity among peoples. At school, other possibilities that are more universal and aesthetic can be explored, such as music and songs, for example. Actually, here in Montpellier, we are working with partners from nine countries on a European Comenius Program EMP (European Music Portfolio) to generate research and tools for primary schools (see European Music Portfolio, 2009–2011). We hope that this approach will provide a stepping-stone so that younger generations will later on feel closer to those who have another language or another culture.

NOTES

1. University town of approximately 300,000 inhabitants, situated in the south of France between Marseilles and Toulouse, 160 kilometers from the Spanish frontier.

2. The French education system is characterized by the separation of political power and religious power; hence, the term *secular.*

3. One example is the mathematician Marie Jean Antoine Nicolas de Caritat, Marquis of Condorcet, who instituted a lifelong learning movement for all citizens.

4. Algeria was annexed in 1848.

5. *Patois* is a pejorative word for a dialect.

6. The languages of the Moroccan Rif region.

7. The laws on secularism were voted in France from 1905.

8. The paradox of complex systems whose parts not only belong to a whole, but whose whole also appears in the parts.

REFERENCES

Abdallah-Pretceille, M. (1999). *L´education* iterculturelle [Intercultural education]. Paris: PUF.

Chaudenson, R. (1998). *Vers une approche panlectale de la variation du français* [Toward variation in French]. Paris: Didier Erudition.

Chaudenson, R. (2000). *Mondialisation: La langue française a-t-elle encore un avenir?* [Globalization: Is there still a future for the French language?]. Paris: Didier Erudition.

Coquery-Vidrovitch, C., & Moniot H. (1974). *L'Afrique Noire de 1800 à nos jours* [Black Africa from 1800 to today]. Paris: PUF Presses Universitaires de France.

Délégation générale à la langue française et aux langues de France. (2011a). *Langues de France* [Lanuages of France]. Retrieved from http://www.dglf.culture.gouv.fr/lgfrance

Délégation Générale à la Langue Française et aux Langues de France. (2011b). *La langue de la République est le français* [The language of the Republic of France]. Retrieved from http:// www.dglf.culture.gouv.fr/

European Music Portfolio. (2009–2011). *Do you speak . . . music?* Retrieved from http://www.emportfolio.eu/emp/

Hardy, G. (1913). *Bulletin de l'enseignement du français en A.O.F.* [Bulletin of the teaching of French in A.O.F] Paris: Colin.

Kern, S. (2005). De l'universalité et des spécificités du développement Langagier [Universality and specificity of language development]. In J.-M. de Hombert (Ed.), *Aux origines des langues et du langage* (pp. 270–291). Paris: Editions Fayard.

Lagrange, H. (2010). Le déni des cultures [The denial of cultures]. Paris: Le Seuil.

Léon, A. (1991) *Colonisation, enseignement et éducation: Etude historique et comparative* [Colonization, teaching and education: Historical and comparative study]. Paris: l'Harmattan.

Morin, E. (2005). *Introduction à la pensée complexe* [Introduction to complex thought]. Paris: Seuil.

Petit, J. (2001). *L'immersion, une revolution* [Immersion, a revolution]. Colmar: Jérôme Do Bentzinger Editeur.

Piatelli-Palmarini, M. (1979). *Théories du langage, théories de l'apprentissage: le débat entre Jean Piaget et Noam Chomsky* [Theories of language, theories of learning: the debate between Jean Piaget and Noam Chomsky]. Paris: Seuil.

Rispail, M. (2004). 75 langues en France et à l'école? [75 languages of France and at school?]. *Les Cahiers Pédagogiques N° 423*, 23.

Semprini, A. (1997). *Le multiculturalisme* [Multiculturalism]. Paris: PUF.

Vermes G., & Boutet, J. (1987). *France, pays multilingue [France, a multilingual country]*. Paris: Logiques sociales, L'Harmattan.

Zarate, G. (2003). Identité et plurilinguisme: Conditions préalables à la reconnaissance des compétences interculturelles [Identity and multilingualism: Prerequisites for recognition of intercultural competences]. In M. Byram, (Ed.), *La compétence interculturelle* (pp. 89–123). Strasbourg: Editions du Conseil de l'Europe.

4

Spanish Students Abroad

An Intercultural Education

Maria Antonia Casanova

Throughout the different stages of the history of Spain, at different times there have been significant migrations of its citizens to various countries and continents. In the last century, the exile of many Spaniards, voluntarily or involuntarily, after the civil war (1936–1939) is noteworthy. Ideological reasons led exiles particularly to the south of France and to Latin American countries that benefited from their arrival. Mexico, for example, afforded a welcome to Spanish intellectuals who, later on, responded generously with their intellectual and educative contributions, and educational work in that country. These intellectuals founded the well-known "Colegio de España," which at present is a pioneer and reference center regarding academic publications and research findings.

At a later time, which leads to the focus of this chapter, during the 1960s and 1970s, and almost always for economic reasons, there was another great migration from Spain to other European countries, mainly to France, Holland, Belgium, Germany, the United Kingdom, Italy, and Switzerland. During that time, the Spanish population wanted to work to gain economic resources, then, in the near future, return to their place of origin. In those early days, neither the migrants nor the government of Spain planned for needs or guarantees beyond those related to the workplace. However, over the years, many of these migrants settled in the country of destination and formed their families there, definitively making a life in their new homeland. This new reality for thousands of Spanish brought about the need to institute a variety of plans for people, not just plans that are work-related. That which is social in its broadest sense, such as, infrastructure for associations and cultural meetings, became part of their demands. Governments that continued after the initial decades of emigration gradually took charge of attending to needs as they arose. Education, in particular, was one of the high-priority areas to be covered promptly.

The children of the first emigrants were incorporated, of course, into the education system of the country in which they lived. Having been born there, the language was not an obstacle for them because they were (at least) bilingual, naturally. They spoke Spanish at home within the family, and German, French, Dutch, English, and so forth, in the street and at school. In this reality, parents' concern was that their children risked losing their native language as well as knowledge of the culture of their ancestors. From this concern arose the first classes, attended by Spanish teachers dedicated to the systematic teaching of the Spanish language and culture, to complement the education system of each host country.

Years have passed and, at present, students who attend the different modalities of the Spanish education system in foreign countries are third and fourth generation, fully integrated into their contextual reality. They are not only bilingual, but children of mixed marriages between people of different nationalities (e.g., Spain and other European countries and, indeed, the whole world) handle at least three languages. Moreover, the new students who join today are not from families who migrated for economic reasons; they are children of European Union officials, or professionals of various kinds who move, as citizens of the EU, to work in any of the constituent countries.

INTERCULTURALISM AND SOLIDARITY AS BASIC APPROACHES FOR ACTION

The actions of different Spanish governments responded, according to circumstances, to different needs and social demands, as has been noted. The model of society in which we live has changed very rapidly in the last 20 years, and if any common features characterize the universal context (at least within the developed countries), we should highlight progress in the field of knowledge, information, and technology. This results in an overall experience of permanent communication between people of different nationalities, languages, cultures, beliefs, and so on, which can be realized either in person or virtually. In every country, every day, very different people live, enriching democratic societies in which minorities are respected and considered valuable in all aspects.

Multiculturalism has become a reality, therefore, in almost all developed or developing countries. In some circumstances, this is because some populations move in search of better opportunities in life and, in others, because there is a high mobility both within the European Union and in connection with other distant environments that share similar cultural and economic visions, where women and men move easily due to interests that may be personal, business-related, arts-related, and so forth. In this social environment, the Spanish administration should seriously consider how to manage coexistence in diversity and coexistence of different cultures, and how to address the notion of solidarity, a concept that lies at the heart of numerous actions in various fields, among which we highlight education. As is evident, the reality of the Spanish population in foreign countries demanded at all times, but even more now, that solidarity be addressed as a foundation and justification for various actions that were in operation and remain in force.

The concept of solidarity takes on many meanings, depending on its origin—etymology, sociology, and so forth. This chapter assumes a generic definition that understands it as adherence to other causes or obligations assumed voluntarily, in connection with the needs or projects of others. This conceptualization views solidarity as unity among members of a society through a common commitment to a path toward a goal. Solidarity does not affect everyone in the same way, but in joint action each group, person, or institution plays a distinct role. Those who empathize with others voluntarily assume responsibility for sharing the goals of others. For some, solidarity helps them to achieve their own goals, but does not exclude them from their original commitments and ongoing collaborative efforts with others. In short, solidarity responds to the human tendency to band together to achieve common goals, to advance in the quality of life that is intended.

In the present case—the education of Spanish who have migrated—the concept of solidarity is closely linked with that of justice, since education is a universal right of the individual and cannot be left unattended. Almost from the beginning, the Spanish governments attended to the children of migrants to prevent them from losing connection with their language and culture of origin, understanding that this was a commitment of all to achieve, which was a common goal desired by the whole population. In this way, the education that each country of residence afforded to Spanish students was combined with attention outside the regular, binding school schedule that Spain provided to its population living abroad, a situation that continues today. The supplementary offering is not required of the Spanish population, but is voluntary; it is true that the majority go to schools where they use the Spanish language and culture. But in any case, and especially now, with children who represent the third generation, there is a population that is no longer interested in the program, which this chapter will address later.

This combination of systems and cultures makes multiculturalism appear as normal life for the children of immigrants in any of the above countries. Therefore, by association, this system promotes the transformation of the reality of pluralism of all kinds in a multicultural society in which everyone gets to know, respect, and live together in a diversity that appears normal in everyday context. For this, education plays a crucial role if we are to achieve this coexistence of equal opportunity and mutual respect, for which the program of Spanish language and culture and the rest of the offerings, as is discussed below, focus all their work from the perspective of intercultural education when developing any of the various programs and lessons.

In short, the Spanish government assumes solidarity with its emigrants abroad, inviting but not requiring children of emigrants to identify in solidarity with Spanish citizens. We can say that solidarity and intercultural education are reflected as the basis of the approach for the care of Spanish students abroad or the children and grandchildren of the first generation of immigrants, as well as for the education of students from other countries and cultures in the schools and programs that the Spanish system has instantiated in foreign countries.

THE EDUCATIONAL WORK OF SPAIN IN FOREIGN COUNTRIES

To facilitate understanding the main actions—but without going into nuances of little significance to the topic at hand—that the Spanish Ministry of Education undertook in foreign countries, we first list them, then explain the rationale and activities of each with respect to offerings of such institutions and programs. The educational activities outside of Spain include centers of Spanish education (Spanish ownership schools, joint-ownership schools, Spanish private schools, and schools of agreement), associations of Spanish language and culture, Spanish and bilingual sections in foreign schools, and European schools. Table 4.1 compares the education models discussed in this chapter in terms of type, ownership, and teachers.

Centers of Spanish Education Abroad

This designation refers to schools that offer the Spanish education system in foreign countries. These centers cover the first four entries in the table above, i.e., Spanish ownership schools, joint-ownership schools, schools of agreement, and Spanish private schools, the latter not belonging to the Ministry of Education (Inspección de Educación, 2009). In total, at present, there are 45 of these centers: 23 of Spanish ownership, 2 of joint ownership with the countries in which they are located, 14 of agreement, and 6 Spanish private schools. Their characteristics vary in regard to both the culture of each country in which they function as well as the curriculum they teach, based on their ownership. The centers are located in the following countries: Andorra, France, Italy, Portugal, the United Kingdom, Equatorial Guinea, Morocco, Argentina, Brazil, Chile, Colombia, Costa Rica, Domini-

Table 4.1: Comparison of Educational Activities Outside Spain

Type of Institution or Program	Owner and Schools' Operator	Country of Origin of Teachers
Centers (schools) of Spanish ownership	Government of Spain	Spain, and country in which the centers are located
Centers (schools) of mixed ownership	Government of Spain and institution of country in which they are located	Spain, and country in which the centers are located
Spanish private centers (schools)	Spanish private organization	Spain, and country in which the centers are located
Agreement centers (schools)	Private organization of the country in which they are located	Country in which the centers are located
Associations of Spanish language and culture	Government of Spain	Spain
Spanish sections	Government of the country in which they are located	Spain
Bilingual sections	Government of the country in which they are located	Spain, and country in which the sections are located
European schools	Supreme Council of the European Schools (governments of the member states)	Spain, and country in which the schools are located

can Republic, Ecuador, El Salvador, Guatemala, Mexico, and Uruguay. The variety of social realities is a fact in all of them, because people from different cultures are woven into their daily work, which requires educational models that provide solutions to coexistence, solidarity, and interculturalism appropriate to each unique situation. Most of the students are from the countries where the centers are located, although the centers all also serve Spanish students as well as those of other nationalities, multiculturalism and pluralism being a reality present today in every nation in the world. The total number of students served is 24,091, of which 50.98% are women and 49.02% are men.

The *Spanish ownership* schools are dependent for all purposes on the Spanish state, in particular, the Ministry of Education and the Ministry of Foreign Affairs, so that in these schools, the Spanish education system is taught for students from age 3 to 18, which is when they finish high school.

Then these students can access any Spanish university just like the rest of the students studying in Spain. The Spanish teachers are civil servants, as the school depends on the Ministry of Education. Teachers arrive at the external schools through a rigorous selection system, after passing several tests and submitting a professional resume, which is scaled and whose score is added to that achieved in the specific required tests. Each teacher stays in the destination school for 6 years, and during this period is evaluated on two occasions (in the second and fourth years abroad) by the central monitoring service of the Ministry of Education, which reviews his or her work at the school, visits the classroom, and issues a favorable or unfavorable report on the person's performance. In the case of an unfavorable report, the teacher returns to Spain, to his or her original post.

These schools provide, as was pointed out above, the Spanish education system plus, in this case, the language of the country in which the school is located: Arabic, English, French, Italian, Portuguese, and so on. Similarly, the curriculum is contextualized in the cultural environment of the country concerned, and intercultural education works with all students: Spanish students, those of the country itself, and those of other nationalities. A diverse student population is a fact in all these places, which promotes solidarity among peoples, provided that a model of inclusive education is promoted that is conducive to mutual acquaintance, respect for differences, and learning to live together in diversity, through the commitment and adequate preparation of the teachers.

Schools of joint ownership follow the curriculum of the country where they are located, adding the components of Spanish language and culture. The schools have both Spanish teachers who work in the school, as well as teachers of the country with which it shares ownership.

The *Spanish private schools* are not of Spanish ownership, so teacher recruitment is dependent on the entrepreneur-professional who is the holder and owner of each of these institutions. Usually, the Spanish curriculum is taught, with the same characteristics as in the Spanish-owned institutions, i.e., adding the language and culture of the country where they settle. These schools require authorization from the Spanish Ministry of Education.

Finally, the *schools of agreement* are schools of foreign ownership, usually private, of the country where they conduct their work; they teach the curriculum set for each nation. However, being schools of agreement, they should also incorporate the materials of Spanish language and literature, geography, and history of Spain during all years of instruction, fulfilling this requirement and others related to facilities, qualifications of teachers, requirements for registration of students, and so forth. When students complete the various stages of education, they will receive Spanish degrees, which gives them two degrees: that of the student's country and that of

Spain, which opens the door to any European Union country with access to the universities of the European Higher Education Area (EHEA). These schools cover schooling from age 3 until the end of high school and university entrance. These are highly valued by the people who attend them, who usually come from many nationalities and cultures.

In these four types of schools where the Spanish educational curriculum is concerned, an intercultural approach is basic and supportive of teaching and educational quality in general, as required by the reality of the societies in which the schools develop and, equally, by the Law on Education of Spain, which promotes in all its provisions attention to diversity and the encouragement of democratic values through the education environment: respect for differences, mutual enrichment of diverse cultures, peaceful coexistence, equality of rights between persons of different sexes, values of solidarity, and so on.

However, it is understood that education for all is not exclusively based on solidarity (understood as a voluntary commitment), but also constitutes the right of the person who is received in the school for reasons of justice. Education for all is a must in the exercise of democracy, which is well recognized in the constitutions of various nations and international conventions. If it would depend on voluntary commitment (as in some developing or Third World countries), many children might go without education, without being able to exercise those rights granted to them by international declarations (among which is that of children's rights), and could constitute a clear and manifest injustice that inevitably could remain, despite their obvious need.

Associations of Spanish Language and Culture

The Associations of Spanish Language and Culture (ALCE, by their Spanish acronym) provide programs of Spanish language and culture targeted to the children of Spanish immigrants, regardless of generation (currently, the schools serve mainly third-generation Spanish abroad). Presently, in many cases, students also include the children of executives, professionals of all kinds, and Spanish officials in the European Union and other international agencies who are living in another country for a certain period. Thus, a change in the type of European migrations is evident at present. Migrants are now no longer motivated by subsistence but rather by mobility into certain specialty areas or for reasons of arrival at EU institutions. The fundamental purpose of these associations is that students maintain or have access to their language and culture of origin (when born abroad), do not lose it in other cases, or continue to outperform their level of competence in these curricular areas as well as in linguistic communication.

As explained at the beginning of this chapter, the genesis of the education model of ALCE emerged from the migration of Spanish, mainly to Europe, for political or work reasons. At first, it seemed to be a matter of Spain's responsibility for and solidarity with its emigrants, but now these associations are being maintained over time, helping to strengthen the Spanish presence on the outside and to respect the right of the individual to strengthen his or her identity in multicultural contexts. These associations are formed through classrooms located in different towns within a country, so that education is carried out as close as possible to the residence of program participants. Countries that have developed the program are: Australia, Belgium, France, Germany, the Netherlands, Switzerland, United Kingdom, and the United States. In total, we are talking about education services in 361 populations of 27 associations distributed in 453 classrooms (there are cities where there is more than one classroom, as seen in figures, for example, in Brussels, New York, or London), involving 14,117 students and 90 teachers.

This is a voluntary program for families, ultimately an offering from the Spanish Ministry of Education (not mandatory for the Ministry; in this case, we view solidarity as a voluntary commitment), free for them, addressed to all who wish to maintain their original language and culture. Students are served by Spanish teachers, which, as in the case of the centers mentioned above, are selected from those who apply for vacant posts in these associations. The scale, selection, and professional evaluation procedures are identical to those applied to the Spanish-ownership centers.

Classes take place during school hours for students, so they can attend easily. Often, they have 3 hours per week over 8 full school years, which results in quite a sufficient curriculum of Spanish language and culture, supplemented by additional activities (theater, cinema, conferences, and so forth) and travel exchanges to Spain, either exclusively cultural or educational in nature, in connection with centers located in different Spanish cities. In addition, regular monitoring of these studies offers the possibility of obtaining the Diploma of Spanish as a Foreign Language (DELE, by its Spanish acronym) obtained through the Instituto Cervantes, now extended to almost every non-Spanish-speaking country in the world and very reputed in professional fields. The DELE constitutes an aggregate of interest and quality for students in the associations, who are enriched by having doors to the workplace opened by having an official certificate accrediting mastery of the Spanish language. The situation in Miami, Florida, presents a paradigmatic example because there is a large population that speaks Spanish but has no official certification that validates this knowledge and functional mastery. Therefore, in the state of Florida, formal study of the Spanish language and achieving the DELE has become an important priority, since possessing it facilitates getting work due to the bilingualism (English-Spanish) that dominates the area.

Spanish and Bilingual Sections in Foreign Institutions

Sections consist of so-called Spanish studies (language and culture) in institutions owned by the country in which they are located, almost always at the secondary level (middle and high school). Some are devoted exclusively to teaching Spanish and others are bilingual, sharing this teaching with other languages. Spanish sections are carried out in France (in 13 cities), Italy (in 7 cities), Germany (in 3 cities), the Netherlands (in Amsterdam), the United States (in 4 cities) and the United Kingdom (in 2 cities). The total number of students served is 8,785, of which 63.61% are from the country, 6.1% are of Spanish nationality, 24.4% are of Spanish descent or dual nationality, and the rest belong to other nationalities. Section teachers are Spanish, depending on the Ministry of Education, the same as in schools and associations of Spanish ownership.

Bilingual sections are located mainly in Eastern Europe; the one created most recently is in China. In particular, they carry out their work in Bulgaria, China, Czech Republic, Hungary, Poland, Romania, Russia, and Slovakia. These sections serve 12,459 students; it is pertinent to note increased interest in learning Spanish and its culture in recent years. During the 1998–1999 school year, only 1,665 students were in bilingual sections, showing that in 10 years there has been an increase of 10,794 students, despite this first year in China having only 87 students. Numbers are estimated to increase exponentially in the coming academic years. Students who, at the end of their studies, pass a test of maturity required by the Spanish Ministry have the degree of Spanish Baccalaureate. Teachers who teach Spanish in this modality are Spanish, employed by the country itself, or native-born but with sufficient qualifications to teach Spanish. As indicated by the figures above, governments are very interested in teaching Spanish to their populations. This interest is demonstrated by the fact that each country hires the teachers and pays their salaries, which does not occur in the models above.

European Schools

European schools serve students who are the children of staff of the institutions of the European Union, covering education from ages 3 to 18. To the extent that vacancies are available, they admit other students whose families are interested in this education model. The native language of each country is compulsory, particularly at early ages, but later shares space and instruction with other language sections. Teaching is organized in the language of each subject taught, not in the specific native language. Therefore, the interesting thing is the multilingual learning model that students acquire naturally, without the problem this poses in traditional models. Intercultural and multilingual coexistence is the norm in European schools. Students who complete these schools get the European Baccalaureate, recognized by all member states of the European Union. Its top leadership rests with the Supreme Council of the European Schools, which are funded by member states.

The first European school was established in Luxembourg in October 1953, and currently 14 schools operate in 7 countries: Alicante (Spain), Bergen (Norway), Brussels I, II, III, and IV (Belgium), Culham (United Kingdom), Frankfurt (Germany), Karlsruhe (Germany), Luxembourg I and II (Luxembourg), Mol (Belgium), Munich (Germany), and Varese (Italy). A total of 21,649 students attend these schools, with Spanish students accounting for 6.44%. It should be noted that only the European Schools in Alicante, Brussels I and III, Luxembourg, and Munich have the Spanish section. Teachers attending the Spanish sections depend on the Ministry of Education and are selected and evaluated the same way as is done for schools and associations already mentioned.

As it is easy to verify, the elements of mutual understanding between cultures, respect for their characteristics, different language skills, and so on are factors of quality of education in any of the education models that Spain now has in foreign countries. The cultivation, therefore, of solidarity among those of Spanish descent, coupled with intercultural values, is present, permanent, and inherent in the school curriculum that is developed at all stages and types of education.

EXAMPLES OF WHAT OTHER COUNTRIES ARE DOING IN SPAIN

Other countries maintain collaboration with Spain for providing education for their own students when they reside in the Spanish state, in a manner that works actively to maintain their native country's language and culture. The examples of Portugal and Morocco are significant, as these are countries with which Spain maintains two programs of collaboration: "Portuguese Language and Culture" and "Arabic Language and the Culture of Morocco." In both, the two countries send native teachers to Spanish schools where they work with Spanish professionals, including Spanish students who are interested in learning these languages and cultures. This situation is totally generalized in the case of the Portuguese language, which is taught alongside Spanish in the schools where it is implemented, as referenced earlier. There are already many years of bilateral collaboration, providing optimal results of solidarity and coexistence between the schoolchildren and the families of these countries related to the schools.

Currently, only in Madrid is there a school population of more than 150 nationalities, but the majority of the home countries do not collaborate in the sense discussed above. In many cases, the administrations of these countries do not take care of these populations, for the very fact that they have emigrated from their country. Nonetheless, some countries maintain a good relationship and facilitate space where students can develop activities that maintain their culture and language, a prime example being the Chinese population that resides in Madrid. Efforts are being made with the embassies to ensure participation and cooperation of the countries of origin of students in the education of their citizens residing in Spain.

BY WAY OF CONCLUSION

This chapter has described Spanish schools abroad and how it is possible to generate and disseminate ideas regarding the importance of education as the source and foundation of models of democratic society that are demanded today. As can be seen throughout this chapter, the Spanish education system is not content to perform its duties and obligations with respect to the population residing in Spain, but is expanding its activities to Spanish students who, for one reason or another, live abroad—at least to those who out of necessity had to leave at a certain time in history to find ways of subsistence due to the prevailing ideology or the poor economy at that time in Spain. In these cases, the education offered is voluntary and free, so it can be considered a joint commitment of the Spanish people, through its government, toward its quasi-exiled population. In other situations where the stay abroad is voluntary due to job mobility or other interests, such solidarity is extended in order to preserve the culture and language of origin, although the students are acquiring other languages and are working with other curriculum requirements that, in any event, enrich a person.

Intercultural and supportive approaches are offered in educational activities outside of Spain, both with Spanish students as well as with foreign students that have access to the activities. This entire system seems to work well. To cite objective data, on all PISA (Program for the International Students Assessment) reports (in the context of the OECD), the Spanish educational system is highly rated in terms of equity. That is to say, through schooling, the population is exceeding its initial social situation, in terms of both cultural and economic levels. Most of the school population in the Spanish state is in a very acceptable learning environment, without strong clusters at lower levels on national data. However, Spain lacks a significant cluster of students who stand out at the top, something that is being addressed now by the education authorities, in a way that would not harm the students who may be able to achieve at higher levels.

Educational activities abroad are extended considerably into everything related to the teaching of Spanish, given the expansion in this area and the enormous interest in learning that exists in other countries, which present Spain with demands to collaborate in the best possible way, that is, with guarantees of quality. It is desirable to maintain the principles of attention to diversity and intercultural education or coexistence with respect for differences, which appear in the activities of the Spanish education system located in different countries. Intercultural education is a basic requirement of the entire population to positively evolve toward higher conditions in their quality of life, personally, socially, and in work. The person in isolation loses humanity; in collaboration with others, he/she reaches his/her individual potential.

REFERENCE

Inspección de Educación. (2009). *Informe-Memoria de la Inspección de Educación. Curso 2008–2009* [Report of the Bureau of Education. Year 2008–2009]. Madrid: Ministry of Education.

Part II

Solidarity as Building Allies
in Contexts of Struggle

5

Multicultural Coexistence in Schools in Spain

New Challenges and New Ways of
Organizing Education Through Solidarity

Encarnación Soriano

Spain is experiencing a transformation of its population. Spaniards had emigrated in the past, but Spain now receives many groups of people coming from different countries and cultures. This chapter discusses the new, complex situation, which developed in only a few years, that was generated by both the country's economic crisis and the increase of immigrants who have not yet been integrated into the native population. The number of students coming into schools from immigrant families is increasing progressively and very rapidly every year, a situation that produces a series of difficulties in the schools.

In Spain, as in other countries, problems of migration are understood as the result of cultural differences between natives and non-natives. However, many people forget that, in addition to cultural differences, there are power differences and social inequalities between groups. Migrants and their new communities need education to serve as a tool to achieve social justice and human rights.

This chapter builds the concept of solidarity and studies its importance for improving the school situation, then synthesizes my research, conducted over the last 18 years, regarding teachers' difficulties working with immigrant students. I argue that Spanish teachers need training and motivation to cope with the multicultural presence in the schools most affected by immigration. Most teachers have not yet learned to transcend the limits of their own culture to understand the culture of their students. Still, motivated teachers who value solidarity and have the skills and attitudes to work in coordination with other teachers, families, and the environment where the school is located, do have the potential to promote learning for all their students (immigrants and natives), and to transform the sociocultural context, promoting a more humane and more caring society that enhances social justice and peaceful coexistence.

THE PLACE OF IMMIGRANTS IN A LAND OF EMIGRANTS

In the last 30 years, Spain has undergone a transformation of its population. This nation, which previously had been characterized as a nation of emigrants, is currently receiving large waves of people from other states who are looking for a place to settle and live with dignity.

Since the last decades of the 19th century until after the 1960s, there were important migratory movements from Spain. During the 19th and early 20th centuries, to the political exiles were added economic migrants who went to countries of the Americas, with Cuba, Puerto Rico, Argentina, Venezuela, Mexico, Brazil, Uruguay, Chile, and Costa Rica being the most important (García López, 1992). Following the Spanish Civil War and military dictatorship, from 1939 began the exodus of political refugees. There was also an economic migration to European countries, motivated by the harsh circumstances in Spain. The young and low-skilled workforce was attracted by good job prospects and higher living standards resulting from economic growth and the reconstruction of Europe after World War II (Liñares, 2009).

According to official figures from the Spanish Institute of Migration (Instituto de Tecnologías Educativas, 2010), between 1959 and 1973, 1,066,440 Spanish migrated to Europe. The end of the 1970s and 1980s marked an important point in the history of Spanish migration: The number of Spanish emigrants who went to work in other countries decreased significantly, while the number of foreigners who came to Spain looking for a job and a place to settle increased. From the 1980s, and more evident since the entry of Spain into the European Union in 1986, immigration to Spain increased.

The European Union country that has experienced the greatest increase in the number of foreigners in the past 10 years, according to Eurostat (2010), is Spain, growing from 648,533 in 1999 to 5,650,968 in 2009, i.e., an increase of 88.52%. Immigrants are usually young people who cannot survive in their home countries and are willing to perform work under conditions that the Spanish do not accept (Liñares, 2009). They come from Africa (Morocco, Algeria, Cape Verde, and sub-Saharan countries), Eastern Europe (Russia, Hungary, Romania, Poland, and so forth), South America (Ecuador, Colombia, Argentina, Brazil, Venezuela, Peru, and so on), and Asia (China).

Spanish society is becoming more pluralistic and, according to Habermas (1999), in Spain there is "daily evidence that departs from the exemplary case of a national state with a culturally homogeneous population. This increases the multiplicity of forms of life, ethnic groups, religious groups" (pp. 94, 96). However, let us not forget the fact that, in addition to ethnic and cultural differences, there are differences of power between the immigrants and native Spanish. Speaking about the situation of immigrants in Spain, Calvo (2000) writes: "Immigrants and native Spanish are two (or more) communities living together, but segregated, in a situation for many of exploitation at work, poor housing, poor social services" (p. 42). For Muñoz Bata (2008), "large-scale migration puts enormous pressure on institutions and social services of the host countries and enhances popular fears and stereotypes of native peoples. Opposition may arise from panic to consider they could be swallowed by foreign cultures and values and also the concern that local people lose their jobs because of immigrants willing to work for lower wages" (p. 38).

The situation Muñoz Bata described is happening in Spain and, moreover, is exacerbated in times of economic crisis. In Spanish society with approximately 46 million people, of whom 5 million are unemployed, many Spanish citizens see immigration as potentially suctioning out the state's economic resources. An example appears in one of the many articles published in national newspapers, in this case, an opinion article published in 2001, when Spain did not have the large number of immigrants we have today. In this article, the author comments on a radio program he heard in which listeners who called blamed immigrants for receiving state benefits that Spanish people do not get:

> People are beginning to weary of the issue of immigrants and making it clear that they are not racist, openly, nobody is racist but, four crazies seize great anger because the caller [referring to a radio program] is an autonomous worker that after 25 years in business and contributing to Social Security, his business was closed and he has no right to receive unemployment subsidy. And a widow calls and talks about a shameful pension she receives. . . . And we could go with a long list of Spanish who feel somehow cheated or neglected by political correctness, that is to say "I do" to immigration . . . and it would be very harmful to everyone if society were to begin to reject immigration. (Aberasturi, 2001, p. 19)

For his part, Delano (2008), confirming the earlier opinion, indicates that the receivers are concerned about economic security; that, and the flow of immigrants into areas that have no tradition of immigration, has generated a powerful backlash against immigration. As Aberasturi and Delano say, it would be very dangerous if Spanish society were to reject immigration and generate racist clashes and outbreaks, like those that have already occurred in several Spanish cities, such as El Ejido and Terrassa. As stated in the Raxen report (Informe RAXEN, 2009), 350 racist and xenophobic acts have taken place in Spain in 2008. Intercultural education is necessary so that this violence will not remain part of the political discourse.

Intercultural education respects, celebrates, and recognizes the diversity in all areas of human life and reflects the belief that this breadth enriches us all. It also promotes equality and human rights (Grant, 2009). Therefore, for immigrants and their communities to achieve social justice and human rights, education that is funded and operated by the state needs to be a tool to promote cooperation and equality, to combat unfair discrimination, and to enable the values of solidarity on which to build intercultural education (Torres, 2001). Solidarity is a contributing factor to achieving the major objectives of intercultural education.

BUILDING SOLIDARITY TO PROMOTE COEXISTENCE AND INTEGRATION IN A MULTICULTURAL SOCIETY

Coexisting—living together—is a process that involves not just being together in a single place, but also engaging in interactive and productive action between people; it requires contact and active, positive exchanges. Learning to live together not only means tolerating the existence of another human being, but showing respect for, knowledge of, and appreciation of the value of individuals from other cultures in an atmosphere of closeness. It is a daily life among people with different cultural backgrounds, interacting with each other in a way that gives rise to social relations, exchanges, and willingness to approach each other (Soriano, 2007). Ortega (2004) says that social integration of the newcomers is a right. The recognition of belonging to a democratic society carries with it equal rights and obligations of the indigenous and foreign, that is, the laws are equal for all and all partake of the same justice. For Young (1990), a goal of social justice is social equality. This equality does not refer to the distribution of social goods, but the full participation and inclusion in all in the major institutions of society, and socially supported substantive opportunity for all to develop their skills and make something of their choice.

In *Public Virtues*, Victoria Camps (1996) argues that justice is the principal virtue in trying to realize the hypothetical virtues of equality of all people and liberty as a fundamental right of the individual. But sometimes justice does not reach all areas of society, and where there is no justice, solidarity can be used to try to work for justice. Solidarity becomes a complement to justice. That is, in a society like Spain, which is in economic crisis, with an unemployment rate of almost 20% and with a population of immigrants that is close to 5 million good feelings such as solidarity help justice but do not replace it.

When the spirit of the laws that pass through Parliament is not enacted in practice, injustice results. In Spain, the laws on paper incorporate good social policy. Here are some examples: Basic-level education from ages 6 to 16 years is free for all children and youth, whether they are native Spanish or arrived with their families from other places; there is a policy of scholarships for children and young people with few economic resources; health care is free for Spanish citizens and new residents; there is grant aid for the unemployed; the Law of Dependency (*Ley de Dependencia*) that supports all people with disabilities has been adopted. Although the laws are intended to serve all citizens of the state, we must recognize that the full development of the laws is reflected more in theoretical political discourse than in good practical application. You could say that there is a dubious equality before the law: While the wealthy can choose alternatives, the poor cannot and thus suffer the consequences of what is or is not made available. Many laws are passed that subsequently cannot be carried out in their entirety because there are no economic resources for doing so. For example, the Law of Dependency, which defines the services that the state will provide to persons with functional incapacity (e.g., paraplegia, serious illness, being very old) and/or low income, is suffering many restrictions: In the health-care system, waiting lists lengthen time for treatment by specialists or for undergoing operations; the education system is undergoing major budget cuts; the salaries of Spanish officials are cut and the pensions of the elderly are frozen; and the more vulnerable (which includes many immigrants) lose their jobs or never attain jobs in the first place. In this situation, we have to emphasize that, to achieve the welfare of all, where justice ends, solidarity should begin.

Camps (1996) defines solidarity as "the value that consists of displaying oneself united with other individuals or groups, sharing their interests and needs" (p. 32). Solidarity involves seeing others with the heart, with brotherhood, and feeling concerned for suffering or injury to others. But solidarity does not only mean sympathizing with wrongs and difficulties; it also requires ethical and responsible behavior in which decisions are made with consideration of the whole of society rather than one's own individual interest (Esquivel, 2006). For Coll (2009), solidarity means recognition, respect, cooperation, and assistance. We cannot build a new society if we do not create a culture of solidarity. Solidarity is not optional; it is a way of living and supposes action. Solidarity is a constant habit of acting in a manner in which we are all responsible for everyone.

If solidarity is always valuable in times of crisis, its cultivation is an urgent need and a huge challenge. The concept of solidarity has two essential components: compassion and the recognition of the value of the existence of the "other" (García Roca, 1994). But not all compassion generates solidarity, only that which recognizes the other in her or his personal dignity. To be supportive, it is necessary to know the situation of the other, his or her status of disadvantage or injustice. The more we know of the other, the more tools we have to understand and act as allies. However, sometimes it is not enough to know; one must also demonstrate empathy and responsibility (Esquivel, 2006).

Tolerance and respect for a new diversity are difficult to achieve, and momentum in that direction does not usually occur without conflicting parties engaging in some form of education and intercultural understanding (Banks, 2004; Grant, 2009). Social justice and solidarity may be achieved through intercultural education. Interaction and learning from encounters with the other are fundamental (Abdallah-Pretceille, 2001). The school is probably the place where we get to reflect all of the cultures and permit communication between them. In education, the first action is the intercultural approach that involves strengthening the individual and the group in order to actively and peacefully coexist, and to exercise solidarity. This action calls for three strategies for teachers to meet the culturally diverse community:

1. *Decentralization.* This is the distance the teacher has to traverse in order to leave the framework of his or her own culture through interacting with students from other cultures. Along the way, there is an appropriation of the principle of cultural relativity, which in this case means considering the various cultures of one's students.
2. *Entrance into the other.* To understand the other, it is necessary to enter into his or her system of values, to stand in his/her place. Entrance is aimed at taking up another culture, discovering ways of thinking that make sense from within that culture, and being able to observe from the point of view of another person, another culture, and another reality.
3. *Negotiation and mediation.* Negotiation means to ensure the exchange of views in order to reach an agreement. Mediation is a way of sharing that allows two parties to reconcile. (Touriñan, 2005, p. 25)

TWENTY YEARS OF EXPERIENCE WITH IMMIGRANT STUDENTS IN SOUTHEASTERN SPANISH SCHOOLS

The first students coming from immigrant families to schools in 1990 were of Moroccan origin. The number of immigrant students has grown rapidly since then. According to the Ministry of Education (Ministerio de Educación, 2010), in the 2000–2001 school year, there were a total of 6,882,363 pupils enrolled in Spanish schools, of whom 141,868 were foreign students; in 2009–2010, the total enrollment amounted to 7,606,517, of whom 762,746 were foreigners (the Ministry of Education used the term *foreign* rather than the term *immigrant*). This rising immigrant student population produced a series of difficulties in the schools. It seems that the incorporation of students from other countries into the schools has been so rapid that the teachers and the schools themselves could not cope with the situation and make the changes that school practice would require. As a result, after a period of 20 years, when the teachers are asked again about the concerns and challenges they are facing due to having immigrant students in their classrooms, as shown in the remainder of this chapter, they still have the same answers as they did initially.

In these 20 years there have been two Basic Laws on Education in Spain, but the day-to-day school situation has not changed. The first, the Organic Law of the Education System of 1990 (Gobierno de España, 1990), makes no reference to interculturalism but mandates, as an end, the training of students in respecting rights and fundamental freedoms, and in the exercise of tolerance and freedom within the democratic principles of coexistence. The law currently governing the Spanish educational system, the Organic Education Law of 2006 (Gobierno de España, 2006), makes explicit reference in its objectives to training for peace, respect for human rights, cooperation, and solidarity among the people, and interculturalism as an enriching element of society. With regard to equity in education, the law says that public administrations have to support entry into the education system of students who, because of coming from other countries, get a late arrival to the Spanish education system. Therefore, specific programs for students with serious deficiencies in their linguistic competence will be developed, in order to facilitate their integration into their respective courses.

Below, I present, first, the conclusions my colleagues and I reached through three qualitative investigations consisting of interviews in 1995, 1998, and 2002, in which we studied the concerns and difficulties of teachers with immigrant students in their classrooms. Second, I discuss more extensively the results of my latest research, which was formulated around the same questions to the teachers. Third, I demonstrate how learning solidarity and being supportive will enhance schooling for all students.

Concerns of Teachers When First Working with Immigrant Students

In the research my colleagues and I conducted in the last 18 years, teachers have identified difficulties in working with immigrants (Cabrera, Soriano, Hervás, García, & Sánchez,1998; Soriano, 1997, 2003). To them, the main problem has been the newcomer students' ignorance of the Spanish language, which has impeded their adequate communication with the teacher during the first months. This lack of knowledge makes it impossible to know about the curricular level of children, according to the teachers, and for the students to learn new knowledge so they can participate in classroom activities. There is also considerable ignorance about the newcomers' culture, which results in conflicts between teachers and students, as well as among students, due to cultural differences. The second problem mentioned by the teachers is caused by the education administration: lack of financing in anticipation of the new immigrant. The teachers report a shortage of material and human resources, and the position of the administration, which is a politics of cuts and savings. The schools need economic resources to acquire materials and support teachers to help students in the classrooms without separating them from their classmates. Other functions of the administration are to finance and facilitate training strategies for teachers who have, in the same classroom, native Spanish students and students of other ethnic and cultural backgrounds. In addition to realizing these difficulties, the cultural diversity in the classrooms motivates and makes the pedagogical activities of teachers more active.

Concerns of Teachers After 20 Years of Experience with Students from Diverse Cultural Groups

Recently, I conducted new research on high school teachers with immigrant students being educated in Spanish schools, taking into account that 1) 18 years have passed, and 2) the state's education system has adopted new measures for managing the situation of immigrant students in schools. The objective of this research was to find out the concerns of teachers with both immigrant and native students in their classrooms. Nonprobability sampling was used; the sample was made up of 42 high school teachers who worked at high schools located in areas of southern Spain characterized by a large number of immigrant students. Data were gathered using in-depth interviews. The interview questions were open and intended to detect the worries and needs of teachers who had students speaking different languages; practicing different religions; coming from different countries; and having different values, attitudes, and cultural practices from the Spaniards.[1]

Teachers' comments were grouped into three main categories. Concerns about immigrant students' cognition (i.e., their knowledge of the Spanish language, culture, and customs, and their knowledge of school academic material) made up about one-fourth of teachers' comments. Concerns about immigrant students' attitudes (expressed in forms such as their relationships with and attitudes toward others, and their willingness to integrate with others) made up about half of their comments. Concerns about school organizational issues (i.e., resources schools made available to help immigrant students directly and to help teachers work with immigrant students) made up about one-quarter of teachers' comments. The following pages will develop in detail each of the categories.

Concerns About Immigrant Students' Knowledge

Teachers expressed five related concerns about cognition or knowledge when discussing the presence of immigrant students in their classroom: ignorance of the Spanish language, school knowledge, the culture of the "other," customs, and the immigrant students' subsequent studies.

Ignorance of the Spanish language. By the time of the interviews, the education authority had developed a policy measure to pay attention to foreign students coming to school without knowing the Spanish language: the language support temporary classroom. The aim of this measure is that the child or young person learns basic tools of the Spanish language to communicate with peers and teachers in these temporary classrooms.

Although immigrant students who do not know the Spanish language attend these classes, the major concern of secondary teachers focused on the ignorance of the Spanish language of immigrant students who are not from South America. The responses of teachers were oriented in various directions. On the one hand, we have teachers who were concerned about the relationship of young immigrants with peers and teachers, and who understand that ignorance of the language creates difficulty in relating to others. In interviews, this category tends to coincide in the teachers' discourse with the categories of communication, integration, and relationship. A teacher told us, "I am concerned that children who come know absolutely nothing about Spanish and there is no way to approach them, that's the main thing, the big problem I see."

On the other hand were the teachers who perceived ignorance of the language as a great difficulty in learning the subjects and continuing their studies. In these cases particularly, in the discourse of teachers, concerns about lack of Spanish overlapped with concerns about integration and studies. A teacher told us, "I worry about the outcomes of these children for university. The level of education and language is lower, expectations are lower due to the above."

Finally, some teachers complained about the situation with reference to the solitude of teachers and the hope that society has placed on them that they alone will solve the complex situation; in the words of one teacher who was interviewed, "do not have translators, for example. There are children who come here without any knowledge of the Spanish language and it is intended that teachers make a kind of miracle or wonder with them."

Ignorance of school knowledge. The teachers spoke somewhat differently about immigrant students' ignorance of school knowledge. On the one hand were those who believed the poor performance of immigrant students would lead to school failure, and questioned whether this was due to limitations of the students themselves (due to the low economy, low housing quality, and so forth) or to a lack of interest in studying.

On the other hand were teachers who said they have great difficulty teaching their subject in their classrooms because there are immigrant students who are unfamiliar with literacy and do not achieve a level of literacy needed to keep learning new skills: "Lately, teachers are having class with immigrant students, you have to remember that they have a different culture, and sometimes have a level of knowledge that is also lower."

Culture, customs, and studies. When speaking about immigrant students' knowledge, teachers made a few references to other things. Two teachers used the term *culture*, noting that immigrant students have a different culture, and that to relate to them it is necessary to be familiar with it. One teacher spoke about immigrant students' customs as follows:

> They separate themselves from Spanish customs because they do not understand many things of our society, because they have a religious society, mostly Arab immigrants, deeply rooted, and there are certain things that they are intolerant of and then they have a hard time assimilating to adapt to the society that we currently have here.

Finally, a teacher expressed concern about immigrant students' studies, their difficulty continuing with higher education, and how to assess these students.

Concerns About Immigrant Students' Attitudes

This dimension signaled the most anxiety for secondary teachers. Teachers expressed concern about the following attitudinal and emotional dimensions: students' integration, students' ability and willingness to live together, student behavior, communication and relationships among students, and the related problems of discrimination, violence, racism, and conflicts.

Integration. Integration of immigrant students was the ultimate concern of the secondary teachers, with 23 of the respondents citing it. Teachers used the term *integration* with two different nuances.

On the one hand, integration is a means for immigrant students not to be excluded from the group. Some teachers argued the need to achieve good relationships in the classroom and school among students, both natives and immigrants. For other teachers, integration is a means to prevent racism and achieve harmony in relations with the "others," i.e., young people of different cultures and backgrounds "learning to live together." Let us see how two teachers expressed this concern:

> That ghettos are not formed is paramount. So I am concerned about the relationship between them, especially the integration and acceptance of students from other countries.

> That young people are accepted as they are and that racism is avoided, since the fact that they have a different skin color makes their peers exclude them, then this must be avoided.

Many teachers used the term *integration* to mean avoiding racism, achieving a relationship between equality and inclusiveness of the group. We observed that teachers never talked about the inclusion of young immigrants in the group, and forgot that integration is understood as an adaptive process by which individuals and groups find their place in a plural society (Soriano, 2004). Living in a society that is integrated rather than fragmented, although it may seem utopian, is the result of the acceptance, recognition, and respect for the person we think differs from ourselves, whether native or foreigner (Soriano, 2006). However, the teacher's words above seem to ignore that the "other" needs to be respected, recognized, and accepted in order to occupy space in the new society. It seems that, because of this ignorance, the teacher above linked integration only to avoiding racism and having knowledge of Spanish.

There was a group of teachers who sensed, because of daily interaction with native and immigrant students, that the difficulty for integration comes not only from the "native" group, but also from the immigrant student or group itself. In the words of one of these teachers:

> They [the immigrants] form a small group in class, four close together in a corner and speaking their language. What are they talking about? The idea is that we, the teachers, are doing nothing to integrate the immigrants. I'm realizing that they are the first to do nothing to integrate, do not you understand?

During the interviews, we also found responses from teachers who had a different opinion. Some teachers understood that a person does not integrate if the "others" do not let him, in this case students perceive that the host group does not let the immigrant join:

> I worry that they are separated by their peers, not welcome, there are groups of immigrant children but not integrated because of the people here.

Living together. In the classroom, the cultural minorities and the majority are in continuous interaction, influencing each other and communicating among themselves (verbally or nonverbally, positively or negatively). However, the perceptions groups have of the other act decisively in establishing interaction, and affect the degree and type of contact, and the type of conduct and emotions that members of each group have with respect to others.

Teachers were concerned about good relations between different cultural groups. Some teachers thought that in the classroom there are problems of communication but not of living together. However, others just expressed the hope that immigrants and natives would live together well, although they did not suggest how one might support making this happen. One of the teachers said, "As for the native, you also need something that would help both immigrants and children of the land (which are Spanish), so they could have a more normal coexistence, so to speak."

Behavior. A few teachers expressed concern about the behavior of immigrant students in the classroom and the school, voicing different opinions. To some teachers, immigrant children behave badly, but the teachers specified that they do not believe that is because they are immigrants. Other teachers indicated that the behavior of immigrant pupils is better than that of the "native." This view depended on where the school was located and the origin of immigrant students. The best behaviors were manifested by newcomer students from authoritarian regimes.

Communication and relationships. For a couple of teachers, communication and relationship overlapped and were related to integration and knowledge of Spanish. One teacher explained that the affective problem immigrant students experience lies in the difficulty the immigrant child has communicating, caused by ignorance of the language, which prevents forming a relationship with the teacher and peers.

Discrimination, violence, racism, and conflicts. Finally, teachers occasionally referred to discrimination, violence, racism, and conflicts as problems. These problems are occurring in secondary schools and their increase is of concern to teachers who demand that the regional government provide strategies to address them.

Concerns About School Organization Issues

Teachers expressed concerns about organizational issues that impacted their work with immigrant students. These included resources, administration, teacher–student ratio, time, temporary classrooms for linguistic adaptation, translators, and mediation.

Resources. What concerned the teachers most was lack of resources. Lack of resources was linked to learning Spanish, the need to work from the students' knowledge level, and promoting knowledge of cultures. The teachers also complained about the "solitude" they experience in working with the students, as the administration only provides access for immigrant students to temporary classrooms for learning Spanish a few hours a week, but no mediators, translators, or more general means. A teacher said:

> It's the nonchalance of people who are competent to providing quality education, really the resources we need to deal with this kind of student, we do not have. There is a person who takes care of it at a specific time, which is few hours a week, but that's not enough; we have no translators, for example. . . . Without any means of mediation or interest from those responsible for this, for the education, to give ourselves the means to address them as they should.

The responsibility for providing this help that the teacher refers to is the Education Council of the Regional Government, which also has the means to contract mediators, intercultural education experts, and so forth.

Additional school organization concerns. Teachers spoke of the indifference of the educational administration toward the issue of schooling for immigrant students. That indifference left them with too many students and too little time and help to meet the needs of immigrant students in their classrooms. The teachers perceived the number of students per class (officially 30) to be high when students' characteristics were so diverse: diversity of cultures, languages, religions, and so forth. In the face of this diversity, teachers lacked the means, lacked translators or mediators, and significantly lacked time to serve all students. This teacher synthesizes what others were saying:

> I think that given the ratio of students per classroom, it is impossible to meet the needs of immigrant students. For obvious reasons, they require more time commitment on our part, that which they can have.

Due to the high number of students in each classroom, along with their cultural diversity, it is impossible for teachers to satisfy students' needs with the present circumstances. For obvious reasons, such as the immigrants' lack of knowledge of Spanish language, students require that teachers dedicate more time to them, but teachers do not have that additional time.

Limits to Well-Intended Laws

After 20 years in which immigrant students have been enrolling in Spanish schools, the teachers still maintain the same concerns they expressed in the early years, augmented by new ones. What is going on when, during these years, two Organic Laws of Education have been in operation? Not only have the problems faced by the teachers not been solved, but with the increased immigration, their magnitude has increased.

Although the education administration has created temporary classrooms that teach Spanish to young immigrants, teachers are complaining that students who have been to school prior to immigration arrive to class without knowing the Spanish language and require time to learn. As a result, first, the immigrant youth retreat and do not relate to their peers because the common language is Spanish, which they do not know, and second, they cannot fully participate in class because of the school curriculum. Even if they attended classes in Spanish for a while, they still have insufficient knowledge of vocabulary and grammatical structures that are required to follow explanations and to do schoolwork that requires mastery of reading and writing.

Teachers complain about the educational administration and feel abandoned by it. Moreover, they complain about the lack of means to address immigrant students, and they have a point, especially since the education system has undergone a major drop in economic resources due to Spain's economic crisis. In schools, in general, there is a reduction of teachers and a lack of support and specialists in the field.

To the concerns that the teachers have been expressing for 20 years, others have been added. Teachers consider the integration of immigrant students the most important concern. But even though they feel great concern, they do not propose how to solve the problems or challenges associated with immigration. In addition, they seem unfamiliar with a number of conditions that would be necessary for this integration to occur, such as showing respect and recognition of the other cultural group. Teachers also hold other concerns that are connected with integration, such as conflict and violence that are occurring in many secondary schools.

Teachers are complaining of poor academic performance of young immigrants and the lag with which many of them come to Spanish schools. We saw the same in the report *Immigration and Students' Achievement in Spain* (Zinovyeva, Felgueroso, & Vázquez, 2008), which shows the differences between children of immigrants and Spanish children in the PISA report of how students are performing internationally on common tests in basic subject areas. The report notes that the children of immigrants have poorer performance than native Spanish children in all subject areas. The authors of the report explain that the performance gap can be attributed to socioeconomic differences observed in parents, the characteristics of the school (such as private vesus public; urban, suburban, or rural), and the nature of interaction among students who may or may not meet each other as equals because of cultural differences.

The culture that immigrant students bring to their arrival schools is considered important by teachers who observe the impact of differences between students' family culture and the school culture, but there are few teachers who take into account the funds of knowledge (González, Moll, & Amanti, 2005) that the immigrant students bring when they arrive in Spanish schools. To bring about school integration, teachers believe that the values taught in the family should be in line with school values; otherwise, they believe that there is a predisposition to school–family conflict.

In view of these considerations, it appears that the solution to the problem depends on the educational administration and their own education agents (such as teachers and parents). On the one hand, we see that the good intentions of the education law in political discourse are not extending to daily practice. The school situation is overwhelming to many teachers who have fallen into a routine, have become textbook transmitters in their approach to teaching, and think that school conflicts fall beyond their competence and must be solved from the outside. Moreover, parents place the burden of educating their children on the school, but few parents overall come there with a collaborative attitude.

In this scenario, in which the law has taken the form of political discourse, and where we see confusion among all the parties involved in education, we must reach for solidarity. So far, we have talked about solidarity with other people who are far away, such as those who make donations to religious institutions or NGOs. But solidarity, coinciding with Camps (1996, 2000), Coll (2009), and Esquivel (2006), must be exercised with those closest, be they native or immigrant, seeing and knowing the needs of those around us and seeking the means to address them. Although doing so looks complicated, it is not difficult to bring into the terrain of the school. To do this, the teacher, students, parents, and local authorities should open the eyes of the heart and look at the suffering of others with fraternity and empathy. The more we know about the situation of another, and about him or her, the more tools we have to understand and help. When we learn more about the other person, we feel empathy with and recognition of others. Let us look at alternatives, some of which have been carried out successfully in a local Spanish school.

THE BEGINNING OF A NEW COEXISTENCE THROUGH SOLIDARITY

Schools are complex places where the individual paths of teachers, students, and families converge under a social and political framework. For humane cultural, social, and supportive reasons, some Spanish schools, cultural associations, and NGOs involved in the schools are carrying out projects to create a real rapprochement between immigrants and native students in order to reduce signs of xenophobia and to promote integration of newcomers. The integration of young immigrants is essential because it can prevent conflict and social injustice, and can also promote human and intellectual values in both the immigrant and native. The important thing about these schools and organizations is finding ways to reach a mutual understanding among students, teachers, families, and society. For the work of solidarity to take place, we are aware that the solution to the lack of motivation among a large number of teachers must be initiated not only by the school. The solution also should come from all those involved in youth education: teachers, families, young people themselves, and organizations that surround the life of the education institution.

Teachers should learn to speak several languages, open themselves to other cultures, be able to work together, be motivated to keep learning, be able to live democracy and social justice intensely, and step beyond their own cultural parameters to interpret the world outside any cultural frameworks (Soriano, 2008; Trueba, 2002). But mostly, teachers should follow the advice of Nieto (2006) when she says that teachers must ask themselves to be people with courage, with preparation, and with heart. Teachers have to live and teach their students solidarity, and engage fully in solving the problems that can arise. They have to become familiar with the needs of their students both in school and at home. School hours must be restructured to support lessons that involve cooperation and participation, in which solidarity is learned and students are prepared to live with people of different ethnicities and cultures, opening a process of self-knowledge and knowledge of others.

In Spain there are teachers with heart, courage, and great human values, but who have not been trained to serve culturally diverse students; valuing solidarity makes these teachers work with the funds of household knowledge, what their students bring to school from home (Gonzalez, Moll, & Amanti, 2005), even without knowing the theory of funds of knowledge. There are teachers who make contact with schools in the countries of origin of students, and organize visits to the country (such as Morocco) with immigrant and native students, enhance contact between students of different countries through email and postal mail, and so on. In the school curriculum, they incorporate works on migration, intercultural classroom lectures, and exhibitions of items from other cultures; they schedule interreligious dialogue activities; share a school magazine designed by students and where all cultures are collected; write notebooks with stories, songs, games, and recipes specific to the different nationalities of students present in schools; show and discuss the topic of movies that include immigration and other cultures; and so forth.

The best method for teaching and learning solidarity is the teacher acting as a model and being supportive. For example, a group of teachers can work with their school's management team to arrange a food bank in the school, to which students (through their families) and teachers contribute food to help families who, due to a crisis, do not have to eat. Service learning should be carried out in institutes and used as a vehicle for teaching solidarity, that is, supportive service that is developed by students, designed to meet the real needs of a community, institutionally planned and integrated into the curriculum, and based on student learning (Tapia, 2005).

In the school itself, the advanced students can teach peers with less knowledge (whether they are immigrant or native), taking responsibility and commitment for the others' learning. Also, both the teachers and the management team can increase the afterschool hours of future teachers, in which they exercise solidarity by supporting students at home, since the low educational level of parents cannot be helped.

The school and the family are two institutions that must work together with the same ideology. School and family, together, have to educate their students and children in coexisting with, evaluating, and recognizing others through democratic dialogue. The school must also ensure that both native and immigrant families come to the school and collaborate with it. There is a supportive experience that takes place in a school with which we work, in which native Spanish mothers teach immigrant mothers the Spanish language, the functioning of the Spanish education system, and how important school is for their children's future.

We should open as many educational fronts as possible. Not only should the family and school be involved, but local institutions and associations should also join and promote the education of citizens. We found solidarity developing through the parents' associations, and through establishing ties of contact between teachers, students, and families. These associations give Spanish courses for immigrant parents, and also support Spanish language learning among immigrant students who have little knowledge of the language. The associations organize courses for parents (immigrants and natives) to teach them what the associations do, and how the bodies of participation and decision making in schools work. These associations teach students to build and strengthen students' associations. Immigrant associations should be involved in schools by supporting the development of the curriculum with input from their culture, knowledge, and materials. They can also perform as mediators and help immigrant parents visit schools. They can teach Spanish and support learning the mother tongue of immigrant youth in afterschool hours. Young immigrants would be aware that their culture as well as their cultural group is valued. This would be a way to empower minorities.

Local institutions should promote the participation of each and all of their members toward becoming genuine public schools that teach the attitude of solidarity. They must promote educating cities, understood in the sense meant by Trillas (1999) as the city that "cherishes the best attributes that you can imagine at both in the context of the city and in education" (p. 45).

Finally, in all educational contexts, the lives of young people must be strengthened. Teachers' have responsibility for strengthening their students' lives, according to Perez Tapias (2000) and Soriano (2007):

1. Teachers and students should have courage and heart, and be educated critically, i.e., releasing prejudices to reach intercultural dialogue.
2. Teachers must be prepared to educate with norms and principles that make them fight for social justice.
3. Teachers and families must educate themselves to be active rather than passive to the suffering of others; where there is no justice, there is solidarity among people working for justice.

NOTE

1. To analyze the data, the interviews were recorded and transcribed, categorized, and codified through the Aquad program.

REFERENCES

Abdallah-Pretceille, M. (2001). *La educación intercultural* [Intercultural education]. Barcelona: Idea-Books.

Aberasturi, A. (2001, August 18). Inmigrantes [Immigrants], *Newspaper Ideal*, p. 19.

Banks, C. (2004). Intercultural and intergroup education, 1929–1959. In J. Banks & C. Banks (Eds.), *Handbook of research on multicultural education* (2nd ed.) (pp. 753–769). San Francisco: Jossey Bass.

Buxarrais, M. R. (2005). Educar para la solidaridad [Education for solidarity]. Retrieved from www.campus-oei.org/valores/ boletin8.htm

Cabrera, A., Soriano, E., Hervás, M. J., Garcia, M., & Sánchez, J. (1998). *La escolarización del alumnado inmigrante* [The schooling of immigrant students]. Almería, Spain: Consejería de Educación y Ciencia.

Calvo, T. (2000). *Inmigración y racismo* [Immigration and racism]. Madrid: Cauce Editorial.

Camps, V. (1996). *Virtudes públicas* [Public virtues]. Madrid: Espasa Calpe.

Camps, V. (2000). *Valores de la educación* [Education values]. Madrid: Anaya.

Coll, P. (2009). El valor de la solidaridad en tiempos de crisis. La responsabilidad de la sociedad civil [The value of solidarity in times of crisis: The responsibility of a civil society]. *Páginas: Centro de Estudios y publicaciones*, 214, 30–32.

Delano, A. (2008) The politics and business of immigrant integration. *Americas Quarterly*, 2(3), 82–88.

Esquivel, L. (2006). *Responsabilidad y sostenibilidad ecológica. Una ética para la vida* [Responsibility and ecological sustainability]. Unpublished doctoral thesis. Universidad Autónoma de Barcelona, Spain.

Eurostat. (2010). Eurostat Statistics. Retrieved from http://epp.eurostat.ec.europa.eu/portal/page/portal/statistics/Themes

García López, J. R. (1992). *Las remesas de los emigrantes españoles en América: Siglos XIX y XX* [Remittances of Spanish emigrants in America: 19th and 20th centuries]. Gijón, Spain: Júcar.

García Roca, J. (1994). *Solidaridad y voluntariado [Solidarity and volunarism]*. Bilbao, Spain: Sal Terrae.

Gobierno de España. (1990). *Ley orgánica de Ordenación General del Sistema Educativo* [Organic Law of General Management of the Education System]. Retrieved from http://www.boe.es/aeboe/consultas/bases_datos/doc.php?id=BOE-A-1990-24172

Gobierno de España. (2006). *Ley orgánica de educación* [Organic Law of Education]. Retrieved from http://www.boe.es/aeboe/consultas/bases_datos/doc.php?id=BOE-A-2006-7899

González, N., Moll, L., & Amanti, C., Eds. (2005). *Funds of knowledge: Theorizing practices in households, communities, and classrooms.* Mahwah, NJ: Lawrence Erlbaum Associates.

Grant, C. (2009). Una voz en pro de los derechos humanos y la justicia social: La educación intercultural como herramienta para promover las promesas y evitar los riesgos de la globalización [A voice for human rights and social justice: Intercultural education as a tool to promote the promises and avoid the risks of globalization]. In E. Soriano (Ed.), *Vivir entre culturas: Una nueva sociedad* (pp. 45–68). Madrid: La Muralla.

Habermas, J. (1999). *La inclusión del otro. Estudios de teoría política* [Inclusion of the other: Studies of political theory]. Barcelona: Paídos.

Informe RAXEN. (2009). *Diálogo intercultural y derechos humanos* [Intercultural dialogue and human rights]. Retrieved from http://www.movimientocontralaintolerancia.com/html/raxen/raxen.asp

Instituto de Tecnologías Educativas. (2010). *Emigrantes-inmigrantes: Movimientos migratorios en la España del siglo XX* [Emigrants-immigrants: Migratory movements in Spain in the 20th century]. Retrieved from http://www.sauce.pntic.mec.es/jotero/

Liñares, A. (2009). *La emigración española a Europa en el siglo XX* [Spanish emigration to Europe in the 20th century]. Vigo, Spain: Grupo España Exterior/ Ministerio de Trabajo e Inmigración.

Ministerio de Educación. (2010). *Alumnos matriculados en el curso escolar 2000/1 y 2009/10* [Students enrolled in the school year 2000/1 and 2009/10]. Retrieved from http://www.educacion.es/mecd/jsp/plantilla.jsp?id=310&area=estadi

Muñoz Bata, S. (2008). We are all immigrants now. *Americas Quarterly, 2*(3), 34–39.

Nieto, S. (2006). Solidarity, courage and heart: what teacher educators can learn from a new generation of teachers. *Intercultural Education, 17*(5), 457–473

Ortega, P. (2004). *Cultura, valores y educación: principios de integración* [Culture, values and education: Principles of integration]. Paper presented at XIII Congreso Nacional y II Iberoamericano de Pedagogía. Valencia, Spain.

Pérez Tapias, J. A. (2000). Una escuela para el mestizaje: Educación intercultural en la época de la globalización [A school for racial mixing: Intercultural education in the era of globalization]. *Aldea Mundo: Revista sobre Fronteras e Integración, 4*(8), 34–43.

Soriano, E. (1997). Análisis de la educación intercultural en los centros educativos de la comarca del poniente almeriense [Analysis of intercultural education in schools in the region of Almería West]. *Revista de Investigación Educativa, 15*(43–69).

Soriano, E. (2003). La educación y escolaridad de niños y jóvenes inmigrantes en Andalucía [Education and schooling of children and youth in Andalucia]. *Educación, Desarrollo y Diversidad, 6*, 41–63.

Soriano, E. (2004). *La práctica educativa intercultural* [The practice of intercultural education]. Madrid: La Muralla.

Soriano, E. (2006). Hablan las mujeres de diferentes culturas [The women from diverse cultures speak]. In E. Soriano (Ed.), *La mujer en la perspectiva intercultural* (pp. 137–165). Madrid: La Muralla.

Soriano, E. (2007). *Convivencia intercultural en la universidad. Propuestas de presente y futuro* [Intercultural coexistence in the university: Proposals for present and future]. Paper presented at Congreso de Modelos de investigación Educativa. San Sebastian, Spain.

Soriano, E. (2008). Formando ciudadanos para ejercer la democracia [Preparing citizens to exercise democracy]. In E. Soriano (Ed.), *Educar para la ciudadanía intercultural y democrática* (pp. 11–133). Madrid: La Muralla.

Tapia, M. N. (2005). *Aprendizaje y servicio solidario: Algunos conceptos básicos* [Joint learning and service: Some basic concepts]. Retrieved from http://web.ucv.ve/humanidades/FHE2005/docscfacultad/SC/SSCFACES/Material%20de%20apoyo/conceptos%20basico%20aprendizaje%20servicio.pdf

Torres, C. A. (2001). Globalization & comparative education in the world system. *Comparative Education Review, 45*(4), iii–x.

Touriñan, J. M. (2005). *Educación en valores, educación intercultural y formación para la convivencia pacífica* [Values education, intercultural education, and preparation for peaceful coexistence]. Retrieved from www.educacionenvalores.org/article.php3?id_article=268

Trillas, J. (1999). La ciudad educadora [The educating city]. *Cuadernos de Pedagogía, 278*, 44–50.

Trueba, H. (2002) Lideres de ayer frente a los problemas de hoy: Corrientes mundiales migratorias y las consecuentes relaciones interculturales, interétnicas e interraciales [Yesterday's leaders face the problems of today: Global migration

flows and the resulting intercultural, interethnic, and interracial relationships].
In E. Soriano (Ed.), *Interculturalidad: Fundamentos, programas y evaluación*
(pp. 19–38). Madrid: La Muralla.

Young, I. M. (1990). *Justice and the politics of difference*. Princeton, NJ: Princeton
University Press.

Zinovyeva, N., Felgueroso, F. Y., & Vázquez, P. (2008). Immigration and students›
achievement in Spain. *Serie capital humano y empleo. Informe Fedea*. Madrid:
Fedea.

6

Oral Histories in the Classroom
Home and Community Pedagogies

Judith Flores Carmona & Dolores Delgado Bernal

Ella me preguntó sobre un familiar que ya falleció y le conté sobre mi papá y le tuve que llamar a mi mamá en México para preguntarle sobre mi padre. Yo tuve que aprender y mi mamá tuvo que recordar para que yo pudiera ayudar a mi hija. Era como una cadenita. . . . Nos hace recordar cosas que a veces las mantenemos en silencio o en secreto porque los papás a veces no lo quieren enseñar o porque ellos no lo saben. Uno descubre cosas junto con los niños. Mi presencia y relación con las maestras y en la escuela es mejor. Uno se involucra y las maestras aprenden sobre uno y sobre nuestra vida y familia. Es importante que ellas sepan mas de mi y de mi hija—nos podemos conocer mas y familiarizarnos mas. Las maestras son bilingües y por eso yo creo que a ellas les interesa saber mas sobre nuestra cultura, no solamente el lenguaje.

[She asked me about a family member who is dead already and I told her about my dad. I had to call my mother in México and ask her about my father. I had to learn and my mother had to remember in order for me to help my daughter. It was like a chain. . . . This makes us remember stuff we have kept in silence or as secrets because maybe our parents did not teach us certain things because they did not know them. I discover along with my children. My presence in the school has bettered my relationships with the teachers. One gets involved and the teachers learn from us and about our lives and family. It is important for the teachers to know about me and my daughters—we can get to know each other more and familiarize ourselves more with each other. Since the teachers are bilingual they are interested not only in our culture but also in our language.]

—Sofia (Spanish-speaking immigrant mother of a 4th-grade student)

The particular project helped me to better understand the relationship that my students and their parents have. Many of the interview answers were very touching and helped me to see how much they love and value their children. It helped me to want to be a better teacher for their child.

—Mrs. Hope, 4th-grade teacher

Sofia and Mrs. Hope's reflections on what teachers and families gained from an oral histories project allude to the importance of the "*cadenita*" (the link or chain) that helps them connect across time, space, generations, and across educational and institutional boundaries. The mothers also acknowledge the value of their children learning about their ancestors, about their family, about who they are, and the significance of collecting and preserving their cultural and familial stories. For the mothers, it was of great importance to have access to teachers who are bilingual and who incorporate and validate their families' culture and language in the school curriculum.

Historically, the persistent marginalization of students of color[1] and students from immigrant communities, especially those who live in poverty, has been replicated in the curriculum. Marginalization in the classroom includes low academic expectations by teachers who view such children through the lens of deficit ideology. This grave problem in the United States precedes test-driven teaching; however, a standardized curriculum further marginalizes these groups of students. Two major issues currently exacerbate this longstanding problem. One is that, increasingly, education, including higher education, is a necessity for young people to gain mobility. The other issue is that in the United States, test-driven teaching has reduced available space for teachers to get to know their students. As a consequence, the histories and lives of students of color, immigrant students, and marginalized communities within the United States are not well represented in school curriculum. Now more than ever, there is a focus on teaching students to the test and an enforcement of positivist types of knowledge in schools (Sleeter, 2005).

To educate and measure intellect based solely on test scores is to deliver an education that does not allow for "new understanding of our history, a fresh vision of the human experience, and also a critical basis for evaluating what we hear and read in courses, and in the society at large" (Rich, 1979, p. 1). An education that is disconnected from one's lived experiences and history is a problem because it further excludes and marginalizes the lives and knowledge(s) of students of color in educational settings. These exclusions also reify the perception of students of color as empty vessels who do not possess cultural, familial, raced, or gendered knowledge, and therefore, cannot be viewed as assets and contributing members in classrooms (Delgado Bernal, 2002).

Sleeter (2005) constantly emphasizes that teachers must recognize the knowledge students bring from home and their community because students do not enter schools as empty vessels. She also asserts that, indeed, it is the responsibility of the teacher to "become familiar with, and respect the knowledge students bring to school, and to organize curriculum and learning activities in such a way that students are able to activate and use that knowledge" (p. 106). Teachers need to be familiar with the communities the students come from; otherwise, they will not know how to activate or utilize the "outside the classroom knowledge" (p. 110). Sleeter's (2005) emphasis can be defined as a call to form relationships based on solidarity and reciprocity.

This chapter looks at an oral history project implemented in an elementary school as one tool to activate the "outside the classroom knowledge" and to form relationships based on solidarity. What happens when the histories, stories, and knowledge of students of color, immigrant students, and other marginalized students are brought into the school curriculum? What happens when teachers, parents, and students begin to form relationships based on solidarity and reciprocity? We opened the chapter with quotes from a Spanish-speaking immigrant mother and a 4th-grade teacher who speak to these two questions and to their experiences in such an oral history project. Sofia and Mrs. Hope speak of optimism and the possibilities that can occur when the knowledge of communities of color is brought into the classroom.

In this chapter, we provide the school and community context in which our research took place and the impetus for the implementation of an oral histories project that is part of a university-school-community partnership named Adelante: A College Awareness and Participatory Partnership. Next, we outline our conceptualization of solidarity and how it relates to the idea of teaching from a perspective that incorporates both culturally relevant pedagogies and the funds of knowledge from Latina/o communities. We then share some of our data from teachers, students, and mothers involved in the oral history project and demonstrate an ongoing process of creating solidarity within schools. After addressing some of the challenges with our work, we conclude with a discussion on how repositioning cultural-familial knowledge has contributed to relationships based on solidarity between students, parents, and teachers.

SETTING THE CONTEXT: *VAMOS ADELANTE* WITH ORAL HISTORIES

Our research takes place at Jackson Elementary School, a predominantly Mexicana/o, and Mexican American urban school on the west side of Salt Lake City, Utah. Jackson's student population includes 59% Latina/o (including immigrant and U.S.-born students with ties to Mexico, Central America, and South America), 26.9% White, 4.9% African American, 4.3% Pacific Islander, 3.4% Asian, 1.3% American Indian, and 0.2% non-declared. Over 90% of the students come from low-income homes[2] (Utah Performance Assessment System for Students, n.d.). There are 26 classroom teachers, and although over one-quarter of the teachers are bilingual in Spanish, the teacher population looks very different from the student population, with approximately 80% of the teachers being White and middle-class. Most, if not all, of the teachers do not reside in the community in which Jackson is located. The new vice principal is White, bilingual in Spanish, and a strong supporter of bilingual education. She and four of the classroom teachers have children who attend Jackson. The current principal is a bilingual Mexican American female who has been at Jackson for 4 years. She is a strong advocate of bilingual education, and in her previous district-level position, she led the effort to create the Spanish dual-immersion program at this school.

In 2005, Dr. Dolores Delgado Bernal, Dr. Enrique Alemán, and Dr. Octavio Villalpando co-founded Adelante: A College Awareness and Preparatory Partnership, and Judith Flores Carmona began working as a research assistant. Adelante's goals are "to prepare students and their families for college by integrating higher education into their school experience and into their personal lives, and to help establish a college going culture within the school culture" (Delgado Bernal, Villalpando, & Alemán, 2005). The partnership was initiated at Jackson because the student population and families in this community, historically, have not had access to or preparation for higher education, and the Adelante team were all new members to the community.

Adelante is grounded in the collective belief that rigorous academics must go hand-in-hand with developing the consciousness of students who will 1) understand who they are as cultural beings, 2) be proud of where they come from, and 3) understand how to draw upon their family and community knowledge (Delgado Bernal et al., 2005). The partnership was started with the kindergarten classrooms in the Spanish and English dual-immersion program, and each year we continue to work with the previous students while bringing in the new kindergartners. At the time of this writing, approximately 250 students in the K–5th-grade dual-immersion classes were participating; however, the ultimate goal is to institutionalize the program in the entire school, K–6th grade.

Although Adelante has five interconnected components (University Visits and Science Camps; University Service Learning and Mentoring; Parental and Community Engagement; Research Informing Practice; and Cultural and Academic Enrichment), in this chapter we focus on the Adelante Oral Histories Project (AOHP), which is part of Adelante's Cultural and Academic Enrichment component. The AOHP reiterates Adelante's belief that there is an abundance of wisdom and knowledge in our community in the form of cultural wealth, and indeed, contrary to the way Latinas/os have been subordinated in U.S. schools, they are holders and producers of knowledge (Delgado Bernal, 2002; Yosso, 2006). It is also guided by the premise that culture and language go hand-in-hand in successful dual-language immersion programs to accentuate prior knowledge that the students bring with them to schools (Fishman, 2000; Gonzalez, 2001; Schecter & Bayley,

2002). The AOHP was developed, in part, because teachers expressed interest in incorporating more culturally relevant content into the curriculum. As
such, there is a purposeful effort to capitalize not only on the culture and
language of the students, but also on the cultural-familial and community
wisdom of marginalized communities and households.

The AOHP creates opportunities for students to engage in the qualitative research method of collecting oral histories to co-produce intergenerational knowledge that centers on the epistemologies of their families. This
is accomplished by introducing the students and their families to curricular
activities that draw from the teachings and learning that take place in the
home via everyday lessons shared through storytelling and family histories
(Delgado Bernal, 2001, 2002; Flores Carmona, 2010). The students and
their families shape various projects via the collection of oral histories and
the sharing of family stories. For example, the students and their families,
with the help of their teachers, are able to produce the story of the student's
name, genealogical research, stories of familial events, a newsletter connecting birth stories to Utah history, and digital stories that are written during literacy time and are produced during computer class. Indeed, through
the collection of cultural-familial knowledge the students have been able
to represent, illustrate, and encompass their understanding of their local
realities as children, students, and contributing members living in Salt Lake
City, Utah. We believe this project has the potential to empower children as
young as 7 and 8 years old "to become researchers, storytellers, historians,
oral historians, and cultural theorists in their own right" (Weis, Benmayor,
O'Leary, & Eynon, 2002, p. 153), as well as knowledgeable in computer
technology. The project is also a way to include the lives of students of color
and marginalized communities in the school curriculum.

SOLIDARITY AND CULTURALLY RELEVANT PEDAGOGIES

Test-driven teaching is a powerful pressure that can further widen the relational gap between teachers, students, and families. Teacher–home connections that persist, and on which both teachers and parents are willing to
work despite counterpressures, are a form of the ongoing solidarity we want
to see at Jackson Elementary School. We understand that relationships of
solidarity are not easily developed nor easily sustained, and we propose that
this is perhaps a result of the way in which the concept of solidarity has
been used and practiced. Solidarity has often been used by conservatives
and liberals to illustrate a situation of dependency, rather than a relationship of reciprocity between equals. In other words, solidarity has often been
invoked to describe situations where one individual is dependent on the generosity or goodwill of another. The two individuals or groups are not aligned

side-by-side, working next to each other. Rather, a missionary approach is mirrored where the person who has (e.g., money or salvation) attempts to give to those who are poor. Solidarity enacted in this manner is superficial because the one who gives to the poor gives enough to be engaged in charity, but not enough to equalize or alter the relationship. Indeed, the concept of solidarity was inherited from the Judeo-Christian concept of charity, which is not grounded in the idea of reciprocity, but the idea of helping those who need help or saving those who supposedly need saving. Charity presupposes a hierarchy in which a superior and inferior are connected through an act that is temporary, not sustainable, reciprocal, or relational (Zeledón, 2010).

Critical education scholar Sonia Nieto (2006) moves us from this common conception of solidarity and asks: "What does it mean to teach with solidarity, courage and heart, and what can we do to change current practices in teacher education programs to reflect these ideals?" (p. 458). Nieto argues that in order to develop and sustain relationships of solidarity with and empathy for students, "teachers must try to understand what is happening in the students' communities" (p. 458) with their families, and in their homes. In fact, these relationships are at the heart of teaching; such relationships can make a difference in the lives of students, in spite of the systemic inequities they might face in schools and in society. Nieto also reminds us that solidarity and empathy are not simply feelings we can have toward students, but that as teachers such emotions must be genuine and transparent in how we value students' identities and their ways of knowing.

> Solidarity with and empathy for students are not simply sentimental emotions. For teachers who think deeply about their work, solidarity and empathy mean having genuine respect for their students' identities—including their language and culture—as well as high expectations and great admiration for them . . . it means trusting them. (p. 466)

In order to better educate and serve students and their families and show respect for the local community, teachers must first learn about the students they teach, about their families, and about the communities where they teach. Teachers must be willing to genuinely include the students' cultures, epistemologies, and backgrounds into the curriculum. This means drawing from the cultural practices, the everyday teachings that are present in communities, and the quotidian teachings that take place at home to better educate all students (Flores Carmona, 2010). Along the same lines, Paulo Freire (1998) emphasizes that "to teach is not to transfer the comprehension of the object to a student but to instigate the student, who is a knowing subject, to become capable of comprehending and of communicating what has been comprehended" (p. 106). Nieto (2006) concludes that "Teaching is not just about reading, or math or art. It is also about *who* is heard, listened to and read about, *who* gets to count, and *who* can paint the picture" (p. 472). Being and working in solidarity with marginalized communities means that teachers need to carefully and critically reflect on their pedagogical and relational practices with the students and community members.

Scholar-activist Cecilia Zeledón (2010) extends this conceptualization of solidarity even further when she urges us to recognize that "*Nadie es mas que el otro, pero si menos sin el otro*" ("Nobody is more than another, but rather less without the other") (personal communication). She is recognizing a type of interdependent solidarity based on the understanding that we are different, yet we can share the same goals and the same struggles. We share duties, dreams, joy, work, and we also share each other's pain. It is through dialogue, listening, and hearing that we become aligned. For example, it is through dialogue, listening, and hearing that a kindergartner shared his pain of crossing the border to a member of our Adelante team who also crossed the border as a child. He described how he and his family were incarcerated and expressed fear, humiliation, and resentment toward "*los puercos policias*" ("the police pigs").

Zeledón argues that really hearing and sharing struggles, pain, and dreams lends itself to a type of interdependent solidarity based on the idea that we are one. The Adelante adult saw herself in the kindergartner and the kindergartner saw himself in her; the young student was not viewed as the "other." There has to be a "we," not an "us" (teachers/school leaders) and a "them" (marginalized students and their families). Too often, well-meaning teachers in schools with low-income students of color are disconnected from the community and send their own children to schools where they feel there are more educational opportunities and higher expectations. When teachers engage in solidarity that aligns them with the communities in which they work, they want the same academic rigor and have the same high expectations for their students as they do for their own children.

One way to move toward this solidarity that aligns teachers with the communities in which they work is to use pedagogies of the home in one's everyday teaching. Pedagogies of the home (Delgado Bernal, 2001) are cultural-familial practices of informal education that take place in the everyday interactions and sharing of experiences in Latina/o homes and communities. These pedagogies are present in everyday practices, contradictions, and teachings such as *consejos* (wisdom passed on through advise), *respeto* (respect for elders and their knowledge), and *educación* (informal education that instills values and includes education based on lived experience), and are at the center of the informal education that takes place in Latina/o homes (Elenes, Gonzalez, Delgado Bernal, & Villenas, 2001). Pedagogies of the home were named out of the necessity to include the epistemologies, pedagogies, and knowledge of Latina/o homes that usually do not make it into school settings, especially in a standards-based curriculum era (Delgado Bernal, 2001). Pedagogies of the home, such as the wisdom passed on through the oral history practices of Latina/o parents, extend critical pedagogies—the centering of knowledge from marginalized communities as legitimate classroom knowledge—by placing "cultural knowledge and language at the forefront to better understand lessons learned from the home space and local communities" (Delgado Bernal, 2001, p. 624).

These everyday lessons and rituals that take place in the homes of Jackson students include parents teaching with stories, legends, *corridos* [ballads], and role modeling. By having the students we worked with collect their family oral histories, the lessons of resilience and of making sacrifices to seek better life opportunities were learned and passed on. By listening and gathering stories that otherwise would not be taught in school, students engage in strategies of resistance that center their family members as holders and producers of knowledge that connects the school, their home, and their community (Delgado Bernal, 2001, 2002; Villenas & Moreno, 2001).

While pedagogies of the home provide a way to include the lives of students of color and marginalized communities in the school curriculum, they also can allow teachers to develop and nurture relationships of solidarity. If solidarity emerges from having genuine respect for students' identities, language, culture, and life experiences, then pedagogies of the home are a tool to share, hear, and learn about the pains and joys of students and their families. Indeed, we propose that the oral history project can contribute to developing solidarity as it clearly aligns teachers with the marginalized communities in which they work. Adelante, and more specifically the oral history project, have the potential to move us away from "us" and "them" and closer to a collective "we." The ideas of an interdependent solidarity and pedagogies of the home shaped the way we understand our data from 3 years of implementing the Adelante oral history project. It is to some specifics of the oral history project that we now turn.

THREE YEARS OF ORAL HISTORIES
AND COMMUNITY KNOWLEDGE

During 2007–2008, the Adelante oral history project began working with all the 2nd-graders in the Spanish dual-immersion program at Jackson Elementary School and has continued to work with them during the last 4 years.[3] One of the goals was to incorporate the epistemologies of students of color by including their lives, their families, and their community knowledge into the curriculum through the collection of family oral histories. While we saw this goal in relationship to the importance of recentering the marginalized knowledge of communities of color, initially we were not framing it as a means to develop solidarity. Judith developed several modules that were designed to bring family cultural knowledge into the school curriculum. For example, one unit was based on each student documenting the history and meaning of his or her name. After reading Alma Flor Ada's (1995) bilingual children's book *My Name is Maria Isabel/Me Llamo Maria Isabel*, students researched their names by talking to family members, and then spent literacy time writing and illustrating their findings. The students wrote the stories of their names to begin to excavate part of their life histories. The teachers also participated in the activities, and by the end of the semester, students, teachers, and Judith produced mini-books on the stories of their names. Adelante held a celebration and presented these books to the families and university co-founders of Adelante.

In another unit, during the second semester in spring 2008, students collected family members' oral histories via short interviews, learned about photography, and organized the narration and images into a "photo story."[4] The students worked with two Latina community professionals who explained to them how to use a camera and do photography, and how to conduct family interviews. They worked with elders in their families to complete the different activities. The families were in constant communication with Judith and/or the classroom teacher. In exemplifying collaboration, the students co-created with their parents and families' new cultural and historical knowledge about who they are and how they are viewed by their families. They became authors and researchers in their own right. The students wrote and converted interview answers from the family elders into a storyboard that took about 1 minute to read. Collaborating with computer instructors, the students then produced digital photo stories. Again at the end of the semester, Adelante organized a gathering to show the 38 photo stories. It is important to note that at each of these culminating events there was tremendous support, with the school's library filled to capacity. It is also important to understand that over the last 3 years, similar types of curricular activities have been developed for each grade level. This provides some continuity to the AOHP and to the idea that familial knowledge is valued in Adelante and is important to the school curriculum, thereby challenging the common practice of devaluing the knowledge students of color bring from their homes and debunking the myth that Latina/o parents are not involved in the education of their children.

Over the last 3 years, Judith has conducted interviews with teachers, mothers, and students to assess how each of these groups views the impact and possible contributions of the oral history project. Now, using a framework of interdependent solidarity, we see how these data suggest that collecting oral histories to produce intergenerational knowledge and to center the epistemologies of parents and their children has strengthened the communication and solidarity between families and teachers. For example, Mrs. Hope, the 4th-grade teacher, commented about how the oral history project in her class, connecting birth stories to Utah history, allowed her to understand parents and students differently and to understand the relationships between parents and students. Mrs. Hope's participation in the oral history project reinforced for her that in order to better serve her students she needed to get to know the parents and the surrounding community at a deeper level. The oral history project became a tool that allowed her to hear and learn about the struggles and the dreams of her students and their parents.

The parents' and students' participation in the oral histories project allowed them to collect multiple truths, share snapshots of their reality, and represent a clearer picture of their lives and their community. The following quotes from two students, Quetzal and Rubén,[5] represent new understandings of their life history that came out in their classrooms through the oral histories project.

My mom was the first in her family to go to college and that's why she wants me to also go to college. (Quetzal)

Mi mamá quiere que yo sea doctor y que ayude a la gente pobre [My mom wants me to be a doctor to help the poor]. (Rubén)

These quotes represent the explicit hopes and dreams of parents that the parents shared with their children, and the children in turn shared with their classmates and their teachers. Rubén's and Quetzal's quotes offer us a glimpse of the importance that education and *educación* have in their households, debunking the myth that Latina/o parents are not concerned with the educational attainment of their children. Importantly, their statements also provide a means for teachers to understand parents and students differently and to understand the relationships between parents and students, as Mrs. Hope suggested. Indeed, the interview data point to the idea that drawing upon familial and cultural knowledge of marginalized communities has the potential to move teachers and parents, and students toward an interdependent solidarity that allows teachers to see commonalities with their students' families and have genuine respect for students, their parents, and acquainted knowledge about the community where they teach.

A number of mothers believed that the impact the project had on them and their family was quite meaningful. Angela, a Mexicana mother, talked about seeing herself as a *libro* (a book) from which she can teach her daughter using home-based knowledge and her past experiences. In doing this, Angela was actively participating and contributing to the education of her daughter Karen.

Pues como si estuviera uno leyendo un libro de historia, se puede decir . . . si habla uno de sus antepasados, o como dice usted, del mas viejito, lo que el vivió, lo que había antes en sus épocas que era lo que hacían ¿verdad?

[Well, you could say it's as if I was reading a history
book . . . if you talk about your ancestors, as you said,
talk about the oldest family member, what he lived, what
existed during that time period, what they did, right?]

During the interview, Angela also talked at length about all the various ways in which she helps and supports Karen, even though she didn't finish elementary school in Mexico.

Lourdes, a Latina immigrant mother of a student in 4th grade, also acknowledged the importance of the oral history project in building a type of solidarity between parents and their children as they look through family pictures and ask about family members.

*Los niños se interesan en saber de sus familiares que; ¿de donde viene
mi abuelita? o ¿de que se murió y de donde venimos? A ella [mi hija] le
gusta y saco el álbum familiar. Les ayuda a involucrarse mas con uno
y hacen preguntas de los familiares de antes, de los antepasados. A ella
le gusta que aprenden en la computadora, las historias y todo eso.*
[The children become interested in learning about their family;
where is my grandmother from? How did she die? And, where
do we come from? She [my daughter] likes the project and she
took out the family album. This helps them get more involved
with us and they ask us questions about our ancestors. She
likes to learn computer skills, the histories and all that.]

The teachers also began to recognize the importance of being able to explore their own life histories to engage in reciprocal learning with parents and students and to better understand their students and parents' pedagogies of the home (Delgado Bernal, 2001, 2002; Sleeter, 2008). It was an enriching experience for the teachers and students to learn about the vast diversity in their classroom, an experience that can build solidarity across various participants because it allows them to have an understanding that we are different, yet we can share the same goals and the same struggles (Zeledón, 2010). For example, in an interview, Karen stated that she was able to connect with her classmates as she remembered the stories of her peers' names and of learning how to use a computer to tell a story. Similarly, another teacher, Mrs. Faith, spoke of breaking down cultural barriers and shared the following.

The benefits of having this Adelante component are plentiful. It
ensures that all of us are taking time to talk about cultural and
ancestral information to help children have a clear understanding of
where they have come from. It builds their self-awareness and self-

esteem. Not only does it help the individual but also breaks down barriers about culture. The stereotyping may still occur in their homes, but once we are able to share who we are with the group there is less judgment and more acceptance. I would hope the ultimate goal is to not just get them excited about their own culture but to realize that we all have culture and we need to celebrate and accept this diversity.

The comments from Mrs. Faith are pedagogically important for at least two reasons. First, she believed the oral history project contributed to increased self-confidence and self-esteem among her students by drawing upon prior knowledge. This speaks to an important outcome of including pedagogies of the home in the school curriculum and of blurring the boundaries between home and school knowledge. Second, she also expressed the cultural knowledge students gained via the oral history project. It exposed students to values, information, and experiences about other cultural and linguistic groups. Mrs. Faith encouraged students to bring a cultural artifact, an object, or to share their cultural traditions before the students presented the stories of their name. These pedagogical practices contributed to nurturing solidarity among the teachers, students, and the families, and between the students themselves. Although Mrs. Faith did not indicate to what extend this might change how she will teach in the future, she is one of the teachers who has continued to implement the oral history project in her classroom. The implications from this project continue to move us to explore the connections between pedagogical practices that draw from familial and cultural knowledge and the nurturing of solidarity.

CHALLENGES AND POSSIBILITIES FOR SOLIDARITY, OR LESSONS LEARNED

In an era of standardized tests and "colorblind" curricula that often exclude the realities of students of color, there are numerous challenges to engaging in work to build solidarity between home and school. Some of the challenges we encountered depended on the interactions, level of commitment, and relationships we had with the parents, teachers, school administrators, or students; others were strictly logistical. An example of a logistical challenge we encountered with parents included time restrictions due to their work schedules. The activities were specifically developed to include the assistance of parents or other family members. However, although long work hours leave parents little time for school-related activities, parents were always willing to contribute to the project in any way they could. If a parent or guardian needed to share a story about the life of a deceased family member, this could create an added strain to parents who worked long shifts or multiple jobs. Therefore, a project like this that strives for solidarity between teachers, parents, and students must negotiate the material realities of parents.

Creative and constant communication between Judith and the teachers made it possible to remain in contact with the families via face-to-face interactions, phone calls, or teachers sending home detailed notes, in English and Spanish, multiple times. On one occasion, Mrs. Faith used the prescribed parent-teacher conference (which has a 95% participation rate at Jackson) to describe and answer questions about the oral history assignment, and hand deliver a letter with instructions. As with other school assignments, some students did not complete every activity, but all participated and were engaged in the process of reconstructing and sharing familial knowledge. Regardless of the families' limited time and work obligations, nearly all parents and families were very generous with their involvement. A demonstration of solidarity is exemplified through the information the families shared, and the overall support and collaboration from the teachers and school administrator. Solidarity was also exemplified despite the various logistical and institutionalized barriers. We were all faced with our commitment and work but the intrinsic interest that teachers, kids, and parents found in this project helped us find ways to work around barriers.

The No Child Left Behind Act and standardized tests play a major role in today's schooling in the United States, and teachers, now more than ever, are forced to teach to the test and focus only on content that will be covered by state exams. Some might view incorporating familial knowledge or oral histories as an extra add-on that is nonessential to classroom teaching. Although there has been much positive feedback from teachers, we believe that teachers sometimes viewed the AOHP as "outside the core" activities that contributed to more work for them and their students, despite our view that this work serves as an important *cadenita* (link or chain) between the teachers, the students, and their parents. It is a tool that can allow teachers to enhance their understanding of students in ways that a standardized curriculum does not offer. Ideally, a deeper understanding of students will lead to understanding the teachers themselves as fellow community members, increasing the possibility of solidarity among families, students, and teachers. And when parents' knowledge and presence is valued in the classroom and school, students often are more engaged and do better in school.

Based on 3 years of implementation of AOHP, we propose that oral histories and intergenerational knowledge(s) are essential components of the core curriculum because they integrate language arts, social studies, and computer technology. We have also learned that the AOHP can be a tool to reposition communities that are seen as marginal or as having little to offer to what is taught in schools. In this way, the project serves to disrupt common or normalized core curriculum and pedagogical practices that continue to perpetuate particular deficit positioning of communities as non-contributing. Teachers' solidarity can be exemplified if they implement the project not as an add-on, but rather as a core pedagogical practice and a way to achieve higher-level thinking skills while focusing on community knowledge and expertise.

CONCLUSION: MOVING *ADELANTE* WITH ORAL HISTORIES AND SOLIDARITY

Home-based funds of knowledge continue to be acknowledged around the work of Latina/o parents in and outside of the household. These home practices serve to educate Latina/o children about the mundane, the quotidian, the motivations and the aspirations that parents have for their children that are exemplified when the children are told, "work hard and get a good education so you don't have to break your back like me."[6] The backbreaking jobs that some of the Latina/o parents of students at Jackson Elementary hold, such as working in the service industry or in construction, allow the parents to modestly teach what they do know, such as figuring out how to build something, social skills in dealing with other people, and making *sacrificios* (sacrifices). The parents teach their children by role modeling, by living life, and using examples of informal *educación* as primer teaching tools, as Angela discussed with Judith when she said she is like a *libro* from which she teaches her daughter Karen.

Sleeter (2005) reiterates that "Household and communities, including those impoverished neighborhoods, have organized funds of knowledge that people use in everyday life, and as children grow up, they become familiar with this knowledge through interaction with adults" (p. 110). Marginalized communities possess cultural wealth (Yosso, 2006) because they are wealthy in cultural-familial resources and assets. Benmayor (2002), in her oral history course, found examples of such cultural wealth and community knowledge among Latina/o parents and college students who were readily available to "help shape the curriculum, the values, and the multicultural life" of their school (pp. 97–98). The students' and families' cultural assets, their bilingualism, their cross-cultural knowledge, and their experiences with transnationalism were drawn into the curriculum to teach culturally relevant pedagogies of the home. Collaboration and demonstration of solidarity, as practiced in the Adelante partnership and specifically in the AOHP, confirms Sleeter's (2005) suggestion that oral history projects have the potential to empower students and teachers alike because such projects facilitate teachers gaining a deeper understanding of knowledge from outside the classroom that can help students in the classroom and affirm that students do bring knowledge from the home. The use of oral histories and family knowledge can build solidarity between families and teachers, where previously relationships between home and school, and pedagogy based on those relationships, had not been as strong.

Sonia Nieto (2006) asks, "What does it mean to teach with solidarity, courage and heart?" (p. 458). In our attempt to answer her question, we recognize that in a partnership and in our commitment to developing relationships of solidarity, we must try to understand students and their families, the community, and the teachings that are occurring in the students' homes. Gonzalez, Plata, Garcia, Torres, and Urrieta (2003) argue that gathering *testimonios de inmigrantes* (immigrants' testimonies) and sharing them with pre-service teachers can better prepare future teachers to address the needs of this growing immigrant population in communities where their presence has been unprecedented. Having students gather their family stories not only strengthens their writing, but the connections to/with cultural-familial knowledge also affirms the *educación* of the home and students are able to see their family elders as *maestras/os* (teachers) with valuable wisdom to pass on to them. These relationships are at the heart of teaching, and such relationships can make a difference in the lives of students.

As the fastest-growing population in Utah and in Salt Lake City specifically, Latinas/os afford the city with the many resources this group brings. New linguistic, cultural, social, and educational assets are present and growing, with a population of nearly a quarter of a million Latinas/os in the state (Perlich, 2004). Given this cultural wealth waiting to be tapped into, what better vehicle to genuinely try to understand the assets that Latina/o students and their parents bring to school settings from this community than through the Adelante Oral Histories Project? The Adelante Oral Histories Project highlights the possibilities of developing and maintaining relationships of solidarity by allowing us to center the epistemologies of immigrant parents and their children, thereby strengthening the communication and solidarity between families and teachers.

NOTES

1. In the context of the United States, we use the term *people* or *students of color* to refer to ethnic/racial populations that have been historically marginalized in this country, especially African Americans, Native Americans, Asian American/Pacific Islanders, and immigrant or U.S.-born Latinas/os. We also use *Latina/o* as an umbrella term to refer to both immigrant and U.S.-born Mexicans, Central Americans, and South Americans.

2. Over 90% of the students are eligible for free or reduced lunch (Utah Performance Assessment System for Students website, 2009).

3. I, Judith, began coordinating and implementing the oral histories project as part of Adelante's Cultural and Academic Enrichment program during the 2007–

2008 academic year and continued fostering and cultivating this program at Jackson with 2nd-, 3rd-, and 4th-graders. In summer 2010, I finished my doctoral degree at the University of Utah and moved to another state, where I began a postdoctoral fellowship. The program continues to be implemented in 2nd through 5th grade, and the original 2nd-graders now participate in the program with their 5th-grade teacher and the new oral history coordinator.

4. Digital or scanned photos are organized in sequence in Windows' Photo Story 3. A slideshow is created and then special effects, such as soundtracks, titles, captions, and animation are added. The students learned the program and did most of the technology by themselves.

5. All the names of students, parents, and teachers are pseudonyms given to the participants to protect their privacy.

6. This *consejo*/advice is often told to children to help motivate them in school. Many parents, including my (Judith's) mother, constantly share advice such as this, using their hard work as an example to derail their children from pursuing similar jobs and to motivate them to stay in school.

REFERENCES

Benmayor, R. (2002). Narrating cultural citizenship: Oral histories of first-generation college students of Mexican origin. *Social Justice: A Journal of Crime, Conflict and World Order, 29*(4), 96–121.

Delgado Bernal, D. (2001). Learning and living pedagogies of the home: The mestiza consciousness of Chicana students. *International Journal of Qualitative Studies in Education, 14*(5), 623–639.

Delgado Bernal, D. (2002). Critical race theory, latcrit theory, and critical raced-gendered epistemologies: Recognizing students of color as holders and creators of knowledge. *Qualitative Inquiry, 8*(1), 105–126.

Delgado Bernal, D., Villalpando, O., & Alemán, E. (2005). Personal communication.

Elenes, C. A., Gonzalez, F. E., Delgado Bernal, D., & Villenas, S. (2001). Introduction: Chicana/Mexicana feminist pedagogies: Consejos, respeto, y educación in everyday life. *Qualitative Studies in Education, 14*(5), 595–602.

Fishman, J. A. (2000). In L. Wei (Ed.), *The bilingualism reader* (pp. 89–106). New York: Routledge.

Flor Ada, A. (1995). *My name is Maria Isabel/Me llamo Maria Isabel*. New York: Aladdin Paperbacks.

Flores Carmona, J. (2010). Transgenerational *Educación*: Latina mothers' everyday pedagogies of cultural citizenship in Salt Lake City, Utah. Unpublished dissertation, University of Utah.

Freire, P. (1998). *Pedagogy of freedom*. Boulder, CO: Rowman & Littlefield.

Gonzalez, N. (2001). *I am my language: Discourses of women and children in the borderlands*. Tucson: The University of Arizona Press.

Gonzalez, S. M., Plata, O., Garcia, E., Torres, M., & Urrieta, L. (2003). Essays and interviews: Testimonios de inmigrantes: Students educating future teachers. *Journal of Latinos and Education, 2*(4), 233–243.

Nieto, S. (2006). Solidarity, courage and heart: What teacher educators can learn from a new generation of teachers. *Intercultural Education, 17*(5), 457–473.

Perlich, P. (2004). Immigrants transform Utah: Entering a new era of diversity. *Utah Economic and Business Review, 64*(5/6), 1–16.

Rich, A. (1979). Claiming an education. Speech delivered to the students of Douglass College, Rutgers University, New Brunswick, NJ. Retrieved from www.pearsonhighered.com/samplechapter/013813202X.pdf

Schecter, S. R., & Bayley, R. (2002). *Language as cultural practice: Mexicanos en el norte.* Mahwah, NJ: Lawrence Erlbaum Associates.

Sleeter, C. E. (2005). *Un-standardizing curriculum: Multicultural teaching in the standards based classroom.* New York: Teachers College Press.

Sleeter, C. E. (2008). Critical family history, identity, and historical memory. *Educational Studies, 43*, 114–124.

Utah Performance Assessment System for Students. (2009). Retrieved from http://www.schools.utah.gov/main/DATA-STATISTICS/Accountability/Accountability-Reports.aspx

Villenas, S. A. , & Moreno, M. (2001). To *valerse por si misma* between race, capitalism, and patriarchy: Latina mother-daughter pedagogies in North Carolina. *Qualitative Studies in Education, 14*(5), 671–687.

Weis, T. M., Benmayor, R., O'Leary, C., & Eynon, B. (2002). Digital technologies and pedagogies. *Social Justice: A Journal of Crime, Conflict, and World Order, 29*(4), 153–167.

Yosso, T. J. (2006). *Critical race counterstories along the Chicana/Chicano educational pipeline.* Routledge: Taylor & Francis.

Zeledón, C. (October 21, 2010). Contra historiadora, zapatista, adherente de la Sexta Declaración de la Selva Lacandona. Personal communication.

7

Community Collaboration in School Improvement
A Case Study of a California Middle School

Gina Elizabeth DeShera

The meeting consisted of a majority of bilingual Spanish/English
speakers and three parents who needed Spanish translation. The
translator did not use headsets so I was able to hear the translation,
which was not always accurate. Even though there was a translator, the
Spanish-speaking parents did not speak in any round-table discussions.
The only time they spoke was during one 10-minute small-group activity
discussing school discipline. The reporting out from the small-group
discussion was by school staff rather than parents. The administration,
principal and vice principal, took up the bulk of the meeting time
presenting the school discipline policy. When parents questioned the use
of suspension as a discipline tactic, administration thoroughly justified
the use, which ended the discussion.

The description above, which was recorded by this author in March 2006, illustrates a huge tension between Spanish-speaking parents and English-speaking school administrators.

The central purpose in this chapter is to detail how a middle school in Watsonville, California, attempted to create a model for including parents in the decision-making processes in order to democratize decision making. To democratize schools, we must open them to authentic participation by parents and the community in planning for, creating, and determining the school's destiny. Community participation in decision making will help build solidarity between marginalized communities and schools, and among marginalized parents with common concerns. Solidarity transcends all political, religious, cultural, and linguistic boundaries, and enables mutual collaboration between school staff and families. Parents hold tremendous power to contribute in meaningful ways shaping the destiny of the school. As Darder (2006) has stated, "Parent and community participation is critical to the liberation of culturally and economically subordinated communities from policies and practices that perpetuate their marginalization and exploitation" (p. i). Often, however, parents are coerced into forms of participation in which their concerns are never heard or are dismissed in repressive ways. This contradiction creates tensions and conflicts, in particular with linguistically diverse communities in which parents struggle for input into their children's education (Olivos, 2006). Olivos contends, "In theory the primary function of schools is to serve the interests of the community and its student population, in reality schools have historically functioned to serve outside interests" (p. 45).

A CALIFORNIA MIDDLE SCHOOL
AND THE POLICIES GOVERNING IT

The middle school where the research took place is nested in the Pájaro Valley Unified School District (PVUSD) in the community of Watsonville, California. The school is real but will be left unnamed. Watsonville, population 48,000, is a community of great wealth and extreme poverty. The region is one the world's most productive and profitable agricultural centers. However, one in five families earns less than the official poverty level, and unemployment (>17.6%) almost triples the California state average. Eighty percent of the population of Watsonville identifies as Latino or of Mexican origin. Forty-four percent identify as foreign-born, 70% do not speak English at home, and 22% speak only Spanish.

Parents of children in the PVUSD find a paradox when it comes to participation in the schools. On the one hand, the most salient legal policy mandates in the United States and California support their active participation. On the other hand are the apparent coercive and meaningless forms of parental involvement manifested in schools. I start with No Child Left Behind and the Public School Accountability Act, then review School Site Councils, followed by English Language Advisory Councils.

No Child Left Behind and the Public School Accountability Act

In 2001, the U.S. Congress approved the No Child Left Behind (NCLB) legislation. This law was intended to reform public schools by raising academic standards and imposing new systems of accountability. In 1999, prior to NCLB, California adopted its own version of reform and accountability called the Public School Accountability Act (PSAA). Similar to NCLB, the PSAA pressured schools in California to produce evidence that all students, regardless of race or socioeconomic status, were making adequate academic progress on standardized tests. Currently, with both NCLB and PSAA in place, schools in California are under tremendous scrutiny to demonstrate that all students are learning. Producing evidence that all students, regardless of race or socioeconomic status, have made progress on standardized tests has proven especially challenging for poverty-stricken districts that historically have experienced great difficulty raising student achievement.

Both NCLB and PSAA are intended to allow the public to hold local school districts accountable for students' academic performance. Under the principle of local control, public schools are supposed to be accountable to a locally elected school board, which is accountable to the electorate. Under PSAA, if schools fail to show progress, the first source of pressure is expected to be from the local community: State intervention is intended as a last resort. Poor communities, however, typically lack the social capital, civic capacity, and other resources necessary to monitor the quality of education at local schools (Noguera, 2004).

According to NCLB requirements, instructional programs, activities, and procedures shall be planned and implemented with "meaningful consultation with parents of participating children" (Section 1118, No Child Left Behind Act, 2001). The section further states, "Parents shall be involved in the joint development of the school plan and the process of school review and improvement." NCLB legislation also states that schools shall build the schools' and parents' capacity for strong parental involvement by evaluating it and identifying barriers to greater participation by parents, especially parents who are economically disadvantaged, and those who have children who are termed disabled, are English learners, have limited literacy, or are of any racial or ethnic minority background. The findings in such an evaluation should be used to design strategies for more effective parental involvement. In addition, Section 1118 details that, "Parents shall be involved in an organized, ongoing, and timely way, in the planning, review, and improvement of instructional programs." Schools receiving school improvement monies shall "provide reasonable support for parental involvement activities as parents may request."

Although the federal NCLB law mandates meaningful parental participation in serious school decisions, it has no practical suggestions for designing and implementing this parental involvement. Furthermore, many school staff members, including teachers and administrators, are unaware of the extent of the NCLB parental involvement mandates.

School Site and English Language Advisory Councils

According to California state legislation, a School Site Council (SSC) shall be established at each school to work with the principal to develop, review, evaluate, and allocate funds for school programs. The council is to be an elected group composed of the principal and representatives of various groups: teachers, other school personnel, parents, and in secondary schools, students. Teachers are supposed to vote for the teacher representatives, parents for the parent representatives, and students for the student representatives. In general, the School Site Council is the local governing body of the school and deals with school policy and the allocation of funds. The School Site Council is supposed to be a major part of the overall decision-making process at each school. At some schools, the School Site Council generally follows the principal's judgment, while at others principals will ask their councils to help develop new programs or oversee changes. School Site Councils are intended to be more than "rubber stamp" committees. Their primary role is to guide the site planning process and to ensure that the needs of all students are addressed in the school plan.

In California, if a school has 21 or more English Language Learner (ELL) students, then the parents of ELL students at the school must elect an English Learner Advisory Committee (ELAC). The ELAC must include a percentage of parents of ELL students equal to, or greater than, the percentage of ELL students in the school population. Others on the ELAC may include teachers, aides, and community representatives elected by the parents of ELL students. The ELAC is responsible for advising the principal and staff on how to address the issues of ELL students in the school plan. In order for the ELAC to communicate and advise effectively on school decisions, it must be represented on the School Site Council. Otherwise, these governing school committees meet in isolation of each other, and advice rarely moves from one committee to the other. In addition, when the principal of the school is responsible for taking concerns raised by the ELAC and articulating them to the SSC, those concerns can be changed drastically.

BUILDING SOLIDARITY THROUGH PARTICIPATORY DEMOCRACY

Considering the high rate of poverty and the high percentage of recent immigrants, many of them undocumented, it was a salient issue for the middle school to build solidarity and trust with the community in order to improve the school. By solidarity, I mean creating a sense of belonging with the most marginalized group of parents, finding a common purpose with the school staff, and simultaneously creating a feeling of being one of us, rather than one of them, thus utilizing collective leadership (Ritchie, Tobin, Roth, & Carambo, 2007). The study I describe here addresses two forms of solidarity: one among parents from a historically marginalized community, and the other between that community and the school. The first form of solidarity does not involve confronting major power, cultural, and language differences, while the second form does involve confronting these issues. In order to build this solidarity, the school needed to create safe spaces for parents' voices to express their opinions, and opportunities for parents to engage in critical dialogue about educational issues. By critical dialogue, I mean public discourse about educational issues, conditions, and problems in the schools, and ultimately, through discourse, offering solutions and alternatives to the problems. The discussions would start from the parents' personal knowledge and, through carefully structured critical dialogue, move from naïve personal knowledge to critical public knowledge. Ideally, the end result from the discussions would be transformative action using the existing democratic processes. This would build solidarity by creating an opportunity for community-driven school reform, linking school reform with the social, economic, and political development of the low-income families and stakeholders who historically had no voice in school decision making.

The theoretical framework used throughout this study distinguishes the extent to which representative and direct participation conceptions of democracy enable participation from diverse groups. Representative democracy can fail to provide frameworks for discussion of the daily, issue-to-issue interactions that bind a community together in solidarity and enable the different segments to understand their different needs and life experiences (Fields & Feinberg, 2001). Thus, certain groups often become underrepresented in the decision-making process. Rather than building solidarity, representative democracy often alienates the most marginalized and powerless groups.

An alternative is direct participation; a group, movement, or organization can attempt to give an equal voice to everyone who wants to participate. According to Fields and Feinberg, this kind of direct participation is usually designed to force a change in policies or systems of decision making. It allows for individuals to take a participatory role in the political infrastructure of their community. Participatory roles can make the formal system of educational decision making more inclusive of people who have not traditionally had much say in the decisions involved in the education of their children. Community members, whether they are parents or not, can actually participate in the making of decisions and in the assumption of responsibility for them. An attempt is made to give everyone who cares to participate relatively equal weight in determining goals, strategies, and tactics. As many decisions as possible are devolved to the grassroots level—to teachers, parents, staff, and community members—rather than to elected or appointed officials. Participatory democracy enables solidarity by allowing diverse groups to resolve universal concerns and issues.

In this model, involvement in the process of decision making has a positive effect on the quality of decisions made and is part of the education of the decision makers themselves (Fields & Feinberg, 2001). As participation grows, it is believed, so does the quality of grassroots decision making.

Participatory democracy is based on the assumption and faith that local people, if given the opportunity, are in the best position and have the best background and collective knowledge to solve differing local educational problems (Hess, 1991).

Participatory democracy's main theorist in the field of education, John Dewey, offers guidance in understanding the conception of democratic schools. Dewey called for participatory publics to engage more directly in public life. As Oakes and Rogers (2006) explained, Dewey suggested a public sphere in which experts and citizens participate together in social inquiry— the gathering, exchange, and interpretation of information, and debates about its meaning and how to use it. Dewey (1916) saw education as a social process. He described a democratic society as one that "makes provision for participation in its good of all its members on equal terms and which secures flexible readjustment of its institutions through interaction of the different forms of associated life" (p. 89). By definition, then, an undemocratic society sets up barriers to free communication of experience. Schools create such barriers when they limit discourse in school meetings to issues of school effectiveness and ignore the ways in which schools are situated in larger structures of inequality. The way in which participation is defined and implemented can also help to maintain rather than challenge the status quo (Anderson, 1998).

Dewey's work does not provide a model of how that inquiry would lead to action and change. Communities contain many complexities that must be considered, including exclusion of various publics from participation in civic activities because of citizenship, language, and/or socioeconomic status. A community's history can influence greatly the capacity and ease of developing a public intelligence as Dewey envisioned it. Schools, under a traditional bureaucratic structure, need guidelines on how to effectively include parents and community groups in decisions that affect the children in those schools. A model for participatory democracy in schools must keep at the forefront these very real obstacles to participation and carefully create processes that will help alleviate these barriers.

In the case study presented in this chapter, I sought to find out what hinders critical dialogue around educational issues on parent councils, what interventions a team of staff and community members would develop and implement to increase critical dialogue and participation in decision making, and what kind of parent and community participation in school councils would create critical dialogue and involvement in decision making.

BUILDING COMMUNITY PARTICIPATION

The research discussed here was intended to be one step in an ongoing long-term commitment to comprehensive change by a combination of community members, educators, and other stakeholders. The study was expected to be an expansive cycle that built the capacity for parent participation and continually drew upon this social capital to include new parents as leaders. The research aimed to "generate a sense that alternative ways of doing things are possible and feasible and to show that some of these alternative ways actually work or that the new ways do indeed resolve problems, overcome dissatisfactions, or address issues" (Kemmis & McTaggart, 2005, p. 590).

This study was not intended to be a magic remedy to the plight of our local schools, but rather a step toward encouraging explorations of the possibilities that would enable teams of parents, educators, and community leaders to address the multiple problems and issues confronting local schools and the surrounding environment. This study arose in response to a larger community social movement where various community members, groups, and organizations shared a concern that there was a deficiency in parental involvement in the decision-making processes at local schools. In order to avoid the pattern of outside experts constructing solutions for local problems, a planning team was formed to develop and implement interventions aimed at increasing critical dialogue in parent council meetings.

The Middle School

The middle school in which this study took place had an enrollment of 750 6th-, 7th-, and 8th-graders during the 2006–2007 school year. Ethnically, 89.3% of the students were Latinas/os, the majority of Mexican heritage; 70% of the total student population was of low-socioeconomic status; and approximately 30% of the student population is labeled as migrant due to their parents' migratory agricultural labor. English Language Learners accounted for 40% of the student population. The students at the middle school did not perform well on standardized tests in English. Only 18% scored at the proficient level on the California Standards Test in English/language arts, and a dismal 14% scored at the proficient level in math on the California Standards Test. At the time of the study, the teaching staff ethnically was 80% White and 16% Latina/o. Only two of the 35 classroom teachers were bilingual certified and provided primary language instruction at the middle school. The administration consisted of one principal and two assistant principals, all three of whom ethnically were White. The majority of the teaching and administrative staff lived in neighboring, more affluent communities, and not in Watsonville. Most of the teaching staff commuted to the middle school and left at the end of the day with no real sense of attachment to or investment in the democratic processes of the community.

As the vignette that opened this chapter illustrates, there was little evidence of critical dialogue among parents, community, and school staff about how to improve this middle school. Most school-directed parent meetings and committees were dominated by the transmission of information, such as how to get children into college, how to communicate with children, and how to eat right. Parents and community were largely viewed through a deficit lens, and parental involvement focused on remedying their perceived deficiencies.

Planning Team to Address
School–Parent Communication

To address these problems, a planning team was created from volunteers who shared the same concerns and desires to widen parental involvement in the decision-making process at the school. The planning team came into existence from a mutual belief that the existing policies, practices, and situations at the middle school were not adequate for authentically engaging the voices of the Spanish-speaking community at the middle school. The team consisted of:

1. The researcher/teacher (myself)
2. The parent liaison of the middle school
3. The bilingual resource teacher
4. The migrant education teacher
5. The assistant principal
6. Three parent leaders

The planning team itself brought a wealth of information and expertise to the table. Several members had been active community members involved in improving local schools for many years, and had participated in parent and community school meetings regularly in the past. The planning team also drew on the expertise and knowledge of the district-level parent coordinator. The planning team, with the power of mutual understanding and consensus, freely and authentically consented to the decisions they made. A shared commitment to transforming the established ways of doing things enabled the group to explore and investigate the social practices and situation at the middle school (Kemmis & McTaggart, 2005). Thus, a unique strategy for increasing parent capacity for participation in the decision-making processes at the middle school was thoughtfully developed based on the knowledge of the existing situation at the school, and the wider sociocultural reality. Strategies for improving community participation in the school's decision-making processes were implemented and evaluated by the planning team.

The planning team decided to use the existing parents councils, the English Leaner Advisory Committee (ELAC) and the migrant parent group (families who work in agriculture and migrate throughout the United States), to implement plans for increasing parent and community involvement in school decision making and ameliorating communication between school staff and the community. Throughout the year, a variety of interventions were designed, implemented, and evaluated at the ELAC/migrant parent meetings.

Gathering Data About What Happened

Data included 14 audio-recorded interviews with eight parents, four school staff members, and two administrators. Data also included audiotapes and notes from 24 parent council meetings and 9 collaborative planning team meetings. The data documented the successes and barriers experienced in the process of attempting to build community participation. The planning team met on a monthly basis to evaluate past ELAC/Migrant meetings, examine data gathered from the meetings, and plan interventions for subsequent meetings. Monthly meetings with the planning team were documented in minutes and field notes, and were audio-recorded. Parent meetings, planned by the group, were also observed by the district parent liaison and documented through notes. Parts of the ELAC/Migrant parent meetings were also audio-recorded. All of the School Site Council meetings were audio-recorded.

SUCCESSES AND BARRIERS

Interventions to Develop Critical Dialogue

The planning team implemented a nontraditional, additive model of parent involvement. Discussions at the ELAC/Migrant meetings started with parents' commonsense knowledge drawn from personal experiences in schools and moved toward more critical and disruptive knowledge. As Olivos (2006) explains, "The process of transformation is possible via the Freirian principals of dialogue and problem posing education that seek to name the problem, understand the conditions creating the problem, and offer alternatives and solutions to the problems" (p. 111). This process contributed to an increase in critical dialogue and participation in decision making.

Parent leadership facilitated communication and articulation of these discussions between Spanish-speaking parents and school staff. For example, the bilingual resource teacher explained:

> The elements of the team approach that make it effective is that it
> is not just the school personnel collaborating, but we are including
> parents really at every step of the decision-making process. They
> help us plan our ELAC/Migrant meetings to the extent that
> they are comfortable that they can conduct and participate.

The parent liaison noted improvement over the year because of including parents in planning for each meeting:

> *Ahora estamos mejorando. No completamente porque nos falta*
> *mucho. Ya estamos mejorando porque tenemos padres aquí ayudando*
> *con la planeación. Y ellos abren las juntas y toman liderazgo.*
> [Now we are getting better, not completely because we
> are lacking a lot. Now we are getting better because we
> have parents here helping with the planning. And they
> open the meetings and take on leadership roles.]

Parent leaders emerged as willing participants to help plan and facilitate parent council meetings. Parent representatives planned each meeting, from choosing the type of food to eat to determining the topic and what format would be used to present it. Parents also critiqued each meeting. Parent leaders demonstrated excellent and impressive rhetorical skills in Spanish, helping to facilitate meetings. Increasing parent talk and decreasing expert or professional talk was a significant step. Parents were nominated and elected by their peers to represent their interests in the School Site Council for the first time. Spanish-speaking parents came to a consensus about numerous recommendations and had a process for voicing their ideas and thereby influencing important school decisions. For example, after compiling the parents' ideas from one ELAC/Migrant meeting, the planning team put the ideas into five recommendations that the ELAC/Migrant representatives would take to the next School Site Council meeting, shown in Figure 7.1. The parents felt these were five important requests that could be attainable, and they hoped for immediate action on some of these items.

This consistent movement from discussion to action helped create a sense of parent empowerment and solidarity. Parent leaders described their work as developing increased trust with disenfranchised families. School professionals working with the parent leaders were simultaneously enlightened by the parents' expertise and knowledge, which is consistent with the "funds of knowledge" theory that advocates perceiving homes and communities in terms of the strengths and resources that they possess (Amanti, González, & Moll, 2005). Also, this study supports Auerbach's (2002) conclusion that "When parents of color generate their own discourse on schooling, rather than passively receive official discourse from the school, they begin to take charge of their participation in education on their own terms" (p. 1385).

Parent meetings can be successfully structured to include parent voices and build on parent expertise. As the study's data show, parents can and want to contribute in meaningful ways to deeper discussions about school curriculum, budget, and instructional practices. The parent leaders participating in this study were able to build networks with school staff and get

**Figure 7.1. Recomendaciones de los Padres de
ELAC Migrant al Concilio Escolar**

[ELAC Migrant Parent Council Recommendations]

1. *Recomendamos establecer un proceso en la escuela de cómo
   hacer conferencias entre maestros y padres. Una persona debe
   organizar las citas cuando queremos pedir una conferencia*

   [Parents recommend that there be an established
   process at school for parent–teacher conferences. A
   staff member should organize the appointment schedule
   when parents want to request a conference.]

2. *Recomendamos pagar horas extras a los maestros que
   puedan asistir a las juntas de padres, visitar familias
   en sus casas, tener conferencias en la noche.*

   [Parents recommend that the school pay teachers for
   the extra time spent attending parent meetings, making
   home visits, and having parent conferences at night.]

3. *Queremos convivios con padres y maestros para
   poder conocernos mejor. En estos eventos se puede
   premiar a los alumnos para motivarlos mejor.*

   [Parents would like there to be informal gatherings with parents
   and teachers so that we can get to know one another better.
   For these events, students should be rewarded to motivate
   better attendance on the part of parents and students.]

4. *Queremos conferencias formales entre maestros y padres
   bianuales. Primero se debe citar conferencias con los padres
   de alumnos que están recibiendo bajas calificaciones.*

   [We want formal biannual teacher–parent conferences.
   First we should set up conferences with the parents
   of students who are receiving low grades.]

5. *Queremos que haya un traductor accesible
   para los padres en la escuela.*

   [We want a translator to be accessible to parents at school.]

closer to the centers of power. Subsequently, parent leaders connected those institutional networks to parents who felt disconnected and unsure of how to approach the school. Three parent leaders described in detail their ability and desire to help build trust with parents who may be reluctant to participate in school activities. The parent leadership that was built will carry on to other schools and contexts within the community. Parent leaders generally stay involved and can be key players in creating social change locally. For this reason, it is worthwhile to create situations that provide parent leaders with the opportunity to represent other parents and to participate in serious decision making, in the process developing their social capital through school governance, decision making, and other forms of collaboration (Braatz & Putnam, 1996; Portés, 2000; Stanton-Salazar, 2001).

Barriers to Critical Dialogue and Participation

The main patterns shown in the data that hindered critical dialogue at parent meetings included the difficulty for school staff to accept the community's constructive criticism, school site and district control and influence on parental input, and parent leaders being co-opted by school administration.

It seems difficult for some school staff to accept parents' recommendations and ideas, especially when those parents are from a different culture, race, and/or socioeconomic background from the school staff. Various times during this study, school staff demonstrated a lack of understanding of the parents' perspectives. For example, when the ELAC/Migrant parents took their first recommendations to the SSC, a couple of teachers became defensive and seemed to get offended. During a discussion on discrimination, the assistant principal repeatedly dismissed the parents' and students' concerns about discriminatory events as typical teasing. Yet, as the data clearly pointed out, teasing was not the problem. Seven out of the eight parents interviewed recounted incidents when they felt discrimination at the middle school and nearby elementary schools. For the interviewed parents, these incidents were profound events that they couldn't forget. Also, at an ELAC/Migrant meeting, students shared with the parents examples of when they felt discrimination at school. Several spoke about teachers who prohibited them from speaking Spanish in class. But when presented with these ideas, the principal denied any wrongdoing by defending the teachers' actions as an effort to promote learning English rapidly.

At various times throughout this study, it seemed that some school staff members were uncomfortable with criticism. Criticism indeed seemed not to be well received even though it was carefully and respectfully worded. It is difficult to critique when the most powerful figures at the school seemed to become defensive and uncomfortable. Consequently, parents tended to blame themselves for any problems rather than examine practices at the school. In contrast, some school staff made general assumptions about the parents' presumed lack of response to their children's academic failure and parents being hard to reach. As the data overwhelming show, parents of the ELAC, as well as the Migrant parent council, were very careful to be non-confrontational with school staff through all their communications, both verbal and written. Yet, any slight criticism from parents appeared to result in a defense of "why we do what we do." The paradox for minority parents is that school staff members criticize parents for their noninvolvement in school affairs, but respond negatively when parents begin to challenge the status quo (Shannon, 1996).

The second barrier was control over parental input. The California state education code specifies how School Site Councils are composed and what their tasks include. In actuality, how the councils are run at each school site varies considerably and depends on the administrator, but there seems to be no oversight of these councils by district personnel. Although there is a district parent liaison in charge of ameliorating the English Language Advisory Committees (ELAC), each school principal implements the School Site Council on his/her own accord. In the case study, school administration controlled the structure, agenda, and implementation of School Site Council meetings, which made it difficult to change any ineffective and/or non-inclusive processes in this council. The principal addressed two-thirds of all items discussed at the School Site Council, speaking during three-fourths of the meeting time. Most of the items brought to vote at the SSC were framed in a way that made it difficult to vote against them. The language that was used, such as "state mandates" and "district mandates," left most parents and school staff speechless. Three of the school staff interviewed mentioned that on the School Site Council there is virtually no disapproval of proposals that are brought to vote. In addition, the parent who was president of the School Site Council also stated that no one ever voted "no" on items brought up for approval by the administration. What happened in the case study school is consistent with previous research on site-based governance councils that revealed the difficulty in creating shared governance that includes a diversity of participants in decision making (Cigliutti & Pini, 1999; Hess, 1991; Malen & Ogawa, 1988). Authorities and professionals influence laypeople on committees with the language they use and their own position of power and status. The SSC seemed to function as an endorsing committee and the school administration appeared to control this partnership.

The third barrier was co-optation. Parent leaders who emerge in this process all too easily became the object of co-optation by administrators. At the end of the 2007 school year, the school administrator offered three of the parent leaders involved in this study work at the middle school helping with the parent center. It is impossible for power to exist without trying to co-opt the other side that is not yet empowered; trying to co-opt is a tactic in the struggle by those who have the power to do so. As Freire (1998) points out, "In order for you not to be co-opted, to be out of the possibility of some power wanting to co-opt you, it's necessary that you do nothing" (p. 206). The dilemma is between doing nothing in order to avoid being co-opted, or doing something and risk becoming an object of co-optation. Parent leaders of the most marginalized parent group are especially attractive targets for co-optation by the powerful. Being employees of the school put these parents in a situation in which they became naturally more favorable to school administration.

Ultimately, district personnel writing the school plan eliminated and discouraged community collaboration in this fundamental document. At the last School Site Council meeting in May 2007, we were informed that a large part of the school plan had already been written by district personnel. A template of the plan, already substantially filled out, had been sent out to the principals of each district school. It appears that school district administration filled out three-fourths of the school plan, leaving little room for community input and collaboration. Dividing the students into three levels according to their standardized test achievement in English/language arts was a district mandate and written into the plan by district administration. The ELAC/Migrant parent council advised against separating the students, fearing that many English Language Learner and migrant children would be tracked into the lower-level English classes. In spite of their opposition, the three-tiered plan moved forward. It seems that the mandate was already in place and most of the school plan was already written when the parent councils were asked for their recommendations. Top-down policy mandates negate the possibility for community input.

CONCLUSION

Building solidarity between the school and the community is complicated because of existing power structures within the school institution. Legislation alone does not ensure democratic schools. Even with laws mandating community input in school plans, the human interactions that actually take place in school meetings determine whether they are indeed democratic. Ultimately, the school and district administrations have the last word in all decisions; other school staff and families can only give their opinions and recommendations. However, if the school staff genuinely were to seek to include the recommendations of parents in collective decision making, solidarity could be achieved.

The first step to building solidarity with the community is to encourage critical dialogue by creating an environment in which parents are free to express their concerns without fear of being criticized or ignored (Olivos, 2006). These opportunities for discussion build critical and transformative knowledge inside the schools and with the families. School personnel should help facilitate and pose questions, but need to hold back from imposing their opinions. School personnel must simply listen to parents' concerns and support parents' efforts to resolve them. Throughout this study, it became evident that it was difficult for school staff to actively listen rather than talk at the parents. Parent meetings must be carefully structured to minimize school staff talk time and equalize parent talk time. Teachers, administrators, and experts, in general, need to be constantly reminded to be succinct while talking and not to dominate meeting time. This question needs to be posed at the conclusion of each meeting: "Who did the majority of the talking?"

It is important that participants in the discussions do not suffer any repercussions for voicing their opinions, and that parents can be critical of practices at the institution and express how those practices could be better. Freire (1998) states, "It is impossible to democratize schools without opening them to the real participation of parents and the community in determining the school's destiny" (p. 24). Building such solidarity creates collective agreements, co-respect, and co-responsibility for goals (Ritchie, Tobin, Roth, & Carambo, 2007). Opportunities to question and critique are imperative for populations that have been historically silenced and marginalized. As demonstrated in this study, immigrant linguistic minority communities can benefit from building institutional social capital under such conditions (Stanton-Salazar, 2001). This was especially significant with the parent leaders participating in this study.

Dewey (1916) envisioned local social spaces where people could learn and exercise the skills of dialogue and debate necessary for the development of a participatory democracy. However, as the data in this study show, the professionals or experts can control meetings to move in favor of their own ideas, thus thwarting participation. Although the parent community represents the checks and balances for the school, in low-income linguistic minority communities it is easier for school personnel to seek endorsement for ideas rather than structure meetings to include critical dialogue about school issues. The data also indicate that some school staff operated under the assumption that the community is neither interested in nor capable of analyzing complicated educational issues. Educators working through a deficit model deny parents the opportunity to voice their concerns and to critically question the structures of inequality at their local schools. When assumptions such as these are present, it is very difficult to build participatory democracy and solidarity, and an antagonistic relationship may persist between marginalized communities and schools.

Parental community involvement that embraces participatory democracy as Dewey (1916) imagined it, where diverse publics are able to dialogue and reach consensus, is more difficult and complex than Dewey theorized. Dewey warned that social class stratification would destroy the possibilities of participatory democracy and collective decision making. Social class, race, language, culture, and history all influence the dynamics of the interactions and dialogue in parent–school meetings. An individual's social class, race, gender, and language play an important role in the unequal distribution of opportunities for entering into dialogue with professionals who control the resources at institutions (Stanton-Salazar, 2001). Moreover, institutions can feel threatened by an informed, energized public that is attempting to collectively change what is and what has become comfortable. The data in this study supported the notion that there exists a voluntary action and a collective intelligence, but the hierarchy of social stratification silences the marginalized and negates their actions for change. The more low-income minority communities remain segregated, the greater the need for professionals to create democratic meeting structures in order to build solidarity with the communities that they serve.

The events in this study are just a small piece of the larger community. This study focused on building solidarity with a Latina/o Spanish-speaking parent community in California who have for many years been trying to build structures of equity in the schools so that their voices may be heard. At times, school parent councils can be platforms for genuine community input. However, these parent councils often serve to reinforce an illusion of democracy by providing opportunities for parents to be represented and voice their opinions, but they are then ignored. It seems that disruptive knowledge—ideas contradictory to the status quo—is neither present nor welcome at parent councils. Thus, the public needs forums outside of the institution for disseminating and accessing knowledge that challenges the status quo.

REFERENCES

Amanti, C., González, N., & Moll, L. (2005). *Funds of knowledge theorizing practices in households, communities, and classrooms*. Mahwah, NJ: Lawrence Erlbaum.

Anderson, G. L. (1998). Funds of knowledge theorizing practices in households, communities, and classrooms. *American Educational Research Journal, 35*(4), 571–603.

Auerbach, S. (2002). Why do they give the good classes to some and not to others? Latino parent narratives of struggle in a college access program. *Teachers College Record, 104*(7), 1369–1392.

Braatz, J. P., & Putnam, R. D. (1996). Families, communities, and education in America: Exploring the evidence. *Center on Organization and Restructuring of Schools*. Washington, DC: U.S. Dept. of Education, Office of Educational Research and Improvement, Educational Resources Information Center.

Cigliutti, S., & Pini, M. (1999). Participatory reforms and democracy: The case of Argentina. *Theory into Practice, 38*(4), 196–202.

Darder, A. (2006). Foreword. In E. M. Olivos (Ed.), *The power of parents a critical perspective of bicultural parent involvement in public schools* (pp. ix–xii). New York: Peter Lang.

Dewey, J. (1916). *Democracy and education an introduction to the philosophy of education.* New York: Free Press.

Fields, A., & Feinburg, W. (2001). *Education and democratic theory finding a place for community participation in public school reform.* Albany: State University of New York Press.

Freire, P. (1998). *Pedagogy of freedom ethics, democracy, and civic courage.* Lanham, MD: Rowman & Littlefield.

Hess, A. G. (1991). *School restructuring Chicago style.* Newbury Park, CA: Corwin Press.

Kemmis, S., & McTaggart, R. (2005). Participatory action research communicative action and the public sphere. In K. Denzin & Lincoln, Y. (Eds.), *The Sage handbook of qualitative research* (pp. 559–603). Thousand Oaks, CA: Sage Publications.

Malen, B., & Ogawa, T. (1988). Professional-patron influence on site-based governance councils: A confounding case study. *Educational Evaluation and Policy Analysis, 10*(4), 251–270.

No Child Left Behind Act. (2001). United States Code Annotated.

Noguera, P. (2004). Transforming urban schools through investments in the social capital of parents. *Motion Magazine.* Retrieved from http:// www.motionmagazine.com

Oakes, J., & Rodgers, J. (2006). *Learning power organizing for education and justice.* New York: Teachers College Press.

Olivos, E. M. (2006). *The power of parents a critical perspective of bicultural parent involvement in public schools.* New York: Peter Lang.

Portés, A. (2000). The two meanings of social capital. *Sociological Forum, 15*(1), 1–12.

Ritchie, S. M., Tobin, K., Roth, W., &. Carambo, C. (2007). Transforming an academy through the enactment of collective curriculum leadership, *J. Curriculum Studies, 39*(2), 151–175.

Shannon, S. M. (1996). Minority parental involvement: A Mexican mother's experience and a teacher's interpretation. *Education and Urban Society, 29*(1), 71–84.

Stanton-Salazar, R. D. (2001). *Manufacturing hope and despair: The school and kin support networks of U.S.-Mexican youth.* New York: Teachers College Press.

8

Build Me a Bridge
Steps to Solidarity Between a School and Its Community

Gilberto Arriaza & Alice Wagner

"Be careful! I can't believe you park on the other side of the tunnel!" Rosie said to me, almost shouting from one end of the school's parking lot. Rosie's words stay with me as I walk down the stairs to the tunnel's opening. As I descend, my ears and eyes adjust to the darkness and the laughter of the women walking together through the lingering smoke of the underage high school smokers. The women help each other to carry strollers down the stairs, their animated conversation brightening the damp interior. As I pass them, they offer cheerful greetings: "¡Maestra! ¡Buenas tardes! ¿Cómo está? (Teacher! Good afternoon! How are you?)" A train rumbles overhead and deafens my ears as the rest of the conversation and laughter continues into the darkness. I begin to ascend and the faint odor of urine fades and mingles with the scents of springtime.

Tall fences separate the houses from the path, but the generosity of nature pushes beyond these man-made borders. An apricot tree decorates this well-used walkway with blossoms that cover the path, hiding random bits of trash that are the usual adornment. Nearby, an urban rooster crows, blending its song with the faint bark of a neighborhood dog. Perfumed teenagers check their cell phones as they slowly make their way home down the path from school. The houses, this side of the tunnel, have many signs of careful tending, yet some, with their dry brown front lawns and empty driveways, show the telltale signs of foreclosure, silent testimony to the economic crisis.

One of us (Alice) jotted the impressions above in her journal. In this chapter, we discuss our qualitative study of a California school's efforts to lay the foundation of solidarity with its parental community. We first briefly discuss the shifting demographics as they relate to the site's social tensions. Next, we discuss what we mean by solidarity and define key concepts, which constitute the core of the theory we used in this chapter. We then examine what constitutes a challenge to teachers' comfort zone, and close the chapter with a discussion and conclusions. We argue that social distance, particularly between teachers and parents, presents a challenge to building solidarity. Without direct attention to factors that underlie social distance—particularly race and social class—progress toward solidarity will remain elusive.

THE PLACE

As the vignette above describes, Golden Prairie Elementary School (pseudonym) is located in what appears a tightly knit working-class community in the south side of Hayward, California, a city known over 100 years ago as "Hungry Town," as Helen Winker, an 80-year-old lifelong South Hayward resident, described it to us (all names of persons in this chapter are pseudonyms). This observation has remained true through the years, even as Hayward strives to become more economically stable and pushes toward more economic vigor. Although some teachers choose to live in Hayward, many others seek more prosperous locales in surrounding cities in which to live and raise their children, some traveling over 30 minutes each morning to teach.

The west side of the train tracks hosts single-family homes that, in fact, house at times more than one family. Golden Prairie is a school with a good reputation among parents. To ensure access, some families find it worth a tight squeeze to share a home with another family, and a white lie to attempt to outwit the school's strictly defined attendance areas.

The other alternative for gaining access to Golden Prairie is to seek housing closer to the school, on the east side of the train tracks, where apartments are more plentiful and houses more affordable. Tall, brown buildings face the well-used cars parked along the straight but broken sidewalks. Walking under fruit trees and past unkempt large yards that surround a trio of small houses, a visitor might hear the band practice of a local group playing Mexicano music. To the right, rows of houses lead down to the train station. These blocks run parallel to the road that houses businesses and restaurants in various stages of economic depression. Beauty is present in the flowers of fruit trees, the architecture of the grandiose Catholic church and its recently rebuilt high school behind the trees and the rolling golden hills that grace the length of Mission Boulevard and beyond.

Golden Prairie's parking lot marks the beginning of the neighborhood park that provides a margin of green grass between the train tracks and the houses that face the street. A walk down the curving path through the well-trimmed grass leads one past the basketball court, through the playground, and past the used syringes tossed into the bushes by illicit drug users. The graffiti tells a story that many members of the community can read. To outsiders, the same paint tells a story of young people searching for meaning beyond the distress they feel with the life they have. Children climb on the play structure with their parents close by as dogs and their owners play and run. Shuddering trains rush by, startling unaccustomed visitors, while habituated locals seem unaware of their passing.

Golden Prairie offers a bilingual education program (as do many schools in the school district) to serve the large population of English Language Learners. Parents may choose between bilingual education in which students study academic subjects in Spanish as they gradually learn English, or Structured English Immersion (SEI) taught wholly in English.

The school reflects the shifting demographics of the United States, and the particular case of California, where more and more there exists a reversed proportional racial representation between teachers and students. In 2007, the school counted 29 teachers: 4 Latina/o, 1 Black, and 24 White. About seven out of every ten students are Latino (mostly children of Mexican immigrant families). More than half of the students are English Language Learners, and most of them speak Spanish. Besides English and Spanish, more than 15 languages are spoken by smaller numbers of English Language Learners, including Tagalog, Hindi, Vietnamese, Tongan, and Urdu.

In a school where teachers commute in to work, everyday solidarity between them and the local community always seems to be difficult to achieve without conscious effort. Close social interaction with parents, whether through formal venues or informal ones (e.g., visiting parents' homes), happens infrequently. Teachers drive through the school's neighborhood en route to and from school, but rarely do they venture on foot through the tunnel or along the sidewalks. The school's leadership has sought to connect—as the tunnel does in actual physical terms—teachers with parents as a central strategy to close the social distance between them in order, ultimately, to improve children's academic performance.

HOW POPULATION SHIFTS CHANGED THE SCHOOL

Parental involvement in children's schooling is rooted in the ideal of public education as a system linked to a pluralistic, local, and secular democracy. The benefits of parents' involvement in schools are so clear and well documented that discouraging parent participation seems to work against a school's function and purpose (see, for instance, the studies by Aspiazu, Bauer, & Spillett, 1998; Collier, 1995; Decker & Decker, 2003; Patall, Cooper, & Robinson, 2008). For years, it has been argued in the United States that students, teachers, and parents constitute the three essential pillars of this system. Yet, somehow, including parents as active school supporters seems to be a source of unproductive tension in the school system as a whole at Golden Prairie.

We can list a long combination of factors as potential explanations for why this school–parent fragmentation still occurs. Instead, we posit that current demographic shifts due in part to the late-20th-century immigration phenomenon (see, for instance, Bouvier, 1991; Cornelius & Martin, 1993; Edmonston & Passel, 1994; LeMay, 1989; Rodriguez, 1996) have profoundly changed the social, cultural, linguistic, and socioeconomic landscape of today's student population, especially in the state of California, while teachers, pedagogy, delivery, and content continue to reflect a society dating a few decades back, when assimilation constituted the predominant pedagogical approach: "sink or swim."

While public schools, such as in California, have increasingly mutated into systems serving predominantly low socioeconomic families, and of Latino, Southeast Asian, and African American heritage, the predominant racial and socioeconomic profile of the teaching force reflects a bygone social order: White and middle-class. According to Knowledge Networks (2010), about three out of every four teachers in the United States are female and eight out of every ten are White. In California, more specifically, White teachers comprise about 72.1% of the total, 14.5% are Latina/o, and 4.5% are Black (EdSource, 2009), rates that may not vary significantly in the near future.

These demographics lead us to wonder about the impact of the current cultural mismatch on the educational system as a whole, and what the social ramifications might be of the cultural disparities between teachers and students. What is clear to us is that at Golden Prairie there appears to be a challenging social distance between teachers and parents.

SOLIDARITY AND SOCIAL DISTANCE IN THE SCHOOL

Solidarity signifies the purposeful actions seeking to eliminate social distance and to redress the tensions it generates. Solidarity can be sustained when and if explicit treatment of race, social class, and gender roles takes center stage. Given that social distance forms the core of our definition of solidarity, we will briefly discuss it.

One of the earliest definitions of social distance comes from Park (1924), who defined it in terms of understanding and intimacy among individuals and groups as measured by grades and degrees. Coleman (1988), Putnam (2000), and Forrest and Kearns (2001), among others, treat social distance as an element associated with social capital. Putman's (2000) study of civic life among U.S. communities shows that generalized reciprocity lies at the base of social capital. Putnam notes that generalized reciprocity exists when people do things for each other "without expecting anything immediately in return, and perhaps without knowing" the other person (p. 134). Putnam observes that a substantial amount of trust and honesty anchors this social behavior.

In social capital terms, when generalized reciprocity exists in a community, the cost of social transactions goes down, and accordingly, social benefits increase. Neighbors watch out for each other's self-interests (e.g., homes, cars parked on the street), and become protective agents—taking care of the neighborhood's children and reciprocating in exchanges of money, information, food, and even tools. As a result, the separation among individuals and groups diminishes. People relate to each other more as acquaintances than as strangers. Even in cases where heterogeneity marks the life of a community, social distance shrinks considerably anytime social capital is strong. Then solidarity, understood as "a feeling of membership or belonging to a group of interlocutors" (Ritchie, Tobin, Roth, & Carambo, 2007, p. 154), can occur.

In cases such as ours, where teachers and the school's parental community live in separate and spatially distant neighborhoods, it is safe to assume that social distance is considerably high, since these separate living arrangements do not allow teachers to attend local, ordinary social functions, or have any ongoing meaningful relationships with members of the community whose children they educate. Conversely, parents may consider teachers and the building where their children spend countless hours of their lives, foreign and removed from their own day-to-day activities. Thus, building solidarity in these circumstances becomes increasingly more important because understandings cultivated in isolation tend not only to be wrong but to nurture false assumptions.

Teacher perceptions and preconceived notions of the families and their neighborhoods often end up primarily shaped by their firsthand contact with children and youths, and to a lesser extent by the occasional meeting with parents (Manning, 1995). Not having other sources to confirm or deny perceptions, the potential for teachers' confusion may considerably increase, because such limited contact may only confirm assumed understandings.

For instance, in her ethnographic study of ten Mexican families living in the United States near the border with Mexico, Valdés (1996) shows how, when social distance exists, key communication breakdown between these families and the schools might take place. The author shows some of the cultural and social ramifications that occur when teachers use assimilation as the frame when approaching these families—teachers dismiss and marginalize the families' cultural specificity, from traditional gender roles, to age, to the functions of education in their lives.

Sending messages home illustrates such communication breakdown. When teachers send evaluative or other types of information through the children, either as written text or orally, the information may be ignored by the family, since legitimate communication with an authority figure (such as a teacher) in that Mexican-origin community only happens face-to-face.

Schools have used a variety of approaches—e.g., home visits, clubs, centers—to shorten the social gap. Since home visits played a central role in Golden Prairie's efforts to build solidarity, we briefly describe what is known about them. Structured and mandated home visits have been used as a remedy to social distance for many years (Harry, Klingner, & Hart, 2005). Visiting families is a way to build solidarity when participants understand that the purpose of these visits is to work with families to build relationships and exchange information (Goodson, Layzer, & St. Pierre, 2000). During home visits, teachers may inevitably expose themselves to their own cultural misconceptions and the social distance between themselves and their students. The most successful visit are those for which teachers prepare by engaging the role that race and social stratification play as mediating factors (Bell, 2002; Manning, 1995). Structured home visits may result in a heightened sense of empathy toward the "child and the child's situation" which, in turn, may influence the teacher's "attitude toward helping that child in the classroom" (Meyer & Mann, 2006, p. 95). Visits may also translate into teachers' increased cultural awareness, which eventually materializes as culturally relevant teaching (Ginsberg, 2007). Approaches that prepare parents and teachers alike for these visits seem to hold greater promise.

De Gaetano (2007) reports that after 3 consecutive years, a program educating parents and teachers about schooling and the community, respectively, the participating Latino families showed understanding of formal and informal active participation in the education of their children at home and the school site, as well as the demystification of the function of schools in their lives and the lives of their children. Likewise, teachers demonstrated an increased awareness about cultural and linguistic issues, which, in turn, aided them to prepare culturally responsive learning experiences for the students. It appears that when schools additionally offer services to the community (such as literacy, English as a second language, dental care, and child care), the potential for sustained involvement increases considerably (Delgado-Gaitan, 2001; U.S. Department of Education, 2001).

Thus far, we have described the immigrant, low-socioeconomic neighborhood to clearly locate our study. We explained how the mismatch between the racial and social composition of the teaching force and the parental community constitute an influential factor in the existing social distance between them. We also defined the nature of solidarity and what is known about some of the actions schools have taken to build it. Now we need to take a closer look at the concrete experience of building solidarity at Golden Prairie elementary.

THE ENCOUNTER BETWEEN TEACHERS AND PARENTS

As a new principal, Ms. Marie Rivas soon realized that the school staff and the parent community had, other than formal encounters, little or no ongoing relations. Ms. Rivas and a small group of core teacher leaders, agreed that organized home visits would help. She then secured a grant to pay teachers for the time they would put into this activity in pre-visit workshops, the actual home visits, and the post-visit debriefings. Visits were voluntary. Twenty-one members of the staff attended the initial preparation and home visit training. Only six teachers went on to do more than one visit. By year 2, only four participated.

We, the authors, documented the experience. Using two different instruments, we surveyed all 29 teachers. One survey focused on teachers who visited homes at least once. The other focused on those who did not participate. To make sure we would have a clear picture of what was going on, we also organized a focus group of seven teachers, and one-on-one informal as well as structured interviews with several teachers, parents, and the school principal. Additionally, we kept close participant-observer journals throughout.

The following journal entry encapsulates the mind-set Ms. Rivas inherited at the time of her arrival to the school:

> Instead of relaxing over a leisurely 30-minute lunch, teachers
> have packed the small, dark mailroom. I'm there with Jasmine
> and Amanda, picking up our mail. Jasmine is a bilingual teacher
> who learned Spanish as an adult. She reaches out to Amanda:
> "I meant to get those books you wanted this morning, but
> a parent came and wanted to talk with me. Then the bell
> rang and I didn't have time to run over to your room."
> Jasmine paused, and continued, "*I* love teaching!" she
> exclaimed. "I just can't stand dealing with parents!"
> The bell rang, drawing all of us outside to where the
> students were lined up in the warm sunshine. The teachers'
> chatting continued as they walked out together to direct
> their students into the classrooms from lunch.

When Ms. Rivas first came to Golden Prairie Elementary as the new principal, the relation between teachers and parents was very much limited to classroom sessions, or to official events such as the Back-to-School Night at the beginning of every school year. The previous principal had recognized the parents' need for a language bridge and hired teachers who spoke Spanish to reflect the language of the community, which was the extent of her efforts to build solidarity between the staff and parents.

Ms. Rivas launched a two pronged initiative consisting of 1) home visits, and 2) formal and informal direct parental involvement in the school's affairs. We define these activities as the steps to building solidarity between the school and its community. We identified three emerging themes throughout our experience at Golden Prairie elementary school: visits, unifying the community, and significance of leadership.

Visits

Jasmine's reaction—captured in the excerpt above—to talking with parents captures some of the class and race tensions we uncovered in our study. While all six teachers who participated in the home visits agreed that "apprehension was relieved" and that "relationships improved" between them and the families, about three out of every four who did not participate stated that their "level of knowledge of the community [was] sufficient." More than half of these same teachers argued that "lack of time is a significant factor in participating in home visits."

Asked about the incentives provided for faculty involvement in the home visits, one of the teacher leaders who participated in home visits said: "We would pay teachers to do something wonderful, that would improve their practice and make families happy." And then she added: "Working with easy families would be easy; we didn't have too many difficult ones."

In addition to being compensated for their time, those teachers who did participate only visited "easy families." Those families considered "easy" were immigrant families, the majority from rural Mexico. No other cultural groups were visited. Teachers were encouraged to begin with families they felt a connection with, where they would feel comfortable. In the end, few teachers pushed their comfort zone into new territory.

Over time, these structured visits left closer relationships between the participating teachers and the families they visited. Despite these attempts, home visits never become a habit, a way the school relates to its community, even among those six participating teachers.

Uniting the Parent Community

As part of Ms. Rivas's attempts to close the social distance between the community and the school, she established both formal and informal structures for both groups to congregate, meet each other, and talk. Between 2006 and 2010, formal leadership committees have been established with greater force and expanded responsibilities. These structures include the School Site Council (SSC), which is, among other things, charged with budget decisions; and the Parents and Teachers Association (PTA), which is charged with coordination of volunteerism and fundraising. These two bodies give parents and teachers parity representation. In fact, the PTA election resembled a true community festive event. Parents and teachers together tallied the votes and a number of people came to watch the process. In the SSC, by establishing seven parents for seven teachers, both parents and teachers will be involved and will work together.

The legally mandated English Learner Advisory Committee (ELAC) has grown in size and influence over the years as well, focusing specifically on the needs and issues of children officially classified as English Learners. These policy-mandated structures are expected to operate on a regular basis, regardless of the school leadership. However, making sure they all function and influence the school depends on whether such leadership—by prioritizing and encouraging attendance, and soliciting parents' views—places them on equal footing with the regular school operations.

Following the school district's policy that requires each school to have a parent center, Golden Prairie has for years had a room equipped with tables, chairs, a microwave, and an electric coffee maker where parents congregate. They use this place to organize activities, stop for a chat, have a cup of coffee, or just sit as they wait for school to be dismissed. The activities are generally unsupervised by school personnel, and as long as what takes place there is not for personal lucrative ends, its uses are open.

Informal structures function parallel to the formal ones. Parents are invited to have *Café con la Directora* (Coffee with the Principal), which is a semiformal monthly meeting where the principal listens to their concerns and ideas, while educating them about their rights and obligations with the U.S. education system. This venue involves almost exclusively immigrant mothers from Mexico who find it convenient to participate. The meetings take place during regular school hours. Working parents, including many fathers, are usually at work during that time. The principal also sends a weekly phone message to all parents, letting them know what is happening at the site and encouraging their involvement. These calls go out to all parents in both Spanish and English.

These informal structures have spawned a few initiatives, including a writing workshop series in Spanish language attended by mothers who used autobiographical material as the basis for essay writing that culminated in a Saturday celebration where mothers read their writings to an audience of children and adults. Another initiative offered by the city police covered a variety of topics, including community safety tips and gang prevention, culminating in a "graduation" for all of the participants. Yet another initiative is the African American parents' club that resulted in the first annual Celebration of African American Culture Through Art and Music in 2010. Parent friendship groups have also emerged. One led to a local women's walk against cancer. Another group of women took a class sponsored by the local community college, which for many was their first foray into higher education.

Finally, parent-organized events of a more leisurely and celebratory nature—e.g., movie nights, carnivals, and dances—run throughout the school year. Parents often ask Ms. Rivas if teachers will attend, if they will bring their children. But their absence is palpable. Moreover, Maria Hurtado, a mother of three, illustrated to us how cultural difference has affected her, and arguably, most mothers like her. She referred to a "coldness" of the school culture:

> *No hay celebraciones. Una que otra. En México siempre*
> *hay algo que celebrar. Es tan diferente aquí comparado a*
> *México. Es frío aquí. Vine una vez a una celebración para*
> *Martin Luther King. ¡Me dormí! Era todo en inglés. Me*
> *aburrí. No volví a venir hasta que cambiaron unas cosas.*
> [No celebrations here. Just once in a while. In Mexico there
> is always something to celebrate. It's so different here in
> comparison to Mexico. It's cold here. I came once to a Martin
> Luther King celebration. I fell asleep! It was all in English. I
> was bored. I never came back until some things changed.]

Ms. Hurtado's comment echoes larger, unspoken feelings that suggest deeper cultural distancing. We wonder whether celebrations offered by teachers that encourage parental involvement and/or increased teacher participation in parents' events could bridge some of the social distance present at the site.

Teachers stated that lack of time was a significant factor in not participating. The surveys showed that they also felt comfortable in their knowledge of the community. These seemingly superficial reasons may belie deeper feelings, not so easily disclosed, as hinted at in the following account in the journal of one of the authors:

> Some of the difficulties for the staff in electing to not
> participate in home visits were fear of the unknown, a lack
> of time. For some, it seemed like "one more thing to do."
> They did not see the benefits of participating. Also, some
> had their own personal reasons for not participating. They
> didn't want to risk having an "uncomfortable moment."

Fear of the unknown—avoiding the risk of uncomfortable moments—codify avoidance, and possibly lack of will and skill in confronting the very issue that may be preventing teachers from building solidarity with a community that most definitely does not mirror them.

Variations of public commentary that refer to parents' "lack of formal education," "dysfunctional homes," or "difficulty talking to them"—as in "I love teaching, but can't stand parents"—as reasons not to establish ongoing solidarity is the manifestation of a behavior that seems, in spite of great efforts from the leadership, quite pervasive.

The Significance of Leadership

Ms. Rivas plays a central role in the school's efforts to build solidarity within the parental community. She mobilized resources to initiate the structured home visits, and created all the venues discussed thus far. "I feel I've been this bridge, always connecting," Ms. Rivas asserted when we asked how she saw herself working with parents. She then elaborated how parents spoke to teachers through her, and vice versa. This function, however, appeared to be consuming her energy and time. She expressed the need for parents to go directly to teachers and wanted the staff to embrace the idea that they needed a direct connection with the parents of the students they serve.

The encouragement to come together to the parent center or to have coffee with the principal has allowed parents to create solidarity among themselves. They talk about their children's schooling; they compare one classroom to another, comment about an issue, and share their experiences. When they encounter differential treatment, they go directly to Ms. Rivas. They actively seek her counsel and advocacy to mediate their relationships with teachers.

Reflecting on her experiences, Ms. Rivas considers her role as a mediator to solve problems, and as an explainer for perceived teachers' shortcomings. "Parents know teachers never attend events, afterschool programs," she stated in one of our interviews. "They [parents] complain to me about that." And then she concluded: "So far I've been a buffer for teachers. I've protected them by excusing them before parents."

MAKING SENSE OF THIS EXPERIENCE

Solidarity—understood here as closing social distance between teachers and parents, and within the different parents' subgroups—is in its very early stages at Golden Prairie. Increased solidarity is happening mostly within the parental community. As parents close the distance gap among themselves, by doing things such as planning events together, they create bonds among themselves, hence improving their social capital.

As the connecting tunnel is metaphorically extended into the school, parents create a stronger base from which to interface with teachers on more equal footing. The teachers who participated in home visits indicated that their relationships with families improved. The teachers' comments replicate what research on home visits has shown. But because so few teachers participated, structured home visits did not translate into the closing of social distance between the school as a whole and parents. Other school efforts, as we showed in the brief literature review in this chapter's first section, seem to have decreased social distance for and within parents' and teachers' groups.

The generally poor teacher participation in the school's efforts to build solidarity reveals deeper school culture issues. Offering "easy families" makes us wonder who are the "difficult families," and whether by providing such choice, unspoken racial and class prejudice was simply relegated to the margins, and treated as something else. Referring to "fear of the unknown" as a reason why so many teachers did not participate seems to avoid precisely that.

The most significant steps taken so far have been toward building solidarity within the parental community; they are interacting together and supporting each other. As parents are increasingly involved in more activities at the school, they inevitably become a larger block from which they can better engage teachers. However, despite the two-pronged efforts of the principal to build connections, teachers continue to be absent.

For a White woman to walk in neighborhoods populated by folks who are ethnically or racially different from her might be perceived as an odd sight to the inhabitants, and it might be anomalous for her, to say the least. But opting out of home visits could simply be too high of a price, for this act may trap teachers in their own assumptions and understandings about the neighborhood's social and cultural makeup. Then, social distance and cultural estrangement will continue to be high and will only increase in the foreseeable future.

In order to last, school-based initiatives must be sustained by actions originating from the community itself. So far, the school principal clearly occupies an indispensable role as the central convener of solidarity work. She brokers solidarity by conveying messages to and from each of the participants (teachers and parents). While this type of leadership may be necessary as an initial phase, it is clearly unsustainable. When asked about this, Ms. Rivas expressed her belief that formal structures will be able to take care of sustainability. Research has shown (e.g., DeShera Rodriguez, 2008; Donato, 1997) that the power of co-optation that institutions exert might overpower the will for transformation of individuals or groups.

CONCLUSIONS

Social distance has been slightly affected at Golden Prairie Elementary School. Solidarity created through the opening of formal and informal structures, which have allowed closeness among parents, seems to be the most significant solidarity work thus far. This kind of solidarity makes it possible for parents to exchange information, organize groups, and forge degrees of social capital. Indeed, social capital appears to have increased because parents have established connections among themselves, and have, so far, begun to stand together around common concerns on issues affecting the education of their children.

Latina/o parents, specifically mothers, seem to have reduced social distance among themselves, yet they still tend to cede their influence to the school principal, and appear to prefer to let her mediate their relations with teachers, so as not to disrupt the status quo. In contrast, the African American parent club was formed after just a year of evening parent meetings. This parent group took the initiative to transform itself from a principal-led group to an independent club, hosting its own events that brought together various community services and educational groups.

The work of the school principal has been crucially important in the creation of solidarity. Her work reminds us of the significance of the role that educational leaders can play as change agents. However, as long as this work primarily comes from the school site and from the principal's office, the sustainability of it all appears vulnerable at best. The imbalance of power between the community and teachers continues to be great. Teachers most definitely benefit from working within the power of the institution, while parents, especially Latina/o, to a degree depend on the principal's advocacy.

If the principal progressively removes herself from her function as convener and as power broker, then she may provide a first step toward building capacity for the long haul. Parallel to this, parents need to actively engage each other, and the schooling of their children. The more parents take the initiative, the more promising the school's efforts for the future.

Parental involvement has overwhelmingly included women—who, for the most part, are housewives—and very few men. Most activities have taken place during the day, the normal working hours for these families' men. By making spaces available that only housewives can use, the school might inadvertently be contributing to keep intact traditional patriarchal family relations.

Solidarity may depend, ultimately, on having open and unambiguous conversations on race and social class. Despite a plethora of published resources people in schools can potentially use, if misconceptions are not corrected, assumptions about economic poverty are not challenged, and racial prejudice is not debunked, sustainable progress toward solidarity will remain elusive. So far, these conversations have been tangential at Golden Prairie.

For sustainability purposes, the small group of teachers that has been more amenable to creating solidarity with the parental community could easily become the school leadership team. As a core group, they could start a process of moving the rest of the faculty in the direction of full solidarity among themselves and between them and the parental community. In the words of a teacher leader:

> Teaching is more than the classroom. It involves the
> community. Especially when the economy is broken. The
> culture of the teachers is changing. It is changing for sure.

REFERENCES

Aspiazu, G. G., Bauer, S. C., & Spillett, M. D. (1998). Improving the academic performance of Hispanic youth. A community education model. *Bilingual Research Journal, 22*(2) 127–147.

Bell, L. A. (2002). Sincere fictions: the pedagogical challenges of preparing White teachers for multicultural classrooms. *Equity & Excellence in Education, 35*(3), 236–244.

Bouvier, L. F. (1991). *Fifty million Californians?* Washington, DC: Center for Immigration Studies.

Coleman, J. S. (1988). Social capital in the creation of human capital. *American Journal of Sociology, 94,* 95–120.

Collier, V. P. (1995). Acquiring a second language for school. Direction in language and education series. *National Clearinghouse for Bilingual Education 1*(4), 1–10.

Cornelius, W. A., & Martin, P. L. (1993). The uncertain connection: Free trade and rural Mexican migration to the United States. *International Migration Review 27*(3), 484–512.

Decker, L. V., & Decker, V. (2003). *Home school and community partnerships.* Lanham, MD: Scarecrow Press.

De Gaetano, Y. (2007). The role of culture in engaging Latino parents' involvement in school. *Urban Education; 42*(2), 145–162.

Delgado-Gaitan, C. (2001). *The power of community. Mobilizing for family and community.* Boulder, CO: Rowman & Littlefield.

DeShera Rodriguez, G. (2008). *Community Collaboration in School Improvement.* Doctoral dissertation, AAT 3318548. Santa Cruz, CA: University of California, Santa Cruz.

Donato, R. (1997). *The other struggle for equal schools: Mexican Americans during the civil rights era.* Albany: State University of New York Press.

Edmonston, B., & Passel, J. S. (1994). *Immigration and ethnicity. The integration of America's newest arrivals.* Washington, DC: The Urban Institute Press.

EdSource. (2009). *Resource cards on California schools.* Retrieved from http://www.edsource.org/pub_resourcecards.html

Forrest, R., & Kearns, A. (2001). Social cohesion, social capital and the neighbourhood. *Urban Studies, 38*(12), 2125–2143.

Ginsberg, M. B. (2007). Lessons at the kitchen table. *Educational Leadership, 64*(6), 56–61.

Goodson, B. D., Layzer, J. I., & St. Pierre, R. G. (2000). Effectiveness of a comprehensive, five-year family support program for low-income children and their families: findings from the comprehensive child development program. *Early Childhood Research Quarterly, 15*(1), 5–39.

Harry, B., Klingner, J. K., & Hart, J. (2005). African American families under fire: ethnographic views of family strengths. *Remedial and Special Education, 26*(2), 101–120.

Knowledge Networks. (2010). Representative panel of teachers for research. Sourced from knowledge panel. Retrieved from http://www.knowledgenetworks.com/ganp/docs/KnowledgePanel-Teacher-Panel-Description-2010-02.pdf

LeMay, M. C. (1989). U.S. Immigration policy and politics. In M. C. LeMay (Ed.), *The gatekeepers, Comparative immigration policy* (pp. 1–24). New York. Praeger.

Manning, M. L. (1995). Teacher reflection and race in cultural contexts: history, meanings, and methods in teaching: understanding culturally diverse parents and families. *Equity & Excellence in Education, 28*, 52–57.

Meyer, J. A., & Mann, M. B. (2006). Teachers' perceptions of the benefits of home visits for early elementary children. *Early Childhood Education Journal, 34*(1), 93–97.

Park, R. E. (1924). The concept of social distance: As applied to the study of racial relations. *Journal of Applied Sociology*, 8, 339–344.

Patall, E. A., Cooper, H., & Robinson, J. C. (2008). Parent involvement in homework: A research synthesis. *Review of Educational Research, 78*(4), 1039–1101.

Putnam, R. D. (2000). *Bowling alone. The collapse and revival of American community*. New York: Simon & Schuster.

Richie, M. S., Tobin, K., Roth, W-M., & Carambo, C. (2007). Transforming an academy through the enactment of curriculum leadership. *Journal of Curriculum Studies, 39*(2), 151–175.

Rodriguez, N. (1996). Immigration and intergroup relations, African Americans and Latinos in immigration: a civil rights issue for the Americas in the 21st century. *Social Justice Journal, 23*(3), 111–124.

U.S. Department of Education Office of Educational Research and Improvement. (2001). *Family involvement in children's education. Successful local approaches.* Washington, DC: U.S. Department of Education.

Valdés, G. (1996). *Con respeto: Bridging the distance between culturally diverse families and schools.* New York: Teachers College Press.

9

Challenges to the Development of Solidarity

Working Across Intersections of Power and Privilege in New Zealand

Anne Hynds

The search for solidarity, which would unify diverse groups both historically privileged and marginalized by Western schooling systems around
issues of equity, is of international concern (Freire, 1997; McLaren, 2000;
Penetito, 2010). This chapter aims to explore notions of solidarity by raising questions about the purpose and complexity of solidarity development
within and between such groups. Using the example of Aotearoa New Zealand (the bicultural way of identifying the country), I highlight specific challenges that have potential to both aid and rupture solidarity development
in colonized countries. By doing this, the chapter reconceptualizes solidarity
development work in ways that move beyond simple process descriptions
and binary notions of group membership.

THE MEANING OF SOLIDARITY
FOR INDIGENOUS PEOPLE

A variety of definitions, underpinned by different epistemological and ideological assumptions, are used within discussions of solidarity development. For example, solidarity is linked to *kotahitanga*, or unity (Penetito,
2010), coalitions or partnerships (Cole & Luna, 2010), moral imperatives within particular communities (Wenger, 1998), and group ethics
within a wider struggle for social justice (Freire, 1997). Solidarity unifies
oppressed groups across international boundaries in a collective struggle
against inequality in all its manifestations. McLaren (2000) described
Freire's notion of solidarity as "anchored" in common positions of hope
and suffering (p. 202).

Wenger (1998) maintains that solidarity in groups is achieved through alignment work, underpinned by common interests, affinity, and moral imperatives. "Solidarity is . . . a source of cohesion that reflects a moral choice [and] . . . commitments [moral imperatives]" (p. 295). Moral imperatives that are shared and understood are essential because they reflect a group's core enterprise and purpose.

For Indigenous peoples in colonized countries, solidarity is often linked to ensuring the survival of language and unique cultural knowledge systems (Batibo, 2005). Since the early 1800s, in Aotearoa New Zealand, the Indigenous Māori tribes have been subjected to European colonization. Schools were designed to produce and reproduce dominant Western knowledge systems and assimilate Māori into the dominant group (Pākehā/White New Zealanders) by eliminating their language and cultural differences (Penetito, 2010). Solidarity within and across Māori tribes is linked to "*kotahitanga* [unity] . . . through being united in a cause" (Penetito, 2010, p. 263). Resistance and decolonizing practices, which work to disrupt and dismantle colonizing systems of oppression, are essential for achieving solidarity across Indigenous tribal communities.

According to Cole and Luna (2010), the degree of solidarity within feminist activist communities is increasingly aligned with partnerships and coalitions that engage diverse community members in owning the problem of gendered privilege and marginalization. These arguments are useful for understanding that solidarity develops through meaningful connections within and across different groups; intersecting boundaries of gender, sexuality, race, dis/ability status, and social class. Consequently, solidarity development occurs through collective consciousness-raising activities that engage partners in critiquing and dismantling oppressive and privileging assumptions of cultural identity.

Although there are differences in interpretations, these authors emphasize that solidarity is an identity process that defines membership for deliberate groups as they undertake coalition work toward commonly valued goals (Cole & Luna, 2010; Freire, 1997; Penetito, 2010; Wenger, 1998). In addition, these authors would argue that solidarity development requires shared imperatives, which incorporate ethical, moral, and political aims. Such arguments raise questions about the purpose and development of solidarity work between mainstream schools and their local Indigenous communities, particularly within colonized countries such as Aotearoa New Zealand.

THE SITUATION IN AOTEAROA NEW ZEALAND

Much of the rhetoric of school–community solidarity is underpinned by alarming statistics that emphasize significant and enduring achievement disparities between minority and majority groups. In Aotearoa New Zealand, this disparity is most evident between *tangata whenua* (Indigenous Māori students) and the dominant Pākehā group. Māori student disengagement in schools is reflected in lower educational achievement and attainment of national qualifications, higher rates for stand-downs or suspensions over behavior, and greater representation in remedial education programs in comparison with the Pākehā (White) group (Ministry of Education, 2006).

The issue of Māori student underachievement is usually framed within a cultural deficit explanation rather than in the enacted racism embedded within schooling systems (Penetito, 2010; Sleeter, 2005). For example, the majority of teachers and principals are Pākehā. Many teacher attitudes and practices contribute to low Māori student achievement, because teachers believe that Māori families and communities are dysfunctional and Māori students require "fixing" or "curing" in some way (Alton-Lee, 2003). In the deficit explanation, the problem of educational failure is located with the child and/or the child's home background rather than in the monoculturalism of schools (Sleeter, 2005). Solidarity work, underpinned by effective learning partnerships between Māori and non-Māori school community members, may be a way to transform mainstream schooling experiences for Māori students.

Within Aotearoa New Zealand, there are various interpretations of the moral imperative needed to underpin solidarity development between Māori community groups and mainstream school communities. There are also different interpretations about unifying processes and the participants who should be involved. For example, in one interpretation, *kotahitanga*, or solidarity, is achieved when there is a clear rejection of the cultural deficit explanation related to Māori student achievement in schools (Bishop, Berryman, Tiakiwai, & Richards, 2003). Bishop et al.'s (2003) interpretation of unity is created through teachers' rejection of deficit theorizing and through teachers' own agency—a belief in the power of teachers to make a difference. This interpretation of unity focuses on the quality of relationships and learning interactions between teachers and Māori students within classrooms. Solidarity development occurs as teachers reposition themselves as co-learners or facilitators of learning experiences as they work to connect with, and value, Māori students and their Māori *tanga* (Māori culture and ways of living).

A second interpretation of solidarity work emphasizes the lack of meaningful relationships and interactions between teachers in schools and their local Māori communities (Biddulph, Biddulph, & Biddulph, 2003). Many Māori parents/caregivers feel alienated from mainstream schools because of past negative experiences. Unity develops as teachers work to involve Māori parents and caregivers in the work of instructional reform. A more welcoming and responsive schooling environment is needed in order to develop school–community alignment work that better supports Māori student learning, both at home and in the classroom. The moral imperative in this interpretation would be to develop affinity, common interests, and mutual commitments between teachers and local *whānau* (family).

A third interpretation is that differences in achievement outcomes are attributable to individual and institutional racism across schools (Penetito, 2010). Educational policies and practices were designed to colonize and assimilate Māori students into the dominant culture by eliminating language and cultural differences. Schools remain responsive to the cultural capital of the dominant Pākehā (White) group, and there is a reluctance to address individual and institutional racism that marginalizes Māori history, knowledge, and custom. Penetito (2010) argues that what is "most damaging to Māori as a people has been the way in which the . . . interpretation of the problem has also contributed to the general public viewing Māori education as a problem area, and Māori blaming themselves for their underachievement" (pp. 58–59). There is an educational debt to the Māori that must be acknowledged. Therefore, solidarity between Māori and non-Māori groups must embrace a particular type of unifying work. The moral imperative within this interpretation would be to disrupt White power and privilege in schools (Penetito, 2010).

These three interpretations raise questions about the development of solidarity work and the types of shared moral imperatives needed to unify New Zealand teachers with local Māori communities in the work of change. But little is said about the complexity of challenges and the obstacles underlying solidarity development when historically marginalized and privileged groups attempt such work. This chapter reports an investigation of that complexity.

A RECENT HISTORY OF SCHOOLING IN NEW ZEALAND

In 2003, the New Zealand Ministry of Education responded to the first two interpretations cited above by initiating new forms of colonial control. The first phase of an exploratory professional development program, "*Te Kauhua*," was implemented in volunteering schools across the country. *Te Kauhua* refers to the supports on the *waka* (canoe), and was used as a metaphor for getting "all on board" and "rowing" in the same direction. The stated aim was to improve teaching practice and outcomes for Māori students based on understandings derived from productive partnerships[1] between Māori and non-Māori groups. Each school involved in the pilot study was supported by an in-school facilitator to:

- collect baseline data on Māori student achievement and identify students' learning needs;
- develop appropriate interventions between schools and *whānau* (families), including professional development programs for teachers to address the most significant of these inteventions;

- implement the interventions;
- observe and record changes in Māori student outcomes; and
- assess the impact the program had on Māori student outcomes and *whānau*–school relationships.

The professional development was facilitated through a process of community consultation that raised teachers' consciousness of alternative perspectives. New spaces were created for Māori students, their *whānau* (parents and caregivers) as well as local *kaumatua* and *kuia* (male and female community elders, respectively) and Māori staff members to speak about their interpretations of mainstream schooling. Participants spoke about teachers attending new professional development *hui* (meetings) together, and setting individual goals to try new strategies. They included cooperative learning approaches, assessment practices, literacy strategies, and co-construction activities (whereby teachers took a "not-knowing" approach in order to encourage student voice and problem-solving). There were increased efforts to involve *whānau* in meaningful classroom and school activities to support Māori students' progress. Teachers made more effort to ensure *whānau* felt welcomed into classrooms and the wider school. Some concentrated on visiting parents/caregivers at home, others on more effective teacher–parent/caregiver meetings to discuss Māori students' progress. Māori and non-Māori teachers worked together in new and different ways to support solidarity work. For example, many Māori teachers supported their non-Māori colleagues to learn *te reo* (Māori language) and *tikanga* (customs) as a way of valuing and using Māori knowledge. Teachers opened up their classrooms for peer observation and feedback. There were new meeting structures whereby teachers presented evidence of Māori students' work, engagement, and achievement. There was a new focus on teachers developing and sharing their knowledge about culturally responsive pedagogies and the impact this was having on Māori students' learning and engagement across both schools.

An initial evaluation, conducted in 2003, indicated positive signs from Māori community consultation within several schools (Tuuta, Bradnam, Hynds, Higgins, & Broughton, 2004). However, recommendations made in the report stated that further research was needed on partnership processes between Māori and non-Māori and the sustainability of such work. Subsequently, a second phase of research (Hynds, 2007) was initiated after consultation with the Ministry of Education, a special advisory group, and school communities. This second phase of evaluation aimed to investigate the challenges that influenced the development of solidarity or partnership work, when Māori and non-Māori participants worked together on school reform.

AN INVESTIGATION OF SOLIDARITY WORK IN AOTEAROA

Culturally responsive research protocols, as advocated by Bishop and Glynn (1999), were used to guide this second phase of research (Hynds, 2007). I have attempted to follow these protocols within a qualitative research process, using inductive analysis. A Māori-centered research methodology was important for establishing trusting and respectful relationships between the researcher and participants.

I conducted semi-structured, in-depth interviews with 77 teachers, students, parents/caregivers, principals, specialist teachers, and in-school facilitators within two schools that had taken part in the government-funded solidarity initiative. Seventeen teachers (7 Māori and 10 non-Māori) from both schools were interviewed twice over the course of 12 months (2003–2004) to track personal experiences and perceptions of change over time. Parents/caregivers (10 Māori and 20 non-Māori) and their children (15 Māori and 15 non-Māori) were also interviewed.

There were particular limitations and gaps within the second inquiry process. Fewer Māori participants were interviewed than non-Māori, and more females were interviewed than males. Teachers were interviewed twice, whereas parents/caregivers and their children were interviewed only once. Information was not gathered on participants' socioeconomic status, country of birth, first language, *iwi* or *hapū* connections, or sexual orientation.

I also kept a detailed research journal, which provided an audit trail for recording hunches and decisions made about interview evidence and data analysis. Evidence from interviews was triangulated to ensure the validity of results. In keeping with culturally responsive research protocols (Bishop & Glynn, 1999), participants were also asked to comment on the trustworthiness of findings.

RESULTS: PERCEPTIONS OF UNIFYING SPACES

The initial results from the first set of teacher interviews indicated positive perceptions arising from the initiation of solidarity work. During their first interviews, 15 of the 17 teachers (6 Māori and 9 non-Māori) reported feeling enthusiastic and optimistic about improving school and classroom practice for Māori students through the development of common interests and a shared moral imperative for change. The action research process developed within schools enabled Māori school-community members to speak about their experiences and interpretations of school life. Ten out of these 15 teachers (5 Māori and 5 non-Māori) from both school communities described how their thinking was transformed when they listened to the experiences of others involved in the whole-school setting; as one non- Māori teacher said:

> It was listening at the *hui* [meeting], and seeing how classes
> were for many Māori students, and from their grandparents'
> perspectives and becoming more aware, of what the cultural
> differences are. . . . It was somebody from . . . the local Māori
> community, a *kaumatua* (elder) who spoke and some of the Māori
> staff spoke, it made me aware of what my downfall had been,
> my lack of cultural knowledge . . . , it made me realize what
> does go on in my classes and rethink how I approach teaching
> . . . and the way I had been treating students prior to this.

Teachers described the process as if they were awakening from a deep sleep, a type of collective unconsciousness (Hynds, 2007). Activities within the initial community consultation process enabled many participants to examine previously unseen biases and assumptions, as described by this non-Māori teacher:

> [H]aving listened to the commentaries, the voices of Māori students
> and realizing now that my whole teaching delivery was uncomfortable,
> suddenly the problem was there for me. . . . I couldn't see the problem
> before. My eyes have been opened to that; I don't think I am alone.
> . . . But let's start identifying what the problem is, and the problem
> doesn't necessarily sit out there . . . it sits here within us as teachers.

Some community members, such as the parent/caregiver of a Māori child below, confirmed the impact of teachers listening to the experiences of others who are not typically heard within the school environment and noted that it had been an "eye-opening" experience for many:

> I have been to a couple of their *hui* [meeting], down at
> the *wharenui* [big house], . . . and basically I think it's
> been an eye-opener for the teachers from their point of
> view, learning about the needs of Māori students.

Twelve of the 17 teachers (6 Māori and 6 non-Māori) stressed that group cohesion, established through a common imperative, was necessary for change. Although the process was exciting, it was also uneasy and unsettling for many. One Māori teacher believed that she had been able to "cleanse" her teaching. She described this as a deeply spiritual process, which enabled her to reconnect with her *wairua* (spirituality):

> There have been changes since our *mahi* [work] . . . , it was like
> a healing process to come out the other side, and it's made big
> changes. . . . I've noticed . . . we respect one another a lot more,
> we share a lot more and we're not afraid to challenge each other.

Because the way we look at things now is different to what it was before. And it was like cleansing, getting rid of the staleness, and for me reconnecting to my *wairua* [spirituality]. . . . I had got to this point in my teaching which was like just, "Do it, turn it over, turn it over," but I wasn't really doing anything for my own growth and I certainly wasn't doing anything for my children's growth.

Some students were particularly enthusiastic about the initiation of solidarity observed within their school, as this remark by a Māori student illustrates:

It's been awesome and really good to see, and like keep on with the *mahi* [work], like . . . it's really good for people to see Māori and non-Māori . . . work together, like it's a partnership thing and it can happen, like often you only get to hear about the bad things, or when there's fighting and arguments but . . . I think it's really made a difference at school, like it's a better place to come now because like you feel your . . . teachers are really trying to understand you and help you to learn so yeah that gives us students a chance to see the two cultures working together.

During the first set of interviews, many participants expressed hope and optimism for the future because of the first signs of unifying spaces developed through initial community consultation. However, this was a very fragile start.

Internal Group Divisions and Disparate Ideologies

Although many teachers believed they had established solidarity through shared imperatives and group cohesion, opposition to reform work emerged over time. Two major obstacles to solidarity development—disparate ideologies and internal group divisions (Cole & Luna, 2010)—became more evident as teachers experimented with new pedagogical approaches identified in research as being effective for Māori students (Bishop, Berryman, Tiakiwai, & Richards, 2003). There was disagreement across staff rooms related to teachers' use of co-construction strategies and approaches, which encouraged students to have a voice and be consulted about classroom processes. Some Māori teachers, such as the teacher below, believed that such approaches contravened deeply held cultural beliefs and protocols:

[I]n my day you had to be white haired, just about bald before you could stand up and speak on a *marae* [meeting house]. Now they've got systems where anybody can go and stand up on the *marae* and *korero* [give a point of view] because this is how they're being taught—"You go to the front"—and yet there's an old Māori saying that, "If it's all right at the back then it's right in the front; if there's no workers at the back then the front will fall down," and a lot of our Māori people are forgetting to learn how to work before they make their way up, because there is a step and our kids aren't going through those steps, . . . you've got to go back to values.

Māori and non-Māori teachers across the two schools were divided about the appropriateness of such pedagogies. Some Māori teachers insisted developing relationships that encouraging self-advocacy among students was central to improving pedagogy for Māori:

The *mahi* [work] is power sharing in the classroom. . . . Teachers need to get off their pedestal . . . and get into the role of their students more. . . . [F]or me, it's about working with them, the students first and stepping into their world and then when you have their trust and some credibility with them, because for a lot of our young people their experience of adults is that they shit on them and just want to disempower them all the time, so if . . . we [need to] work alongside our students and really build that relationship and our understanding of them as people . . . but that means letting go of the power . . . and teachers like power.

A few Māori teachers asserted that reform work could be achieved only through shared power and reciprocal learning between teachers, students, and their families and that this was an important part of building solidarity:

We think that it's easy to know what's best at this school as teachers, 'cause we're seen as experts, and maybe others aren't seen that way, you know, but we can learn off everybody and you should never ever say that you know lots and never ever assume and judge, 'cause our parents here have got knowledge that they can hand on, kids have, too, kids have got knowledge that they can hand on that they know something about, so you should never cut those links or cut off that line of communication. There should always be a reciprocal sharing of knowledge, so as teachers—Māori and non-Māori—we don't hold the power, it's a shared thing, you know, and I think maybe teachers do think that they have all the power, and that knowledge is power, but it can also be ignorance.

Within each school's local Māori community, there were also differing views about who should be consulted about the work. Nine of the 15 parents and caregivers of Māori students who were interviewed believed their children needed to be involved in order to bring about change:

Kids know what's happening at school, even young kids . . .
we need to be asking them what they think. . . . I know if
my boy is happy at school, and if he's happy with his teacher
. . . so I think we need to be asking the kids more.

However, 13 caregivers also believed that reform (improving practice
and outcomes for Māori students) could not be undertaken without including *whānau* members:

We've also had a number of projects designed to help change
things for our *tamariki* [children] which don't seem to last so
people think this is just another project. How many times have
we been involved in projects? About 15 years now at that school,
and I've gone to different *hui* [meetings] over those 15 years . . .
the school needs to be serious about the *kaupapa* [purpose]
and that means partnership with *whānau* [families], and that's
more than having a token Māori voice here and there.

Other parents and caregivers of Māori children felt there should be
more specific involvement from older *whānau* and community members
who held status in their community:

I'd like to see them [teachers] ask our *kaumatua* [elders] and get them
more involved. Why I say the *kaumatua* is they have been here in
this community a lot longer than, say, some of our Māori teachers.

It was evident that within and across both school communities
there were internal group divisions fueled by different ideologies about
what counted as culturally responsive pedagogies. There was clear
disagreement about who should have a voice and be consulted, and
there were different interpretations about the goals of solidarity work.
Subsequent member checks revealed that some teachers, students, and
parents/caregivers across both school communities wanted to debate
these issues on their local *marae* (meeting house). However, other more
powerful forms of opposition emerged, which challenged any further
hope of achieving solidarity.

Racism, Power, and White Privilege

There was evidence that racism embedded within systems of marginalization
and privilege existed within and across both school communities. Twelve of
the 15 non-Māori parents/caregivers who were interviewed saw the reform
program as threatening their own children's cultural identity and academic

progress. These participants were very vocal in their opposition, as they believed their own children's learning opportunities were now threatened by the increased focus on Māori language, customs, and protocols.[2] During interviews, some non-Māori parents/caregivers appeared quite comfortable to express racist views and assumptions:

> [I]t's not good if there's too much of a Māori influence in the school . . . the kids that come into school now are more needier, there's more theft in the area, there's more direct disobedience towards their elders and a lot of that has to do with the kids and where they come from. The lives that their parents have had. I mean, you might have a Māori woman who has five or six kids from different fathers and they're all in or out of jail. And the kids are living with their grandparents and they're swapped around, they don't have good role models.

Consequently, the principal of one school received a delegation of angry non-Māori parents and caregivers who threatened to "pull their children out of school" if the work of solidarity was not stopped. There were attempts to appease non-Māori community members by diluting and/or reducing culturally responsive practices.

Evidence of racism was not isolated to just Pākehā parent/community groups. A particular stereotype emerged across both staff rooms and related to "lazy" and "greedy" Māori. These constructions of Māori were contrary to other evidence. For example, the majority of Māori teachers were supporting non-Māori colleagues in Māori language classes and/or attending extra and additional *whānau hui* and giving up their own time after school to do so. Messages within participant stories emphasized racist beliefs, as well as a lack of respect among some for Māori teachers' views, as the following comment by a parent/caregiver of non-Māori child illustrates:

> I have seen teachers being basically racist and that troubles me. At that school there was a general consensus among some of the non-Māori teachers that the Māori teachers didn't work as hard, like they were really laid back, and these teachers hoped the Māori teachers would come up to everyone else's standard, not the other way around.

Racism and power imbalances, within both school communities, prevented any possibility of achieving solidarity. Cole and Luna (2010) note that groups who attempt to forge coalitions across historical relationships of privilege and power encounter significant internal and external threats. Study results confirmed such arguments.

Divisions in the Playground

While debates appeared confined to particular adult groups, students had unique perspectives on community divisions and tensions. The inclusion of diverse student perspectives is important because it has implications for curriculum development needed to address solidarity work in schools. According to Cole and Luna (2010), childhood experiences associated with the development of empathy "toward people whose social identity categories were different from theirs" was a common experience of social justice activists engaged in solidarity work (p. 81).

Some students had their own concerns about racism within their school community and the attitudes of students toward different ethnic groups. For example, a non-Māori student said:

> I think there's racism [in this school] and it would be good to see less racism . . . there are some people who don't hang out with Māori . . . it's just how they act around Māori students . . . they act as though they are better than students from other races like Māoris and Asians in the way they talk about them like they're looking down at them.

Interviews emphasized that existing social divisions within school playgrounds were linked to wider school and community discourses and practices. For example, one Māori student knew of tensions within his school's wider community about the use of *te reo* (Māori language). He was particularly concerned that friends might get into trouble and be disciplined at home for learning Māori, as their parents would disapprove, and that these adult disagreements could impact on existing student friendships:

> Some people might not want to learn *te reo* because they might think it's bad for them . . . their parents might growl at them if they learn it, the Māori, and if they don›t tell their parents they're learning it, they might get an even worse growling.

Others believed that cultural divisions were a way of life that students needed to prepare for. There was also a general apathy expressed toward solidarity between Māori and non-Māori groups. As the following statement by a non-Māori student illustrates:

> Oh no, it [Māori and non-Māori solidarity] doesn't really bother me. I don't see how it works. I've never seen it happen, like with the kids at school the Māori and the Pākehā are really split, one side is on one side of the school and the other on the other, there's hardly any mixing, there are little glings [groups]. Like there's the

Māoris who want to play touch and the White jokers who want to play touch and then the Māori smokers and the White smokers and then the people who just don't enjoy that sort of stuff, and then all the Chinese dudes and people just stick together in their group.

Some participant interviews revealed prejudices toward those perceived as different, including homophobic and heterosexist attitudes, and ableist attitudes toward children with forced "special needs" identities (Hynds, 2007). Labels such as *fag*, *gay*, and *special needs* were used as derogatory descriptions, as in this remark by a Māori student:

[My hope] is that this work keeps going and teachers don't give up. My concern is about the younger ones. Some of them think it's gay to be in *kapahaka* [Māori performing arts], like it's dumb, special needs, touchy-feelings, like somehow you're a fag if you're in *kapahaka*.

Deficit schooling practices perpetuated stereotypes and low expectations toward students labeled as different. Interview evidence indicated that many Māori students across both school communities were located within "remedial," "special education," and/or "alternative" education classes. These school practices contributed to negative stereotypes that labeled Māori students as "dumb," which students like the Māori student below viewed as impacting on students' motivation and engagement:

Well, most of the Māoris just say non-Māori, they're brainy, if you're Māori, you're dumb, and you're going to end up working in the bush, yeah. That's why they just drop out of school.

Individual and institutional racism intersected with other forms of marginalization and oppression and contributed to "forced identities" or stereotypes (McIntosh, 2005, p. 48). Interview analysis showed a lack of awareness among participants that school structures produced and reproduced practices of privilege and oppression for particular student groups, and were developed from particular ideologies about difference (Artiles, 1998).

THE ELUSIVE MORAL IMPERATIVE

Study results revealed the depth and significance of challenges to the development and achievement of solidarity work within and across Māori and non-Māori school-community groups in both schools. Findings confirmed arguments put forth by others that substantial obstacles include conflicting ideologies, internal group divisions, and unequal power relationships (Cole

& Luna, 2010; Penetito, 2010). Although the first stage of community consultation initiated the perception of unifying spaces, important for solidarity development (Cole & Luna, 2010), such activities were not enough. Interviews with various teachers and *whānau* (family members) emphasized that there were different interpretations about the moral imperative needed to underpin solidarity work. Some believed that traditional knowledge systems should be adhered to, and that this would be the basis for Māori students achieving "as Māori." Others argued that contemporary teaching and learning approaches would stimulate student engagement in class and increase achievement levels. Divisions fueled by disparate ideologies existed across groups of teachers, students, and parent/caregivers within and across both school communities and presented significant challenges.

Culture is not static (Durie, 2005). There are many forms (systems) of knowledge, linked to identity and language, location and position. Yet modern and traditional concepts of culture lead to fixed definitions of cultural identity (McIntosh, 2005). Fixed and normative identities emphasize unity at the expense of diversity and hybridity. One challenge to solidarity between schools and their local Māori communities lies in the acceptance and inclusion of diverse identities. Māori youth identities are particularly fluid, with multiple expressions and literacies that can be very different from those of traditional culture (McIntosh, 2005). Consequently, there are multiple identities, valued achievements, and ways of knowing within and across unique cultural groups. Penetito (personal communication, September, 15, 2010) agrees that the degree of solidarity is closely linked to how much diversity and difference is accepted and embraced within and across school communities. Within solidarity work, a common problem can be to turn a "blind eye" toward difference and the power imbalances within groups that intersect positions of privilege and oppression (Cole & Luna, 2010).

Analysis of participant stories indicated that the moral imperative remained elusive in the work of solidarity within and across both school communities. All communities are made up of diverse groups that can simultaneously experience positions of marginalization and privilege across intersections of race, gender, social class, sexuality, and ability status (Cole & Luna, 2010). Unless schools and their local communities actively work to disrupt racism and other forms of oppression and marginalization, they will only get so far in solidarity development (Cole & Luna, 2010; Freire, 1997).

The purpose of the initial change program was to establish unity between teachers and their local Māori communities, in order to improve practice and learning outcomes for Māori students. As discussed earlier in this chapter, there are different interpretations within Aotearoa New Zealand about "what counts" as the moral imperative needed to underpin solidarity work. In the first interpretation, Bishop, Berryman, Tiakiwai, and Richards (2003) argued that unity is achieved through teachers clearly rejecting deficit theories about Māori students and through the development of shared power and co-construction activities within classrooms. Although this is clearly an important process in the establishment of solidarity work, study results revealed disagreement among participants about whether such approaches "were Māori" and appropriate within the school setting. Disparate ideologies about the moral imperative needed to underpin solidarity work existed within and between Māori and non-Māori participants.

In the second interpretation, the moral imperative was concerned with constructing meaningful relationships and interactions between schools and their local Māori parent/caregiver groups (Biddulph, Biddulph, & Biddulph, 2003). However, results indicated that Pākehā (White) parent and caregiver communities disrupted attempts at partnership and coalition. Interview evidence revealed that racism and prejudice were alive and well within each school. There was no attempt to make visible or disrupt Pākehātanga (White) privilege, maintained through unequal power relationships. Nor was there a moral imperative to uncover or disrupt oppressive colonizing ideologies and epistemologies that encouraged and perpetuated participants' deficit thinking.

Study results presented in this chapter align with the theories put forth by Penetito (2010). The present schooling system within Aotearoa New Zealand is designed *to be* culturally responsive, but only to the culture of the dominant Pākehā (White) group. The moral imperative, so important within solidarity work, must be to make such issues visible within and between our school communities. Solidarity must be viewed as a collective struggle (Freire, 1997; McLaren, 2000) that engages diverse groups of students, teachers, and parents/caregivers in understanding that we are all "connected to a great deal of suffering in the world" and "we . . . begin with what most people don't want to look at, which is what privilege, power and difference has to do with us" (Johnson, 2006, p. 75).

Collective consciousness-raising activities initiated as part of the initial community consultation appeared to promote some unifying spaces, but these activities needed to be extended and developed further if solidarity was to have a chance. Solidarity can develop through collectively owning the problem of power, privilege, and difference, a conversation that can occur through the creation of "third space" where competing knowledges and discourses can be brought into conversation with each other to enable new learning (Gutierrez, Baquedano, & Tejeda, 1999). This is not easy work because solidarity development is not uniform. It develops through "multiple bonds of belonging but also conflicting positions within collectivity" (McLaren, 2000, p. 202). Conflict and resistance can produce productive spaces where change and transformation can occur (Hynds, 2010). Participants involved in solidarity work must be prepared to navigate both the visible and less visible values, beliefs, and identities that participants bring into such work (Cole & Luna, 2010; Hynds, 2007) and challenge racism and other forms of oppression and marginalization. There are implications here for capacity development that ground the practice of solidarity across communities of difference in understanding the multiple ways that power, privilege, and suffering plays out in schools. By doing this, solidarity work is reconceptualized in terms of intersectionality, in ways that move beyond binary descriptions of group membership, and expands engagement to include multiple groups of students, teachers, and parents/caregivers.

NOTES

Kia ora koutou, I would like to acknowledge Professors Wally Penetito, Alfredo Artiles, and Emerita Professor Christine Sleeter for their feedback and assistance in writing this chapter. I would also like to thank the many teachers, students, and *whānau* (parents/caregivers) who made this study possible.

1. Partnership work between Māori and non-Māori has particular significance in New Zealand and usually refers to the partnership principle in the Treaty of Waitangi. This treaty was signed in 1840, and formed an agreement between Māori and the British Crown about governance of the country.

2. I have spoken about this previously. See Hynds (2008).

REFERENCES

Alton-Lee, A. (2003). *Quality teaching for diverse students in schooling: Best evidence synthesis.* Wellington, New Zealand: Ministry of Education.

Artiles, A. J. (1998). The dilemma of difference: Enriching the disproportionality discourse with theory and context. *The Journal of Special Education, 32*(1), 32–36.

Batibo, H. M. (2005). *Language decline and death in Africa: Causes, consequences and challenges.* Clevedon, Canada: Multi-lingual Matters.

Biddulph, F., Biddulph, J., & Biddulph, C. (2003). *The complexity of community and family influences on children's achievement in New Zealand: Best evidence synthesis.* Wellington, NZ: Ministry of Education.

Bishop, R., Berryman, M., Tiakiwai, S., & Richards, C. (2003). *Te kotahitanga: The experiences of year 9 and 10 Māori students in mainstream classrooms.* Hamilton, New Zealand: Māori Education Research Institute (MERI), School of Education, University of Waikato.

Bishop, R., & Glynn, T. (1999*). Culture counts: Changing power relations in education.* Palmerston North, New Zealand: Dunmore Press.

Cole, E. R., & Luna, Z. T. (2010). Making coalitions work: Solidarity across difference within U.S. feminism. *Feminist Studies, 36*(1), 71–98.

Durie, M. (2005). *Ngā tai matatū: Tides of Māori endurance.* Melbourne, Australia: Oxford University Press.

Freire, P. (1997). A response. In P. Freire, with J. W. Fraser, D. Macedo, T. McKinnon, & W. T. Stokes (Eds.), *Mentoring the mentor: A critical dialogue with Paulo Freire* (pp. 303–329). New York: Peter Lang.

Gutierrez, K. D., Baquedano-Lopez, P., & Tejeda, C. (1999). Rethinking diversity: Hybridity and hybrid language practices in the third space. *Mind, Culture and Activity, 6*(4), 286–303.

Hynds, A. S. (2007). Navigating the collaborative dynamic: Teachers collaborating across difference. Unpublished Ph.D. thesis, Victoria University of Wellington.

Hynds, A. (2008). Developing and sustaining open communication in action research initiatives: A response to Kemmis (2006). *Journal of Educational Action Research, 16*(2), 149–162.

Hynds, A. (2010). Unpacking resistance to change within school reform programs with a social justice orientation. *International Journal of Leadership in Education 13(4)* 377–392.

Johnson, A. G. (2006). *Privilege, power and difference* (2nd ed.). Boston: McGraw-Hill.

McIntosh, T. (2005). Māori identities: Fixed, fluid, forced. In J. Liu, T. McCreanor, T. McIntosh, & T. Teaiwa (Eds.), *New Zealand identities: Departures and destinations* (pp. 38–51). Wellington, NZ: Victoria University Press.

McLaren, P. (2000). *Che Guevara, Paulo Freire, and the pedagogy of revolution.* New York: Rowman & Littlefield.

Ministry of Education. (2006). *Nga haeata matauranga: Annual report on Māori education.* Wellington, NZ: Author.

Penetito, W. (2010). *What's Māori about Māori education?* Wellington, NZ: Victoria University Press.

Sleeter, C. (2005). How white teachers construct race. In C. McCarthy, W. Crichlow, G. Dimitriads, & N. Dolby (Eds.), *Race, identity and representation in education* (2nd ed.) (pp. 243–256). New York: Taylor Francis Group.

Tuuta, M., Bradnam, L., Hynds, A., Higgins, J., & Broughton, R. (2004). *Evaluation of the Te Kauhua Māori mainstream pilot project: Report to the Ministry of Education.* Wellington, NZ: Ministry of Education.

Wenger, E. (1998). *Communities of practice.* Cambridge, UK: Cambridge University Press.

10

Building Solidarity Between the Tribal Community and the School in India

The Case of Srujan

Mahendra Kumar Mishra

All men are intellectuals, one could therefore say: but not all men have functions of intellectuals in society. There is no human activity from which every form of intellectual participation can be excluded.
—Antonio Gramsci, cited in Monasta, 1993

India, a multilingual and multicultural country with a diversity of cultures, languages, customs, faiths, and beliefs, offers a new spirit of living together. M. N. Srinivas (2002), mentioning the diverse cultures of India, says that "there are literally hundreds of such relatively homogenous regions in India, and the culture of each of them cut across caste and class" (p. 428). Farmers, artisan groups, and landowners, despite their diversities in caste, language, religion, and customs, live together. The social categories of urban, rural, and tribal have intertwined in the web of diverse languages and cultures, which has created a composite culture in the country.

This chapter discusses the community school linkages in the tribal villages of the state of Odisha through Srujan (creativity), a program adopted in the primary schools by the government of the state of Odisha (also known as Orissa) in India. The objective of the program is to explore the funds of knowledge from the community and to help children learn from their cultural context. It further aims to create culturally responsive schools that would reverse tribal children's alienation from school. In the program, the community acts as the cultural resource, contributing to the school through activities that include storytelling festivals, arts and crafts, music and dance, nature study, village exploration, and math and science festivals. In this chapter, I examine how Srujan has been instrumental in building solidarity between the community and school by breaking the dichotomy that casts the school as the abode of knowledge and the community as a nonentity in knowledge creation.

BACKGROUND AND CONTEXT OF EDUCATION IN ODISHA

Although the constitution of India safeguards the education of minority children in their languages and cultures, there is little evidence that the Indian states have addressed the educational issues of marginalized communities. Thus, the democratic spirit of education is violated by way of imposing the dominant culture and language on the state curriculum. Social exclusion leads to educational exclusion as well, not just physically but also intellectually. The dominant state language is used as the medium of instruction. Uniform textbooks are written by the upper-caste curriculum designers who have little knowledge of the cultural values of linguistic and ethnic minorities. Teachers' structured knowledge from the textbook and use of fixed teaching methods impede children's creativity. Thus, the diverse cultural resources of race, gender, language, religion, and ethnicity are ignored in the school system. Instead, discrimination is found in the school and classroom, and the behavior and attitude of the teachers perpetuates these inequities in schools. Mainstream education subjugates the learning of the marginalized (Kumar, Ahmed, & Singh, 2010).

Odisha, whose total population is approximately 42 million, is a tribal-dominated state: its 62 scheduled tribes (ST)[1] constitute 23% of the total state population (Taradutt, 1994). The tribes are divided into three language groups: Austric, Dravidian, and Indo-Aryan. While the state's literacy rate is 63.5%, the state's tribal literacy rate is 37.37%. The male tribal literacy rate is 51.48%, while the female rate is 23.37% (Ministry of Home, 2001).

The Scheduled Caste (SC) community in Odisha constitutes 16% of the state population. Thus, the ST and SC communities constitute about 39% of the state population. Historically, they have been marginalized from the upper caste/class. While the STs are forest dwellers and live geographically secluded from the plains, SCs used to live with other caste groups in the plains. They were considered untouchables, and were living separately on the outskirts of the villages. In post-independence India, they have asserted their rights as being equal to other caste groups.

There are 30 revenue districts in the state, distributed by 314 bocks, with 4,742 clusters, and each cluster serves a unit of 8–10 schools. The state has 51,668 primary schools and 22,042 upper primary schools (Management Information System Unit, 2010). Seven out of 30 districts have a female literacy rate that is less than 30%. The interdistrict disparity in the state's literacy is more than 50% (Ministry of Home, 2001).

Ninety percent of the teachers in tribal areas are nontribal. Their role is to "mainstream" the tribal children by imparting the uniform curriculum to make them capable of writing and reading the alphabet in the state language. The nontribal teachers consider the tribal language and culture "uncivilized" and "uncultured" compared with state language and culture (Mishra, 1997). About 10% of the teachers in the state belong to tribal communities. But since they were also educated in the Oriya medium schools, they, too, do not use their mother tongue to teach tribal children.

Children in tribal areas do not understand the language and content of the textbooks and, therefore, face serious learning difficulties. Tribal children do not find their experiences reflected in their classroom. The content and language of the teachers and textbooks are non-contextual. As a result, a majority of tribal children in tribal areas drop out of school.

Parents and community have little to do with school functioning except to send their children to schools. The functioning of the school, in both management and academic domains, has weak community participation. There is a huge gap between the literate teachers, on one side, and the nonliterate parents and school committee, on the other side, in creating a common understanding of school functioning.

Developing a More Creative Curriculum: Opportunity and Challenges

The basic philosophy of India's National Curriculum Framework 2005 (NCF) is to bring revolutionary change by building solidarity between the school and community. The guiding principles of NCF are to connect knowledge to life outside the school, shift learning away from rote methods, enrich the curriculum to provide for overall development of children rather than remaining textbook-centric, make examinations more flexible and integrated into classroom life, and finally to nurture an overriding identity with India's diverse cultures and foster democratic values. NCF offers a great opportunity, in the context of challenges. To understand both the opportunity and the challenges, it is important to consider the meaning of solidarity and differences. Many cultures coexist in a given space, but that does not mean that they form an integrated multicultural society unless they see that doing so is mutually beneficial. Thus, solidarity means understanding different cultures, enriching each for a common goal of respecting and understanding them all, and thereby reducing disparities among caste, language, and gender groups, and fostering democratic values.

Defining the dynamics of multiculturalism, Bikhu Parekh (2001) is of the opinion that cultures are internally plural and dynamic in nature, changing as they relate to other cultures. He further says that "Multiculturalism doesn't simply mean a numerical plurality of different cultures, but rather a community which is creating, guaranteeing, and encouraging spaces within which different communities are able to grow at their own pace. At the same time, it means creating a public space in which these new communities are able to interact, enrich the existing culture, and create a new consensual culture in which they recognize reflections of their own identity" (p. 337). This public space in which diverse communities interact suggests what solidarity might mean.

According to Dobbie and Richards-Schuster (2008), solidarity has most often been treated as a latent quality—implicit in shared interests or cultural backgrounds—that only needs to be uncovered. An organizer's task is thus to show people how their true interests are connected to each other, how those interests can be achieved through collective action, and to maintain this solidarity during struggles. This traditional model associates solidarity with commonality and unity, and the process of building solidarity is viewed as consisting mainly of pointing out similarities. Similarly, Dean (1996) explains that traditionally, solidarity has been conceived of oppositionally, on the model of "us versus them." But this traditional conception overlooks the fact that the term *we* does not require an opposing *they*; *we* also denotes the relationship between *you* and *me*. Reflective solidarity, which Dean proposes, provides spaces for difference because it upholds the possibility of a communicative "we." Once the term *we* is understood communicatively, difference can be respected as necessary to solidarity. Dissent, questioning, and disagreement no longer have to be seen as tearing us apart, but instead can be viewed as characteristic of the bonds holding us together. Dobbie and Richards-Schuster (2008) show that building solidarity involves a long-term process of communication that includes building inclusive organizational structures and space for people to work out their differences.

Currently, the Odisha school curriculum does not develop a communicative "we." Semali and Kincheloe (1999) wrote that the Western benchmark curriculum has been universal in schools, and knowledge of the marginalized has been subjugated. According to them, "the power struggle involves who is allowed to proclaim truth and to establish the procedures by which truth is to be established; it also involves who holds the power to determine what knowledge is of most worth and should be included in academic curricula" (p. 3). There has been a deliberate blunder in which the people with the power to construct curriculum ignore the marginalized. Non-representation of the indigenous cultures in the state curriculum not only violates the democratic spirit but also leads to cultural genocide and self-hatred, thereby maintaining existing power relations. In this way, the system becomes responsible for creating disintegration and preventing solidarity among diverse cultural groups through the schools.

In India, communities and teachers have never based their relationship on solidarity, even after 60 years of independence. Thus, the hegemony of educated school people over the non-literate parents and community prevails. Apple (2004) asserts that curriculum is itself part of a selective tradition. That is, from the vast universe of possible knowledge, only some knowledge gets to be official knowledge. This means that community knowledge is not properly represented and children of many marginalized communities are deprived of their history and culture. They are forced to follow a curriculum that may not be from their own cultural context. Unfortunately, teachers who belong to the marginalized groups also become instrumental to domination, because they hardly understand the dynamics of power. Semali and Kincheloe (1999) write that, "when history is erased and decontextualized, teachers, students and other citizens are rendered vulnerable to the myths employed to perpetuate social domination" (p. 31).

If we look into the state of school–community relations in Odisha, it would be evident that the histories of the marginalized, such as tribal peoples, Dalits,[2] Muslims, and women, were not mentioned in the state curriculum. While Indian villages, having different castes, classes, languages, and ethnic groups, form a transcommunal nature and maintain solidarity among members in their public sphere, there is a lack of solidarity between the adults and children of the community, on one hand, and teachers on the other. In a state like Odisha, the hierarchy of the mainstream curriculum ignores the community's funds of knowledge, and the unequal relationship between high and low cultures is maintained, inviting injustice.

In the public domain, the people of India share common beliefs and customs irrespective of their caste/class differences. The symbols of such solidarity are visible in their cultural practices and performances, like annual festivals and fairs, where everyone takes part regardless of caste and class. But school as a modern institution offers little to invite the community to take part. There is a gap between the literate teachers and the illiterate community members. Schools are an alien place for most of the parents in tribal areas. This is equally applicable to the semi-literate and literates as well. In a tribal village, the schoolteacher is a much-respected person in comparison to the illiterate chairman of the village school committee. Thus, the historic gap between the community and school is perpetuated due to illiteracy.

The Community as a Resource for School Curriculum

Respecting the funds of knowledge that diverse communities have, Sleeter (2005) discusses how community knowledge is in absorbed into children's minds; teachers have the opportunity to explore it together with the children. She writes that, since children bring diverse funds of knowledge to school with them, teachers should make use of what children know in order to engage them in learning the curriculum, as well as in exploring their diverse backgrounds. Allowing for the development of diversity in expertise can serve as a constructive intellectual resource for a multicultural democracy and a diverse world. It is to our benefit that we do not all learn the same thing, beyond the basic skills. Helping next generations acquire intellectual knowledge of diverse communities, including those that have been historically silenced, can enable creative dialogue and work from which we might better address problems that seem intractable.

In a state like Odisha, where the disparity between tribal and nontribal peoples is highly visible in cultural practices, the tribal people are marginalized. According to Sleeter (2005), historically knowledge systems as well as everyday knowledge have been subjugated as peoples have been subjugated. Defining peoples and knowledge as "backward," "uneducated," or "nonscientific" historically served as a rationale for exerting power over them and claiming access to their resources (p. 83). If community knowledge is not respected, then the curriculum has become discriminatory. Curriculum framers need to build on children's experiential learning. Secluding classroom knowledge from local knowledge is a cultural loss.

Vygotsky (1930) writes, "That children's learning begins long before they attend school is the starting point of discussion. Any learning a child encounters in school always has a previous history" (p. 84). Children learn through oral and physical activities that are purposeful for productive work. The work may be storytelling during supper, listening to stories before sleeping, playing games in the peer group, singing while planting a sapling, or singing lullabies to put younger children to sleep. Each activity in which the children take part is supported with an elder's participation. The community has created a space for children to play and to enjoy and learn. Learning is intergenerational in the community, irrespective of gender differences. In a traditional society, learning is not an isolated or competitive activity. It never creates distinctions/disparities among children. The concepts of "winning" and "defeat" are not part of their community life. This is evident from the dance, music, song, arts, crafts, and many more practices of everyday life of the community. Inside and outside the home in rural and tribal India, parents and children work together at productive activity. Elders do their part, but the children also contribute according to their physical ability. While fetching water from the pond in her big pitcher, a woman is also well aware of the small girl fetching water in a small pitcher, thus symbolizing the social responsibility of elders toward the younger generation. When a woman goes to the forest to collect wildflowers (mahul and basia litifolia) or mango, she also is aware that the little 3-year-old girl also collects flowers or mangoes in her small bamboo basket. This indicates that the community has adequately thought about children's capabilities.

Even in the absence of a school, the children learn in the community. Parents do not teach their children; their children work with them and learn. Nothing is taught didactically. Parents do not identify for the children the trees, fruits, and flowers, but the child learns these things from contexts that have purpose and meaning.

Play is a most interesting representative of culture that children enjoy. According to Butler, Gotts, and Quisenberry (1978), play as part of curriculum has three major strengths. First, play incites curiosity and physical development. For example, from kitchen and household materials children learn the shapes and sizes of items they use every day, as well as counting and measuring. Second, through dramatic and sociodramatic play, children learn the customs of society. For example, children imitate the events and characters of the family and village in their games. Third, play has the potential to teach rules. Traditional games replicate the customs of the society. By playing games with their peer groups, children learn to take part in role-playing, and they learn social dynamics and social rules.

Let us look in some detail at arts and crafts, another aspect of culture that community members use meaningfully and that requires complex knowledge. Tribal women draw wall paintings for two purposes: beautification of their houses and ritual purposes. They learn how to prepare the color from the objects in their natural environment. The art they draw is meaningful in their cultural context, full of cultural symbols and meanings. The women folk used to paint inside the houses, and for this they did not charge money, since their painting is a part of community knowledge in which everybody shares learning. In modern times, this form of folk art—Saora art—has become popular, and it has become a market for selling and earning money.

Craft is a productive activity that is equally important for earning and learning. Craft can employ the most complex technology: mathematics and use of natural resources. Building the house; melting iron; doing wood-, earthen-, and bamboo work; weaving; and engaging in many other crafts are highly intellectual, but teaching them is not found in the state curriculum.

The artists and artisans of the community depend on local resources. Their creative expressions and skills are not copyrighted. A story, a song, a wall painting, or a piece of art is not owned by the creator in the community; thus, the sharing of knowledge is democratic. Children help their parents while making a bamboo mat and basket, and they gradually learn by participating. Take any example of traditional weaving and explore how, although weavers may live in adverse conditions, while making clothes they show the best creative art imaginable from that social situation. The creative mind is better expressed among them, and interestingly, if a textile engineer has to learn this knowledge, it will take many years. It is easy to borrow the motifs of art, but difficult to create a piece of art from one's own mind.

Based on these theses, it is now important to examine how the Sru-jan program in Odisha has represented the culture of marginalized communities in the schools as the means of fostering multiculturalism and building solidarity.

THE SRUJAN PROGRAM

The program I directed—Srujan—is conceptualized to establish community and school linkage through child-centric activities, thereby building solidarity between community and school. Its main objective is to create a common platform where community, teachers, and children work together to understand the environment outside the school as a source of learning. Its aim is to create a child-friendly atmosphere in the school that is familiar to the children so as to bring out the inherent talents of each child, using community knowledge (oral and material resources) for curricular support.

Beginnings

The Odisha Primary Education Program Authority (OPEPA), the main body of the state education program, adopted Srujan as a flagship enterprise to build a bridge between the community and schools. Between January and March 2007, three workshops were conducted, inviting creative teachers to conceptualize Srujan's basic objectives. The workshops focused on exposing teachers to the community's knowledge and cultural methods of learning.

These questions were discussed in the workshops:

1. When there is no school in our village, how were the community members learning? Do you believe that the villages that have no school still have an education system?
2. How is knowledge generated? What are the methods of dissemination of knowledge in the school and in the community?
3. Why do you need culture? Do you think that our culture is lost? If yes, how can you regain it?
4. How many of you have read the National Curriculum Framework 2005? What is the NCF saying about the community's role in the school?
5. What do the children like? If you had to make your school child-centric, what would you do for the children?

Briefly, the findings were as follows. First, school is run by teachers who do not involve the community in schooling except during the monthly meeting on school management. Teachers have very little knowledge about the community knowledge system. Teachers feel that since the community is non-literate, community members cannot understand school knowledge, and therefore, teachers do not share what they are teaching with the community members/parents.

Second, while community knowledge is generated and taught intergenerationally, school knowledge is disseminated through reading and writing. But the practice of reading and writing is not a part of tribal culture. Therefore, parents cannot help their children with their learning outside of school hours. Nontribal educated people consider tribal culture to be inferior to the mainstream culture.

The third finding, however, showed that children come to school with many experiences and much knowledge. They come with many languages learned from their home and society. Children like to sing, dance, play, listen to stories, draw pictures, travel to the forest and fairs, and so on. In order to make the school culturally responsive, teachers suggested adopting these types of activities.

Preparing for Implementation

Before the Srujan program was started, the teachers collected oral traditions from the community to use in schools. Teachers collected cultural resources from storytellers, singers, musicians, and artisans. Oral tales, songs, myths, legends, proverbs, and riddles were collected and documented in the schools or local cluster to be edited and prepared as bilingual and multilingual reading materials. This work led the teachers to understand that the oral tradition offers language resources that are useful for teaching language skills as well as comprehension.

Implementation of Child Friendly Activities

During 2007, six activities were adopted for the children: 1) a storytelling festival; 2) a workshop on arts and crafts; 3) song, dance and music; 4) traditional games; 5) a nature book (study of nature through direct observation); and 6) a village project. (As the project has developed, science and math were added later.) Each program was represented by all the schools under the cluster. Because Srujan is a state-driven program, about 300,000 children, 14,000 teachers, and 12,000 community members took part in the program in 523 clusters. Children were given an opportunity to take part in all the activities; 600 children from each cluster took part in the six activities according to their own choice, and teachers helped identify children with specific talents. About 15,000 community members took part in storytelling to 75,000 children, and the oral stories were written down by the children. These six activities were conducted during six national holidays in six different schools. Community resource persons such as storytellers, musicians, artists, artisans, and other knowledgeable persons took part in the six programs, depending on their interest and expertise.

The process of enacting each activity varied. The storytelling festival was initiated by a storyteller with five to six children around him in a group. After he told the story, children wrote it down in their own language. Then they drew a picture based on the theme of the story. Thus, one story that had been narrated by the storyteller was then expressed in five to six variations in children's writing, in addition to five or six variations in the pictures the children drew to go along with the story.

The workshop on arts and crafts was based on the raw materials available in the environment. For art, children collected raw materials from their home and village, such as bamboo, clay, wooden particles, palm leaf and sticks, ropes, and bird feathers. Using these natural materials, they prepared different craft materials. Some children used their parents' help to prepare indigenous colors from the local materials, such as charcoal and castor oil for preparation of black color, rice powder and water for white color, green leaves from beans for green color, and turmeric for yellow. After that they prepared floor and wall paintings in the school. (This art form had been found only in the home.) In this way, the children in the arts and crafts workshop transformed raw materials from nature into cultural materials. They produced handicrafts made of bamboo, clay, wood, rope, straw, leaf, fruits, flowers, and roots—creative work that they had learned from their parents and elders. The shapes and sizes, mathematical calculations, higher skill of counting, and complex weaving were known to the school children.

Supported by community musicians, the children performed traditional dance, with costumes, music, and songs. The most important aspect of musical instruments is the craft of making them. Children learned from the musicians both the techniques of making instruments from local sources and a bit about the art of music.

Traditional games, both outdoor and indoor, for boys and girls, were played during the game festival. Physical activities, socialization, learning the rules of the games, and active participation were the outcomes.

In the nature study activities, children were taken to observe the natural environment in order to understand the importance of the natural objects from the elders. Led by the elders, students learned to identify the different kinds of trees and berries in the forest and nearby areas, and uses of these resources. Students listed the names of the trees, flowers, and fruits along with the birds and animals they saw from the nature study. Then they prepared a chart for trees, flowers, fruits, birds, and animals for discussion in schools. Children also prepared lists of natural objects with their medicinal values.

For the village project, children were taken to a village to do a simple survey of its geography, location, direction, institutions, households, roads, and communications. They also prepared a village map with the help of the teachers and villagers who took part. This activity involved discovery of the knowledge system of the village, such as making of pots by the potter, axes and cutters by the blacksmith, and doors and windows by the carpenters. Even though the students saw these everyday, they had not attached meaning to what they saw. Similarly the students could explore the musicians and singers of the villages. For instance, although they were used to listening to the musicians in their village, the children had not given due attention to the structure and construction of the musical instruments, how one learns to play the instruments, in what occasions the music is played, how much the musicians earn from playing music, and so forth. This means until Srujan was introduced, students had not thought critically their everyday culture.

Table 10.1 shows the learning outcomes from each of the activities in relationship to activities prescribed in NCF 2005.[3] Through Srujan, teachers and educators learned to recognize community members and parents as resources for knowledge. This program demonstrates that in a non-literate/semi-literate and multicultural society, linkages can be established between community and school to reduce the differences of caste, class, gender, and language and bring solidarity.

The Impact of Srujan

The two major outcomes of Srujan are 1) building solidarity among the teachers, the community, and the children for a common cause; and 2) engaging the learning potential that comes from embedding community knowledge that was recognized and shared among everybody (but that has been historically ignored in school) into the school curriculum.

Involving literate people with illiterate people in the sharing of oral knowledge is a major point of departure from exclusion and a step toward solidarity. Marginalized illiterates can create and share knowledge that can become a source of curricular knowledge. Doing this gives the listeners the firsthand impression that any language has the power of expression, and that the school has finally recognized the languages that are spoken in the community. Many people who differed from each other by language and culture shared with each other: Teachers and community members shared their experiences, and community resource persons such as artisans recognized that their knowledge can be important for schoolchildren. This sharing was a unique experience for both the teachers and the villagers, who had never met before to share community knowledge. The children, parents, and other community members came to accept the teachers and the school as a social institution. In short, many communities listened to each other.

Table 10.1. Learning Outcomes from Srujan Activities

Activity*	Learning Outcomes
Storytelling Festival	Reading, creative writing, picture story, capturing community oral tradition, fluency of speaking, use of local language style, body language, comprehensive discussion, concentration, attention
Song, Dance, and Music	Creative expression, physical movement, use of musical instruments, developing dancing skill, psychomotor development, understanding of the role of music in society, group solidarity, art of singing, leadership and group behavior, phonetics, structure and function of musical instruments
Arts and Crafts Festival	Understanding of natural and material resources, preparation of useful productive materials from raw materials, intergenerational learning, understanding seasonal productive activities, income-supportive materials such as paper, art of making different colors, love for manual work, aesthetic beauty, geometric shapes and sizes, preparation of meaningful teaching/learning materials for the classroom, expression of ideas
Traditional Games and Sports	Games for boys and girls, indoor and outdoor games, socialization, concepts of shapes, size, and time, counting, measuring, group behavior, imitation of social rules and practices, mathematical calculation, role-playing, meaningful use of local resources, compensation, leadership, physical development, group dynamics
Nature Study	Exploring the local environment and nature, collection of words related to flora and fauna, medicinal plants/ herbs, agriculture
Science Quiz	General science knowledge, observation, experimentation, truth, logic, problem-solving, reasoning, exploration, analytic thinking, mental exercise, competition
Math Festival	Truth, logic, reasoning, geometrical concepts, mental exercise, mental math, concepts of time and shape, mathematical calculation, arithmetic, cultural mathematics, math magic, puzzles, quiz

*Note: These categories were adapted from National Council of Educational Research and Training (2005).

Teachers explored the idea that tradition has its methods—learning and teaching that cannot be excluded from context. In the storytelling festival, Dalit elders, tribal elders, and Muslim elders felt honored while articulating their tales and songs. While the children were amused with play, storytelling, music, dance, and arts and crafts, teachers and community members were relinquishing their respective myths about disconnections and developing a relationship of mutual learning and understanding. Teachers discovered that anything, including the music, stories, dance, and so forth of community traditions, can be treated as a part of learning since it has come from a human intellectual activity. Thus, solidarity between teachers and community began as teachers learned to respect the community language.

Before Srujan, the community had little opportunity to take part in any intellectual activities in the school system. For instance, a potter said that the school only remembers him when the school needs new tiles during the rainy season. Through Srujan, for the first time, he was called in by the school as a potter to share his craft, which gave him immense pleasure; he felt honored. Another old man was invited to the school and was given 10 minutes to tell a story. As he stood and started to tell the story, he became so energized by speaking before a loudspeaker that he elaborated the story. Thirty minutes later, when he was asked to complete the story, he was still not ready to leave the loudspeaker. He narrated the whole story, which was full of energy, eloquence, oral narrative style, and body language, thereby making it enjoyable. It was a new experience for a man in his 70s to get recognition from a school for being a storyteller. When the story was then written and showed to him, he could not believe that his story could be written down. Similarly, women artisans, storytellers, dancers, and musicians had a new experience. The whole set of activities conceptualized in Srujan produced a web of connectivity that combined the creative activities of children, community, and teachers.

Srujan transformed teachers' perceptions of community knowledge. Prior to this program, teachers from the target schools were almost ignorant about the community. The storytelling program was an eye-opener for the teachers, prompting a transformation in their approach to language teaching. The oral formula of storytelling in the villages was revealed when the storytellers started performing in the storytelling festivals. Observing this oral formula, the teachers discovered that the community has its own methods of storytelling that, although oral instead of written, are participative and interactive for the children. Teachers also found that children could write down the story along with a picture to create texts. Teachers found the texts meaningful when the community discussed why and how the stories were important and meaningful in their cultural context. Other activities, such as playing games, were also highly productive for learning because they involved rules, socialization, and physical expression. Music, dance, and arts and crafts were complex aspects of culture that were connected to the natural environment.

Teachers played their role as facilitators between the children and the communities in conducting the activities, showing awareness that knowledge created by the community is as important as school knowledge. They came to understand that community knowledge acquired by the children prior to school should be connected to school knowledge. Community members, irrespective of age and sex, attended the school activities and took part. Teachers recognized and honored them as knowledge-givers. The gap between the teachers, children, and community was bridged. Teachers found that school had become a center for community interaction. In the follow-up program of Srujan, teachers and community resource persons were engaged in the preparation of bilingual materials such as storybooks, picture-dictionaries, story charts, big books, and small books. Changes that participation in Srujan brought about are reflected in Table 10.2.

CONCLUSION

The rural and tribal communities in India have been historically marginalized and isolated from the school curriculum because it was widely assumed the members were illiterate. But the funds of knowledge actually created by the community form the foundation of children's development. Diversities of castes and tribes, and of languages and beliefs, need to be addressed through a critical multicultural education school system. Inclusion of the community as the prime actor introducing knowledge from the social domain into the school domain, and recognition of community resource persons as intellectuals in the construction of child-friendly curriculum and materials, is a small initiative adopted by the government of Odisha.

Communities in the rest of the world may be different from those of tribal and rural India. A program like Srujan, from the Orissa context, may not be suitable in other contexts. But the culture and knowledge created for the children by the community, irrespective of diversity, is universally common. All communities create knowledge. Therefore, the experience of Srujan may help in conceptualizing how to learn and incorporate local knowledge. Some of the methods of storytelling, for example, may be useful to other locations.

Due to global migration, states reflecting monocultural and monolingual hegemony have been challenged by multiculturalism. In this case, understanding another's culture in relation to one's own, and respecting the values of another's culture, help bring peace and harmony to the world. School, as an agency of social transformation, must nourish community knowledge and values to create solidarity among the oppressed and marginalized, and solidarity between the children of the marginalized and their teachers. Creating solidarity would help ensure that all children receive the benefits from a high-quality and equitable quality education.

Table 10.2: Reflections on the Impact of Srujan on Teachers, Children, and Community

Before Srujan	After Srujan
Teachers	
Teacher's table acts as the barrier between teacher and students	Barrier-free and two-way learning is made possible
Teachers are actors and children are silent viewers	Children are actors and teachers are helpers
All classroom time is consumed by the teacher; the students are passive receivers	Teachers and students are fully involved in classroom transactions
Learning is limited to blackboard	Learning from outside the classroom is being taken up
Teachers are unable to understand the language, culture, and tradition of the children	The teacher is well versed in the language, culture, and tradition of the children
Importance is given to curriculum and prescribed text	Importance is given to both text and local knowledge
Hidden talents and creativity are not recognized	Hidden talents and creativity are duly recognized and given importance
Children	
Individual talent and creativity not explored	Exploration of children's creativity and hidden talents
Stage fright found in every child	Children become fearless speaking in and outside the classroom
No scope for development of leadership qualities	Leadership qualities gradually developed
No spontaneous, fun participation among children	Spontaneous participation in all activities
Lack of curricular integration of cultural elements with educational elements	Local cultural elements are now integrated with the educational elements

Before Srujan	After Srujan
Children are passive and their talents are not discovered by the teacher	Children become active
There is no child-dominated activity	Child-centered activities are being conducted
Both the parents and children are not involved in the school curriculum	Much more involvement of parents and children in school curriculum
Self-respect of SC/ST children is not considered	Self-respect is being honored
Voice of the children is ignored and suppressed	Children have freedom to express their thoughts
Parents do not give attention to aspirations or expectations of children	The parents are giving importance to the aspirations of children
Caste discrimination is found in the classroom	Caste discrimination in the classroom is being eradicated
Nonuse of cultural resources	Cultural elements are being used in classroom transactions
Children absent from school	Absenteeism reduced
Community	
Little involvement of community members in school intellectual activities	Active participation of community members in Srujan activities
Local storytellers, traditional musicians, artists, carpenters, craftsmen, and folk singers are ignored by society	Local resource people feel good that their culture, tradition, musical instruments, songs, and dance, which might be forgotten by society, are used in the Srujan program
Community is ignorant about the creative skills of their own children	Community has opportunity to recognize their children's creativity
Less scope for community, teachers, school, and children interaction	Through Srujan, interaction between community members, teachers, school, children is increased

NOTES

1. Scheduled Tribes are the tribes that are officially recognized by the constitution of India.

2. *Dalits* means "oppressed." In earlier times, these castes were considered untouchables.

3. It has been helpful to match the community knowledge learning activities with activities that are suggested or prescribed in the National Curriculum Framework 2005. Once the bureaucrats can see how a Srujan activity fits with what is prescribed in NCF, they feel more comfortable adopting the Srujan activity.

REFERENCES

Apple, M. W. (2004). *Ideology and curriculum*, 3rd ed. New York: Routledge Falmer.

Butler, A. L., Gotts, E. L., & Quisenbery, N. L. (1978). *Play as development.* Columbus, OH: Charles E. Merrill.

Dean, J. (1996). *Solidarity of strangers: Feminism after identity politics.* Berkeley: University of California Press.

Dobbie, D., & Richards-Schuster, K. (2008). Building solidarity through difference: A practice model for critical multicultural organizing. *Journal of Community Practice,16*(3), 317–337.

Kumar, S., Ahmed, R., & Singh, P. D. (2010). *Inclusive classroom, social inclusion/exclusion and diversity: Perspectives, policies and practices.* Delhi: Deshkal Publications.

Management Information System (MIS) Unit. (2010). *Orissa Primary Education Programme Authority OPEPA.* Govt. of Odisha, Bhubaneswar, India: Orissa Primary Education Programme Authority. Retrieved from http://www.opepa.in

Ministry of Home. (2001). *Census of India.* New Delhi: Government of India.

Mishra, M. K. (1997). *Final report of the workshop on attitudinal issues of tribal area teachers 1997.* Govt. of Odisha, Bhubaneswar, India: Orissa Primary Education Programme Authority. Retrieved from http://www.opepa.in

Monasta, A. (1993). Antonio Gramcsi. *Prospects: The Quarterly Review of Comparative Education, 23*(3/4), 597–612.

National Council of Educational Research and Training. (2005). *National Curriculum Framework 2005.* New Delhi: NCERT Publications Division.

Parekh, B. (2001). *Rethinking multiculturalism: Cultural diversity and political theory.* Basingstoke, UK: Macmillan.

Semali, L. M., & Kincheloe J. L. (1999). *What is Indigenous knowledge? Voices from the academy.* London: Falmer Press.

Sleeter, C. E. (2005). *Un-standardizing curriculum: Multicultural teaching in the standards-based classroom.* New York: Teachers College Press.

Srinivas, M. N. (2002). *Complete works of MN Srinivas.* New Delhi: Oxford University Press.

Taradutt, P. (1994). *Tribal education in Odisha in the context of education for all, 2000 AD: A status paper*. Govt. of Odisha, Bhubaneswar, Odisha, India: Tribal Welfare Department.

Vygotsky, L. (1930). *Mind and society*. Retrieved from http://www.marxists.org/archive/vygotsky/works/mind/chap6.htm

11

Building Solidarity for Education in Complex Societies

What Have We Learned?

Christine E. Sleeter

Diversity and equity in education are concerns all over the world, particularly with the rapid increase of immigration resulting from shifts in the global economy that propel people to seek work elsewhere, and with the growing imperative to broaden universal access to education. Further, democracy movements frequently bring to light injustices rooted in culture, language, religion, and gender that have far-reaching implications for schooling. Questions about how to involve and respond to diverse populations in schools have become global concerns.

Although the concept of solidarity is often evoked in discussions of diversity and equity in education, as explained in the Introduction to this book, solidarity has been greatly under-theorized and under-researched. Importantly, however, this concept speaks to how people might connect and work together, both within and across communities of difference. The purpose of this book has been to explore what solidarity means for equity and diversity in education from the vantage points of various national and cultural contexts, social locations, and theoretical positions. In this concluding chapter, I seek to extrapolate what we can learn from the chapters, when taken as a whole

FROM COMMUNAL TO MASS, COMPLEX SOCIETIES

Solidarity is not a new concept, but what it means derives partially from the social context in which the concept is being used. Conceptualized as interdependence, communitarianism, and mutual support, solidarity has long been necessary for human survival in small communities with subsistence economies (Pérez, 2006; Zibechi, 2009).

In this book, we see examples of solidarity in small-scale societies. In Chapter 2, José Luis Ramos documents that solidarity, understood as people mutually supporting each other toward the common good, is a core component of the identities of the indigenous peoples of Mexico, Mixtec peoples in particular. Similarly, in Chapter 10, Mahendra Kumar Mishra describes members of traditional villages in India as being bound by an ethic of solidarity that is rooted in the interdependence that is needed for survival (such as growing and gathering food). Mishra points out that community solidarity is most visibly displayed in community festivals and celebrations. Even in mass societies, on local levels the kind of communalism that traditional village life depended on can be fostered, although perhaps on a more limited scale. In Chapter 1, Verónica López, Carmen Montecinos, José Ignacio Rodríguez, Andrés Calderón, and Juan Francisco Contreras portray schools in which effort was invested in building a sense of solidarity and inclusion among students and teachers, with the result that students learned to treat each other with more respect than in schools that had not invested this effort.

Humans are very capable of building solidarity in the form of communal interdependence, as such examples show. However, in large and complex, diverse democratic societies, there is considerable disagreement about what solidarity means or even whether it has value today. In societies where capitalism and neoliberalism strongly reinforce individualism, solidarity is often elusive (Buxarrais, 2005; Camps, 2000; Zubero, 1996). Thus, one challenge in mass and complex societies is confronting individualism when it thwarts efforts to advance human welfare that would require empathy and collaboration.

Although building empathy and creating community across differences requires work, an even more significant challenge is confronting power disparities. One might posit that the greater the disparities of power among groups, the more important and the more difficult solidarity work becomes. Indeed, as studies by Janmatt and Braun (2009) and Korab-Karpowicz (2010) show, how strongly members of a society support common human rights may be more significant to social solidarity than how ethnically and culturally diverse they are. The question then becomes: In diverse and complex societies characterized by individualism and significant power disparities, how might solidarity work contribute to building an ethic of human rights and strengthening democratic participation?

Education is central to building democratic participation and social justice; schools, classrooms, and local communities can serve as important sites for learning the practice of democracy in diverse societies (Dewey, 1916). However, there is a tension between viewing education as an agent of social transformation, and understanding it an agent of the status quo. In hierarchical and unjust societies, individuals with power construct schooling as a means of shaping young people for the existing society. As Chomsky (1987) wrote, "The process of creating and entrenching highly selective, reshaped, or completely fabricated memories of the past is what we call 'indoctrination' or 'propaganda' when it is conducted by official enemies, and 'education,' 'moral education,' or 'character building,' when we do it ourselves" (p. 124).

Building solidarity through education, then, may be highly progressive or highly regressive, depending on who is being bound to whom, and for what purpose. What solidarity means depends at least partially on the extent to which one views society primarily from the perspective of those with the most or the least power. From the perspective of those who occupy positions of power in large, complex societies, solidarity often means broad identification with the state, no matter what a resident's social position is. After considering this meaning, I will turn to perspectives of those who are marginalized, for whom solidarity involves identifying with a community or movement directed toward challenging marginalization.

SOLIDARITY AS IDENTIFICATION WITH THE STATE

Three chapters in this book speak to national solidarity in diverse societies. Although usually we think of such solidarity as an imposed identification with the state, the state can also encourage national solidarity on a voluntary basis.

Two chapters discuss solidarity imposed in the context of nation-building, with schools being important agents in that process; they probe fractures that are inherent when a powerful group works to absorb others through processes of colonization and cultural imposition. In their critique of French Republican solidarity, in Chapter 3 Isabelle Aliaga and Martine Dreyfus ask what happens when a colonial power addresses culture and language differences by defining its own language and culture as synonymous with civilization and progress, offering everyone it governs equal citizenship (on paper, at least), on the condition that they adopt the dominant language and culture. The authors point out that what we know as French today was imposed not only on the African and Asian peoples that France colonized, but also on speakers of other languages and dialects within the borders of what is now France. Their case studies of immigrant children show how this system fosters feelings of rejection and hostility as the children sense the exclusion of their home language, and ultimately the exclusion of the identity of their family and community. In other words, the system of imposed national solidarity masks differences and identities that matter to people, as well as the racism that African immigrants experience. Equal citizenship in a diverse and unequal society is not actually equal; Aliaga and Dreyfus suggest that imposed solidarity breeds social violence and instability.

José Luis Ramos takes up a similar issue in his discussion of nation-building in Mexico in Chapter 2. Mexico's official policy had been one of Hispanicizing both indigenous Mexicans and immigrants. When a new bilingual policy was developed for indigenous Mexicans, it was practiced—even by indigenous teachers—in a way that continued the assimilationist policy of devaluing indigenous cultures. Looking into why this was the case, Ramos points out that the disparity in social power between indigenous and nonindigenous people undergirds a continued devaluation of indigenous cultures and identities. Hispanic Mexican culture need not be forcefully imposed, since it is the culture of power. Ironically, part of what is devalued by nonindigenous Mexican teachers is solidarity, or mutual support. Although homogenizing Mexicans might be seen as promoting solidarity, it promotes an identification with the state that embraces individualistic rather than communal conceptions of solidarity.

In Chapter 4, Maria Antonia Casanova shows that national policy promoting identification with the state can be offered voluntarily. In her discussion of Spanish education abroad, she details a variety of configurations that are designed to induct Spanish emigrants, their descendants, and students in countries in which they reside, into Spanish language and culture, often in the context of intercultural education. The intended result is that many Spanish emigrants globally will continue to feel a sense of solidarity with Spain. One assumes that the continued growth of these various programs attests to their popularity among Spanish emigrant communities.

In pluralistic nations, individuals who benefit from existing relationships and arrangements often worry that pluralism is a threat to national unity. Feinberg (1998) notes the example of a New York school superintendent a century ago who argued that schools should not be teaching immigrant children who their ancestors were, but rather should teach loyalty to the United States and an "absolute forgetfulness of all obligations and connections with other countries because of descent or birth" (p. 18). Taken together, the three chapters that examine solidarity as meaning national unity question the wisdom of suppressing ethnic and community identity, but on the basis of different arguments. For Casanova, national solidarity can be encouraged voluntarily, quite effectively, and without fostering backlash. For Ramos, national solidarity that devalues indigenous peoples is unjust, and "solidarity" that attempts to replace communalism with individualism is contradictory. For Aliaga and Dreyfus, imposed national solidarity that teaches children to devalue themselves and their communities breeds violence.

SOLIDARITY FOR SOCIAL JUSTICE SUPPORTED BY LEGISLATION

Solidarity in diverse and complex societies is commonly understood as a process of collective identity formation around work on behalf of social justice. The remaining chapters in this book take up questions about building solidarity in ways that support rather than negate ethnic and community differences. In the process, these chapters also grapple with what happens when confronting power disparities. Legal frameworks sometimes complement solidarity work for equity and justice, although legal frameworks by themselves have limited impact. Legal frameworks are usually the result of social struggle and, as such, embody compromises. And, there are always gaps (perhaps large chasms) between what legislation supports and what actually happens on the ground, which is generally shaped by longstanding and institutionalized power relations.

In Chapter 10, Mahendra Kumar Mishra points out that in India, the National Curriculum Framework 2005 (National Council of Educational Research and Training, 2005) aims to connect school with community, supporting flexibility to enable curriculum, pedagogy, and assessments to reflect and support India's diverse cultures. NCF 2005 is the result of struggles over who counts as Indian, given India's huge cultural diversity and its caste system that had long locked millions of people out of education as well as many other sectors of public life. But, despite NCF 2005, in rural areas the reality is that huge gaps remain between schools and communities. Most teachers are from elsewhere, and even those who teach where they grew up have learned implicitly to devalue local cultures through their formal education. In Chapter 8, Anne Hynds explains that in New Zealand, the Māori (the indigenous peoples of New Zealand) struggled to achieve legal recognition of the rights of land ownership and citizenship. The Treaty of Waitangi, first signed in 1840, provided the legal basis for power-sharing between the Māori and everyone else. Yet, as Hynds's chapter makes clear, biculturalism and power-sharing are still goals to work toward rather than a reality in schools. The authors of both chapters ask how solidarity can be built between teachers from the dominant groups and local indigenous communities, so that education actually reflects legalized principles. While Hynds probes fractures in solidarity work, Mishra shares a program that has had considerable success.

In the United States, some states such as California require schools to have English Learner Advisory Councils that will represent immigrant parents whose first language is not English, and these councils are supposed to advise the principal and staff. In Chapter 7, Gina Elizabeth DeShera shows that in practice, these councils may be constructed in a way that keeps them fairly powerless. In Spain, Basic Laws on Education support teaching for peace, intercultural education, and solidarity among people in the context of immigration. Yet, Encarnación Soriano in Chapter 5 shows that most teachers she surveyed had not been trained in these areas, and largely saw immigrant students as problems to be served mainly in supplemental language classes. DeShera and Soriano ask how schools can build solidarity with parents and immigrant communities in ways that are supported by law but undermined by traditional power relations.

In Chile, Verónica López, Carmen Montecinos, José Ignacio Rodríguez, Andrés Calderón, and Juan Francisco Contreras, writing in Chapter 1, explain that due to the growing concentration of hard-to-teach students in municipal schools, schools are required to develop a Convivencia Rules and Procedures Handbook to improve school climate, and that this is supposed to be developed through participatory processes. Yet, in many schools, official documents were simply handed down rather than created from the ground up; these were the schools with the greatest amount of peer-to-peer aggression. The authors show the relationship between the process by which a school develops its rules and procedures for *convivencia*, and relationships of solidarity that do or do not develop among people within the school.

The work of Cheung and Ma (2011) helps to analyze gaps between what is legislated and what is practiced. Cheung and Ma differentiate among three forms of solidarity: distributive solidarity (policies and practices that support equity), inclusive solidarity (shared identity through inclusive relationships), and dialogic solidarity (communication). The implication is that, while distributive solidarity may exist, bringing it to life requires engaging in inclusive and dialogic solidarity. Distributive solidarity provides a foothold to those seeking to develop a living inclusive and dialogic solidarity. Sometimes that foothold works; other times it does not. In what ways do chapters shed light on what seems to matter most?

BUILDING SOLIDARITY AROUND MARGINALITY

Most chapters in this book examine possibilities of building solidarity between professional educators and members of historically marginalized communities. This work is complicated by overlapping differences in culture, language, education level, and social position. While most teachers in most of the studies in this book are members of the dominant ethnic or racial group, speak the dominant language, and are reasonably well educated, parents in communities are often immigrants, of color, poorly educated, and/or working in low-skilled wage jobs. With or without policies that support equity, bridging these gaps in power is treacherous.

In two chapters, it was among the parents themselves that solidarity emerged. In DeShera's study in Chapter 7, parents who participated in the English Learner Advisory Council and migrant parent group, who initially had not been organized, developed their use of critical dialogue: getting to know each other and talking through concerns in a way that moved from personal stories to public knowledge, coming to consensus, and making their recommendations to the School Site Council. Similarly, in Chapter 8, Gilberto Arriaza and Alice Wagner document how, through a combination of formal and informal venues, parents—including immigrant mothers from Mexico and African American parents—established clubs and activities that served both recreational and advocacy purposes.

More's (2009) use of Sartre's framework is useful for interpreting these examples. Recall from the Introduction that Sartre distinguished among seriality (social collective of individuals passively united by something fairly inconsequential), group (collective consciously united toward common end), group-in-fusion (individuals in the process of becoming aware of sharing a fate), and pledge group (a group that is becoming institutionalized). The parent groups in Chapters 7 and 8 can be regarded as groups-in-fusion, as the individual parents, through participation in organized communication venues, became aware of shared concerns related to culture, language, and racism. They were able to move from sharing stories and identifying common concerns to taking collective action because of the "common fate" they perceived for their children in the school.

The more difficult problem is building solidarity that involves getting those who do not directly share a group's fate to act as active allies in work for justice and rights. This problem is particularly challenging because it requires directly confronting power disparities. In addition to differences of race and class, the fact that those who are formally well educated received their education in the dominant language and culture reinforces a distinction between those who "know" (i.e., the professional educators) and those who do not (i.e., the parents and their children). How, then, can solidarity be built among partners who are so unequally positioned? Cole and Luna (2010) maintain that while an individual may be born into social location and social identity, he or she acquires a political identity through political work. They suggest that solidarity work for allies can be constructed as people work together on common issues.

Katsarou, Picower, and Stovall (2010) write that for educators, those common issues revolve around care and concern for the well-being of children, both in the school and the classroom, and in the community. Deep concern for children's well-being rests on a moral imperative that is based on respect for others as full human beings, and translation of that respect into actions that seek to alleviate the sufferings of others (Buxarrais, 2005; Camps, 2000). Attaining a shared moral imperative requires considerable dialogue. Indeed, in the absence of a shared moral imperative that grounds political work for justice, there may be limits on the extent to which solidarity can be developed. In Chapter 9, Hynds illustrates that, as long as solidarity work is somewhat easy, people may be enthusiastic, but as it becomes more challenging, in the absence of a shared moral imperative, those who benefit from the status quo tend to back away from solidarity work.

It appears, however, that some educators willingly embrace the work of building solidarity with families who are poor and from a different background, nondefensively accepting a shared moral basis for the work. Soriano, in Chapter 5, refers to these educators as teachers "with heart" who are willing to set aside fear of the unknown and comfortable assumptions in order to make things better for the children they teach. Chapters by Soriano, Mishra, and Flores Carmona and Delgado Bernal illustrate teachers who engage personally with families, and through that engagement, develop empathy and a growing sense of solidarity with them that results in co-constructed actions to link families, students, and school. Chapter 1 by López and her colleagues illustrates principals and teachers learning to build inclusive school climates, and involving children in that process. In all of the above chapters, face-to-face communication was the main process through which solidarity was built.

Several chapters, however, examine breakdowns, failures, or lacks of initiative to develop solidarity between professional educators and families. In DeShera's study (Chapter 7), while members of the parent groups developed solidarity with each other, the White administrators and most of the White teachers dismissed parents' concerns. DeShera points out that most of the White English-speaking professional educators had difficulty taking criticism or another point of view from Brown people who were immigrants, poorly educated, and spoke Spanish. In Arriaza and Wagner's study (Chapter 8), most of the White teachers did not go beyond their comfort zones in getting to know parents through the structured home visits the principal encouraged them to make. Although some volunteers did engage in home visits, they selected families they felt most comfortable with; the authors point out that underlying their decision about which families to visit was "fear of the unknown." In Hynds's study (Chapter 9), while the European New Zealander (Pākehā) and Māori teachers initially worked to build solidarity, over time efforts eroded as Pākehā parents and students pressed to retain their dominant position. As Hynds points out, participants in her study were unaware of, and unprepared to challenge, the forms of institutional racism that were part of the school structure and its community, and that pressed toward a reproduction of racialized privileges and ideologies.

Yet, other chapters in this book point toward initiatives that give hope for involving more educators than the few who approach solidarity work intuitively and "with heart." The common factor in these initiatives is that a leader structured ongoing processes that enabled people from diverse and unequal backgrounds to communicate, and particularly for those from dominant communities to listen to and learn from marginalized communities. The leader also connected solidarity work with a moral imperative to serve all children well, and helped educators to see positive impacts of this work on the well-being of the children, and consequently on the well-being of the teachers.

The study in Chapter 1 by Verónica López and her colleagues highlights the importance of the principal's vision and actions. Case study principals were able to build solidarity among members of the school community by taking on and changing policies of exclusion that engender violence, and by developing among everyone a sense of responsibility for the community. Further, the principals helped make clear that inclusive policies and practices, grounded in an ethic of *convivencia*, produced marked reduction in violence and peer-to-peer aggression. Not only did the schools become better places for students, but they also became better places for teachers. The oral histories project discussed in Chapter 6 by Judith Flores Camona and Dolores Delgado Bernal took place in a school that had strong and consistent principal leadership on behalf of bilingual education. Although the authors did not describe the principals' leadership in much detail, the fact that they supported the larger Adelante project of which the oral histories curriculum was a part attests to their active leadership. Conversely, the school DeShera discusses in Chapter 7 did not develop solidarity with its parent community primarily because the school's leadership served as an obstacle rather than a support to that goal.

Leadership can come from outside as well as inside schools. In Chapter 10, Mishra's project Srujan involves a structured process for teachers in rural communities to interact with and become familiar with the funds of knowledge in the local community, and on that basis, to develop solidarity with the community—a sense of "we"—that supports reworking curriculum and pedagogy. Table 10.2 in Chapter 10 illustrates the impact that participating in that process has on teachers, and the subsequent impact on children as teachers learn to work with rather than against the community in the classroom. Like in the study in Chapter 1 by López and her colleagues, children's shift from being passive nonparticipants who were frequently absent from the classroom, to becoming enthusiastic participants who have knowledge and talents on which academic learning can be built, served as a motivator for teachers to continue solidarity work with the community.

CONCLUSION

Although one commonly hears that diversity is a threat to stability, and that schools should treat all students as much the same as possible, the authors in this book show that this is not a sustainable position. People do differ in culture, religion, language, and life experience, and families do want the best for their children. This book has advanced the concept of "solidarity" as a tool for considering how to forge alliances that work toward equity and justice, in the process respecting the diversity of families and communities that increasingly bump shoulders in complex societies. Perhaps the chapters in this book can best be connected through Childs's (2003) analysis of his own work to build what he terms *transcommunality*:

> Rather than being an abstract call for "unity," transcommunality relies on concrete interpersonal ties growing out of what I refer to as shared practical action from diverse participants. From such practical action flows increasing communication, mutual respect, and understanding. (p. 11)

It is the hope of all of the contributors to this book that readers will gain both a sense of hope that solidarity across difference is possible, and some direction for building the kind of communication, shared actions, and moral grounding that makes the work possible.

REFERENCES

Buxarrais, M. R. (2005). *Educar para la solidaridad* [To educate for solidarity]. Retrieved from www.campus-oei.org/valores/ boletin8.htm

Camps, V. (2000). *Valores de la educación* [Education values]. Madrid: Anaya.

Cheung, C., & Ma, K. M. (2011). Coupling social solidarity and social harmony in Hong Kong. *Social Indicators Research*, 103(1), 145–167.

Childs, J. B. (2003). *Transcommunality: From the politics of conversion to the ethics of respect*. Philadelphia: Temple University Press.

Chomsky, N. (1987). The manufacture of consent. In J. Peck (Ed.), *The Chomsky reader* (pp. 121–136). New York: Pantheon Books.

Cole, E. G., & Luna, Z. T. (2010). Making coalitions work: Solidarity across difference in U.S. feminism. *Feminist Studies* 36(1), 71–98.

Dewey, J. (1916). *Democracy and education*. New York: Free Press.

Feinberg, W. (1998). *Common schools/uncommon identities: National unity and cultural difference*. New Haven, CT: Yale University Press.

Janmatt, J. G., & Braun, R. (2009). Diversity and postmaterialism as rival perspectives in accounting for social solidarity. *International Journal of Comparative Sociology*, 50(1), 39–68.

Katsarou, E., Picower, B., & Stovall, D. (2010). Acts of solidarity: Developing urban social justice educators in the struggle for quality public education. *Teacher Education Quarterly*, 37(3), 137–153.

Korab-Karpowicz, W. J. (2010). Inclusive values and the righteousness of life: The foundations of global solidarity. *Ethic Theory Moral Practice*, 13, 305–313.

More, M. P. (2009). Black solidarity: A philosophical defense. *Theoria: A Journal of Social and Political Theory*, 56(120), 20–43

National Council of Educational Research and Training. (2005). *National curriculum framework 2005*. New Delhi: NCERT Publications Division.

Pérez, P. M. (2006). Valores y pautas de crianza familiar en los Montes del Pas [Values and family upbringing in the Monts du Pas]. *Teoría de la Educación*, 18, 115–136.

Zibechi, R. (2009). Time to reactivate networks of solidarity. *Socialism and Democracy 23*(2), 110–112.

Zubero, I. (1996). Construyendo una sociedad solidaria: Una propuesta para el análisis y la acción [Building a caring society: A proposal for the analysis of action]. *Cuadernos de Trabajo Social*, 9, 303–327.

About the Contributors

Isabelle Aliaga teaches Spanish as a foreign language for primary and secondary education in the Institut Universitaire de Formation des Maitres (IUFM) of Montpellier and University of Montpellier II, France. Her research interests focus on intercultural competence of communication, language acquisition in children less than 6 years old, and bases for a new global didactic in language based on Edgard Morin's theory of complexity. She explores the use of music to create complexity in learning language. She is a member of France's steering group in a Comenius program that creates tools to develop language and music skills simultaneously in European primary schools.

Gilberto Arriaza is professor of educational leadership in the College of Education and Allied Studies at California State University East Bay in the United States. His teaching and research interests include transformative leadership, organizational culture, and the social dynamics of schooling. His latest book (coauthored with F. Briscoe and R. C. Henze) is *The Power of Talk: How Words Change Our Lives* (2009).

Dolores Delgado Bernal is professor of education and ethnic studies at the University of Utah. Her research contributes to the fields of education and Chicana/o studies by examining the sociocultural context of the educational pipeline for Chicanas/os and other students of color, and investigating alternative conceptions of knowledge, teaching, and learning. She is co-editor of *Chicana/Latina Education in Everyday Life: Feminista Perspectives on Pedagogy and Epistemology* (2006), which received the American Educational Studies Critics Choice Award, and she is the author of numerous chapters and articles, some of which have appeared in *Harvard Educational Review, Urban Education,* and *Social Justice.* She is co-director of Adelante, a university-school-community partnership at Jackson Elementary School, which is dedicated to creating educational opportunities and college-going expectations through community engagement, research, and reciprocity.

209

Andrés Calderón recently obtained his undergraduate in Psychology at Pontificia Universidad Católica de Valparaíso, Chile. He currently works as a school psychologist in two schools.

Judith Flores Carmona is an Andrew W. Mellon postdoctoral Fellow in Critical Literacies and Pedagogy at Hampshire College (2010–2012). She earned her doctorate from the University of Utah in the Department of Education, Culture, and Society. Her research interests include Latina mothers' pedagogies of the home, *testimonio* [testimony] as method and communal-reciprocal methodology, Chicana/Latina feminist theory, and oral history. She was born in Veracruz, Mexico, raised in Los Angeles, and is a first-generation college student. Her academic and community work are guided by a sense of responsibility and commitment to social change.

Maria Antonia Casanova is professor of education at the University Camilo José Cela, Madrid, and director of Training at the Higher Institute of Educational Advancement (Madrid). She has held the positions of educational inspector, assistant director general for Special Education and Attention to Diversity (in the Spanish Ministry of Education), and director general of educational promotion (Community of Madrid Government). Her recent publications include *Diseño Curricular e Innovación Educativa* [Curriculum Design and Educational Innovation] (2009) and *Educación Inclusiva: Un Modelo de Futuro* [Inclusive Education: a Model for the Future] (2011).

Juan Francisco Contreras recently obtained his undergraduate in Psychology at Pontificia Universidad Católica de Valparaíso, Chile. He currently works as a school psychologist in two schools.

Gina Elizabeth DeShera lives and teaches in Watsonville, California. Over the last 20 years, she has taught 3rd grade through high school. For the last 13 years, she has been teaching middle school dance and Spanish for Spanish speakers. She is an experienced practitioner in implementing multicultural education, culturally relevant pedagogy, and critical pedagogy in the bilingual secondary classroom. She completed her Ed.D. degree at the University of California–Santa Cruz, and teaches part-time at San José State University.

Martine Dreyfus is a research professor in sciences of language (General and Applied Linguistics) at the Institut Universitaire de Formation des Maitres (IUFM) of Montpelier, and the University of Montpellier II. Her thesis and research relates to multilingual and multicultural communities or societies, language learning or teaching issues, especially French as a second or foreign language in different sociolinguistic contexts. She currently teaches at the IUFM of Montpellier and at the University of Montpellier III, and she is involved, in particular, in a Comenius European program on European music and language portfolio and in an academic program on norms and variations in language used by youth at school.

Anne Hynds is a Pākeha (European New Zealand) researcher/senior lecturer in the School of Educational Psychology and Pedagogy, Faculty of Education at Victoria University of Wellington, Wellington, New Zealand. She is also a research associate for the Jessie Herrington Research Centre at the Faculty of Education. As a teacher, Anne taught in elementary and secondary school settings, and in mainstream and Deaf education. She has a real interest in collaborative research/action research methodologies and has worked in a number of bicultural evaluation projects. Her research interests are focused on issues of diversity within education, the relationship between teacher understandings of culturally responsive and inclusive pedagogies, and resistance to change in equity-minded school reforms.

Verónica López is associate professor at the School of Psychology at Pontificia Universidad Católica de Valparaíso, Chile, and associate researcher of the Center for Advanced Research in Education (CIAE). Her research focuses on classroom and school influences on student victimization, and on how to create inclusive classrooms, schools, and policies in Latin America.

Mahendra Kumar Mishra is the founder of multilingual education in elementary education in the state of Orissa, India. He has worked to apply culture to the primary school curriculum. He is also a well-known folklorist of India, and is the author of *Oral Epics of Kalahandi* (2007). He is associated with many national and international organizations on community knowledge, multicultural education, and critical pedagogy.

Carmen Montecinos is a professor of educational psychology at the School of Psychology, Pontificia Universidad Católica de Valparaíso and principal investigator at the Center for Advanced Research in Education. She has published extensively on topics related to the improvement of teacher education, multicultural education, and school leadership. Her most recent co-edited book, *Mejoramiento Escolar en Acción* [School Improvement in Action] (2011), brings together Chilean school practitioners and university researchers, as well as international authors, exploring exemplary practices in teacher education, school leadership, school climate, and science and mathematic education.

José Luis Ramos is a professor of anthropology at the Escuela de Antropología e Historia, Periférico Sur y Zapote, Mexico. His research focuses on indigenous identities, conceptions of intercultural education, and professional education of anthropologists. His most recent publications appear in *Zona Próxima*, *Revista de Antropología Experimental*, and *Gazeta de Antropología*.

José Ignacio Rodríguez recently obtained his undergraduate in psychology at Pontificia Universidad Católica de Valparaíso, Chile. He currently works as a consultant in organizational development and human resources.

Christine E. Sleeter is professor emerita in the College of Professional Studies at California State University–Monterey Bay, where she was a founding faculty member. She currently serves as president of the National Association for Multicultural Education. Her research focuses on anti-racist multicultural education and multicultural teacher education. She has published extensively in journals such as *Journal of Teacher Education*, *Race Ethnicity & Education*, *Teaching and Teacher Education*, and *Curriculum Inquiry*. Her recent books include *Professional Development for Culturally Responsive and Relationship-Based Pedagogy* (2011) and *Teaching with Vision* (2011) (with Catherine Cornbleth). She has been invited to speak in most U.S. states as well as several countries. Awards for her work include the American Educational Research Association Social Justice Award and the Central Washington University Distinguished Alum.

Encarnación Soriano is professor of research methods in education at the University of Almería (Spain) and director of the research group Research and Evaluation in Intercultural Education. She is the author and editor of numerous books and articles on issues of intercultural education, cultural identity, intercultural citizenship, and interculturality and gender. Her recent publications include the books *Education for Democratic and Intercultural Citizenship* (2008), *Living Between Cultures: A New Society* (2009), *International Challenges in Front of the Interculturality* (2010), and *The Value of Education in a Globalized World*. Among her articles are "Emotional Competencies of Secondary Education Native and Immigrant Students" (Soriano and Osorio), "Objectives and Content on Interculturality in the Initial Training of Educators" (Soriano and Peñalva), and "The Impact of a Values Education Program for Adolescent Romanies in Spain on Their Feeling of Self-Realisation" (Soriano, Franco, and Sleeter).

Alice Wagner holds a master's degree in educational leadership from California State University–East Bay. She is a bilingual teacher (Spanish/English) who has taught adults and primary students for over 14 years; she is also an education consultant. Alice co-founded an independent public library in rural Oaxaca, Mexico, as well as co-coordinated a cultural immersion program for California pre-service teachers from Mills College in rural Oaxaca. She currently teaches bilingual kindergarten in the San Francisco Bay area of California.

Index

Note: page numbers followed by "t" or "f" indicate a table or figure, respectively; an "n" refers to a note.

Abdallah-Pretceille, M., 66, 98
Aberasturi, A., 95
Abric, J. C., 51
Abu-Luban, Y., 12
Acevedo, A. M., 5–6
Adelante: A College Awareness and Participatory Partnership program, 116, 117. *See also* Adelante Oral Histories Project
Adelante Oral Histories Project (AOHP), 114–129
Aggression
  addressing peer-to-peer aggression, 23–41
  inclusion-oriented schools, 39–40
  INSEBULL [Instrumentos para la Evaluación del Bullying], 41n3
Ahmed, R., 181
Ahumada, L., 25, 38
ALCE [Associations of Spanish Language and Culture], 85
Alcudia, R., 59n1
Alemán, E., 117
Aliaga, I., 13, 200–201
Allies in contexts of struggle, solidarity as building, 10–13, 91–197

Almonacid, C., 25
Alter-identification, 50, 57
Alton-Lee, A., 165
Amanti, C., 107, 108, 140
Ambivalences, West African education, 68–69
Anderson, G. L., 136
AOHP (Adelante Oral Histories Project), 114–129
Aotearoa, New Zealand, 163–178
Apple, M. W., 184
Arón, A. M., 40
Arriaza, G., 15, 205
Artiles, A. J., 175
Artists and artisans, Indian tribal community involvement, 186
Arts and crafts, Indian tribal community involvement, 186, 189, 191t
Aspiazu, G. G., 150
Assimilation
  and colonial peoples, 65
  shifting demographics and social distance, 151
Associations of Spanish Language and Culture (ALCE), 85
Astor, R. A., 37

Atria, F., 25
Auerbach, S., 140
Avilés, J. M., 41n3
Ayala, A., 25–26

Bakan, A. B., 12
Balibar, R., 64
Banks, C., 98
Baquedano-Lopez, P., 177
Baraúna, T., 6
Basic Laws on Education, Spain,
    202–203
Batibo, H. M., 164
Bauer, S. C., 150
Bauman, Z., 26
Bayley, R., 117–118
Behavior. *See* Student behavior
Belfield, C. R., 24
Bell, L. A., 153
Bellei, C., 24
Benbenishty, R., 37
Benmayor, R., 118, 127
Berryman, M., 165, 170, 176–177
Bicultural educational program,
    Mexico, 52–60
Biddulph, C., 165, 177
Biddulph, F., 165, 177
Biddulph, J., 165, 177
Bilingual education
    social distance and, 148–160
    teachers in Mexico, 52–60
Bishop, R., 165, 168, 170, 176–177
Bonfil, G., 52
Boutet, J., 64
Bouvier, L. F., 151
Braatz, J. P., 142
Bradnam, L., 167
Braun, R., 8, 9, 199
Broughton, R., 167
Bryk, A. S., 38
Buckley, J., 25

Bullying
    inclusion-oriented schools,
        39–40
    INSEBULL [Instrumentos para
        la Evaluación del Bullying],
        41n3
    peer-to-peer aggression,
        addressing, 23–41
Burkas, 75
Bustos, S., 25
Butler, A. L., 186
Buxarrais, M. R., 8, 199, 204

Cabrera, A., 99
Calderón, A., 13, 27, 199, 203,
    205, 206
California schools. *See also* English
    Learner Advisory Committee
    (ELAC)
    community involvement and
        collaboration, 131–146,
        148–160
    Public School Accountability Act
        (PSAA), 132–133
    School Site Council (SSC), 133,
        155–156, 204
    social distance and, 148–160
California Standards Test, 137
Calvo, T., 95
Camps, V., 9, 96, 97, 107, 199, 204
Carambo, C., 4, 6, 134, 145, 152
Carrasco, C., 25–26
Casanova, M. A., 14, 201
Caste system, Indian, 181–182
Castro, L., 40
Celebrations
    oral history curriculum program,
        122
    social distance and, 157
Centers of Spanish education
    abroad, 82–85, 83t

Centre for Advanced Research in Education (Chile), 40–41n
CGEIB (Coordinación General de Educación Intercultural y Bilingüe), 59n2
Chaudenson, R., 68
Chávez, J., 59n4
Cheung, C., 38, 203
Childs, J. B., 2, 11, 207
Chile
    exclusion and Chilean school practices, 23–27
    Ley General de Educatión (LEGE), 24–26
    peer-to-peer aggression, addressing, 23–41
    socioeconomic status of students, 26
Chilean National Fund for Scientific and Technological Development, 40–41n
Chomsky, N., 70, 200
Churchill, D. S., 7
Cigliutti, S., 143
Cohen, J., 34, 41n1
Cole, E. G., 11, 163, 164, 170, 173, 174, 175–176, 178, 204
Colegio de España, 79
Coleman, J. S., 151
Coll, P., 97, 107
Collier, V. P., 150
Colonized societies
    indigenous groups in New Zealand, 163–178
    multiculturalism in French education model, 67–70
Communication. *See also* Home visits by school staff
    barriers to critical dialogue and participation, 142–144

criticism as barrier to critical dialogue and participation, 142–144
dialogic solidarity, 38–39
    and immigrant students' attitudes, 104
    planning team to address school-parent communication, 138–139
    social distance and, 148–160
    teacher-home relationships, 118–121
Community collaboration and involvement. *See also* Parental involvement
    building community through solidarity, 4
    civic virtue for participatory citizenship, 5–6
    India, solidarity between tribal community and school in, 180–196
    indigenous groups in New Zealand, 165, 166–175
    oral history curriculum program, 114–129
    in school improvement, 131–146
    and social distance, 148–160
    social distance and, 148–160
Contreras, D., 25
Contreras, J. F., 13, 27, 199, 203, 205, 206
Convivencia, 23, 41n1, 203
    leadership for promoting social inclusion in, 31–37
    peer-to-peer aggression and, 27–37
    questionnaires and reports relating to, 28–30, 29t
Cooper, H., 150

Co-optation as barrier to critical
    dialogue and participation,
    143–144
Coordinación General de
    Educación Intercultural y
    Bilingüe (CGEIB), 59n2
Coquery-Vidrovitch, C., 67
Cornelius, W. A., 151
Craft, Indian tribal community
    involvement, 186, 189
Criticism as barrier to critical
    dialogue and participation,
    142–144
Cultivation of diversity, 97–98
Cultural diversity and differences.
    See also Interculturalism
    and intercultural education;
    Marginalization and
    marginalized people;
    Multiculturalism
    compared with social inequality,
    45–46
    immigrant students and, 102,
    106–107
    Indian tribal community, 182
    indigenous groups in New
    Zealand, 165, 170–172

Dance, and Indian tribal
    community involvement, 189,
    191t
Dart, J., 69
Davesne, A., 68
De Gaetano, Y., 153
de la Fuente, L., 25
Dean, J., 7–8, 183
Decentralization as strategy for
    teachers and cultural diversity,
    98
Decision making and parental
    involvement, 131–132
Decker, L. V., 150

Decker, V., 150
Defensive reactions to criticism as
    barrier to critical dialogue and
    participation, 142–144
del Carmen, M., 59n1
Delano, A., 95
DELE [Diploma of Spanish as a
    Foreign Language], 86
Délégation Générale à la Langue
    Française et aux Langues de
    France, 64, 65
Delgado Bernal, D., 14, 115,
    117, 118, 120–121,
    124, 205, 206
Delgado-Gaitan, C., 153
Democracy and parental
    involvement, 131–146, 199
Demographic shifts, social
    distance, community
    involvement and
    collaboration, 149–151
Derpman, S., 8
DeShera, G. E., 15, 159, 203, 205
Deslandes, A., 11
Dewey, J., 136, 145–146, 199
DGEI (Mexico) [General
    Directorate of Indigenous
    Education], 47, 52
Dialogic solidarity, 38–39
Diploma of Spanish as a Foreign
    Language (DELE), 86
Direct participation parental
    involvement, 135–139
Discrimination and social bias.
    See also Marginalization and
    marginalized people; Racism
    France, multiculturalism and
    education in, 62–77
    and immigrant students'
    attitudes, 104
    Spain, multicultural coexistence
    in schools in, 93–110

Disparities in power, 199
Distributive solidarity, 38
Diversity. *See also* Cultural diversity and differences
  comparisons and explanations, 65–66
  importance of tolerance and respect for, 98
  indigenous groups in New Zealand, 176
  strategies for teachers, 98
  valuing students' diversity, 72–74
Dobbie, D., 3, 11, 183
Donato, R., 159
Dreyfus, M., 13, 200–201
Durie, M., 176
Durkheim, E., 59n7
Duro, E., 5–6

Early childhood language acquisition, 71
Edmonston, B., 151
EdSource, 151
Educational policy implications, inclusion-oriented school, 39–40
EHEA (European Higher Education Area), 85
ELAC. *See* English Learner Advisory Committee (ELAC)
Elacqua, G., 25
Elenes, C. A., 120
Elices, J. A., 41n3
ELL (English Language Learner) students, 134, 137. *See also* English Learner Advisory Committee (ELAC)
EMP (European Music Portfolio), 76

Empathy
  differences in culture and power, 4–5
  entrance into "the other" as strategy for teachers and cultural diversity, 98
English Language Learner (ELL) students, 134, 137. *See also* English Learner Advisory Committee (ELAC)
English Learner Advisory Committee (ELAC), California, 134, 138–139, 143, 156, 202, 203
  ELAC Migrant Parent Council Recommendations, 141f
  ELAC/Migrant meetings, 139
Entrance into "the other" as strategy for teachers and cultural diversity, 98
Epstein, S. E., 5
Escobar, A., 59n4
Esquivel, L., 97, 98, 107
Estrada, J. N., 37
Ethnic identity, 45–60. *See also* Social identity and identification
Ethno-political indigenous identity, 52
Europa Press, 2
Europa Press/Barcelona, 2
European Baccalaureat, 88
European Higher Education Area (EHEA), 85
European Music Portfolio (EMP), 76
European Schools (Spain), 87–88
European Union, 85
  European Schools, 87–88
  multiculturalism effect, 80–81
Eurostat, 94

Exclusion. *See also* Marginalization and marginalized people; Segregation
and Chilean school practices, 23–27
Eynon, B., 118

Family/student solidarity, oral history curriculum program, 123–124
Feinberg, W., 135, 201
Felgueroso, F. Y., 106
Feminism, 10
Fendler, L., 7, 10
Fields, A., 135
Fishman, J. A., 117–118
Flament, C., 51
Flor Ada, A., 122
Flores Carmona, J., 14, 117, 118, 119, 121–122, 205, 206
Forrest, R., 151
France
history of education system, 63
monolingualism, 64
multiculturalism and education, 62–77
plurilingual school context, 71–74
republican model of solidarity, 62–77, 200
Frankowski, R., 41n3
Freire, P., 119, 144, 145, 163, 164, 176, 177

Games, Indian tribal community involvement, 186, 189, 191t
Garcia, E., 128
García, F. J., 46
Garcia, M., 99
García López, J. R., 94
García Roca, J., 97
García-Huidobro, J. E., 24

Gavilán, P., 59n1
General Board for the French Language, 65
General Commission for the French Language and Other Languages of France, 65
General Coordination of Intercultural and Bilingual Education (Mexico), 59n2
General Directorate of Indigenous Education (DGEI) (Mexico), 47, 52
General Education Law (Chile), 24–26
Generalized reciprocity, 151–152
Gil, F., 4
Giménez, G., 51
Gimeno Sacristán, J., 59n1
Giné, N., 59n1
Ginsberg, M. B., 153
Glynn, T., 168
Gobierno de España, 99
Goldsmith, T., 2
Gonzalez, F. E., 120
González, N., 107, 108, 117–118, 140
González, R. (Chilean congressman), 39
Gonzalez, S. M., 128
Goodson, B. D., 153
Gotts, E. L., 186
Gould, J. L., 12
Gramsci, A., 180
Grant, C., 96, 98
Grau, I. M., 5–6
Guerrero, A., 51
Gutierrez, K. D., 177
Gutiérrez, N., 53

Habermas, J., 95
Hall, K. A., 6
Hardy, G., 68

Harry, B., 153
Hart, J., 153
Hayward (California), 148–160
Hervás, M. J., 99
Hess, A. G., 136, 143
Hetero-identification, 50
Higgins, J., 167
High Council for the French
    Language, 65
Hispanicization and acculturation
    in Mexio, 48
Home visits by school staff
  ELAC Migrant Parent Council
      Recommendations, 141f
  social distance and, 153, 154–
      158, 159
Horne, A., 39
Hoston, W. T., 10
Hui, T. K., 2
Hui (meetings), *Te Kauhua*
    professional development
    program, 167, 169, 172, 173
Humphrey, K., 2
Hynds, A., 15, 167, 168, 169, 175,
    177, 178, 202, 204–205

Identity and identification.
    See Social identity and
    identification
IEEPO (Instituto Estatal de
    Educación Pública de Oaxaca),
    59n1
Immigration and immigrant
    populations. *See also* Latino/a
    communities in the United
    States
  attitudes of immigrant students,
      102–104
  deficiencies in students'
      performance, 100–105
  economic resources, 100, 105
  former French colonies, 67–70

France, 62–77
  language and language
      instruction, 70–74, 99–100,
      101, 109
  Mexico, 46–49
  oral histories and curriculum,
      Mexican immigrants, 114–129
  rapid increase in numbers, 98–99,
      105
  Spain, multicultural coexistence
      in schools in, 93–110
*Immigration and Students'
    Achievement in Spain,* 106
Inclusion-oriented schools
  in dealing with peer-to-peer
      aggression, 23–41
  policy and professional
      development implications,
      39–40
Inclusive solidarity, 38
The Independent Schools, 2
India, solidarity between tribal
    community and school, 180–
    196, 199
Indigenous and non-indigenous
    persons
  deficiencies in students'
      performance, 164–165
  definitions and descriptions of
      terms, 46
  ethno-political indigenous
      identity, 52
  Indian tribal community, 180–
      196
  Mixtec indigenous teachers of
      Mexico, case study, 52–60,
      59n10
  moral imperative, 175–178
  in New Zealand, 163–178
Informe RAXEN, 96
INSEBULL [Instrumentos para la
    Evaluación del Bullying], 41n3

Inspección de Educación (Spain),82
Instituto Cervantes, 86
Instituto de Tecnologías Educativas,
    94
Instituto Estatal de Educación
    Pública de Oaxaca (IEEPO),
    59n1
Integration
    building solidarity to promote
        coexistence and, 96–98
    and immigrant students'
        attitudes, 102–104
Interculturalism and intercultural
    education
    comparisons and explanations,
        65–66
    and immigrant students in Spain,
        98
    Mexico, 45–60
    Spanish students abroad, 79–90
Interdependence, communal, 199
Interpersonal relations. *See also*
    Communication; Home visits
    by school staff
    and promotion of social
        inclusion, 36
Inzunza , J., 25
Islamic headscarves, 75
IUFM of Montpellier (Teacher
    Training Institute), 62, 70,
    77n1

Janmatt, J. G., 8, 9, 199
Jodelet, D., 51
Johnson, A. G., 177
Joint-ownership schools, Spanish,
    82, 83t, 84
Jover, G., 4
JUNAEB (Junta Nacional de
    Auxilio Escolar y Becas), 34

Justice
    legislation, solidarity for social
        justice supported by, 201–202
    and relation to concept of
        solidarity, 81, 85, 96, 98
Juul, S., 8

Karmy, M., 25–26
Katsarou, E., 4, 204
Kearns, A., 151
Kemmis, S., 137, 138
Kern, S., 70, 71
Kincheloe J. L., 183, 184
Klingner, J. K., 153
Knowledge Networks, 151
Korab-Karpowicz, W. J., 8, 199
Kotahitanga, achievement of, 165
Kraemer, K. R., 13
Kruidenier, J. F., 10
Kumar, S., 181

Labrador, J., 50
Lagrange, H., 64
Language and language instruction,
    72–73. *See also* Bilingual
    education
    early childhood language
        acquisition, 71
    French monolingualism, 64
    immigrant children, 70–74, 99–
        100, 101, 108
    Indian tribal community, 182
    plurilingual school context,
        71–74
    standardization and assimilation,
        65
Latino/a communities in the United
    States
    oral histories and curriculum,
        114–129

school improvement
collaboration, 131–146
social distance and, 148–160
Law of Dependence (Spain),
97
Law on Education of Spain,
85
Layzer, J. I., 153
Leadership
principal's role in bridging social
distance, 158, 160
solidarity as core value for school
leadership, 37–38, 206
Leadership for promoting social
inclusion, 31–37
LEGE *(Ley General de Educatión)*,
24–26
Legislation
Basic Laws on Education (Spain),
202–203
critical dialogue and
participation, 132, 133, 143,
144
French education system, 63
and immigrant students, 105–107
inclusion-oriented schools, 39–40
Law of Dependence (Spain), 97
Law on Education of Spain, 85
Ley General de Educatión
(LEGE), 24–26
Ley of Depedencia (Spain), 97
No Child Left Behind Act
(NCLB), 126, 132–133
Organic Education Law of 2006
(Spain), 99, 106
Organic Law of the Education
System of 1990 (Spain), 99,
106
Public School Accountability Act
(PSAA) (California), 132–133

social justice supported by
legislation, solidarity for,
201–202
Spain, 85, 97, 99, 105–107,
202–203
LeMay, M. C., 151
Léon, A., 68
Levin, H. M., 24
Ley General de Educatión (LEGE),
24–26
Ley of Depedencia (Spain),
97
Liñares, A., 94
López, J., 25–26
López, V., 13, 25–26, 39, 41n3,
199, 203, 205, 206
López Rodríguez, F., 59n1
Luna, Z. T., 11, 163, 164, 170,
173, 174, 175–176, 178, 204
Lunchrooms and social inclusion,
35–36

Ma, K. M., 38, 203
Malen, B., 143
Mamadou and Bineta (textbook
series), 68
Management Information
System (MIS) Unit, India,
181–182
Mandates. *See also* English Learner
Advisory Committee (ELAC)
critical dialogue and
participation, 132, 133, 143,
144
home visits, 153
No Child Left Behind Act
(NCLB), 126, 132–133
Spanish law, 99
Mann, M. B., 153
Manning, M. L., 152, 153

Māori people, challenges to
    development of solidarity,
    163–178
Marginalization and marginalized
    people, 12. *See also*
    Discrimination and social bias;
    Racism
    building solidarity around,
        203–206
    and cultural isolation in France,
        74–75
    France, multiculturalism and
        education in, 62–77
    identification with one's own
        marginalized community, 6
    Indian tribal community, 180–
        196
    New Zealand, indigenous people
        in, 131–146
    oral history curriculum program,
        114–129
    parental involvement, 131–146
    unity in the face of
        marginalization, 9–10
Martin, P. L., 151
Mass societies, solidarity in, 199
Math festival, Indian tribal
    community involvement, 191t
Mauss, M., 59n7
McCabe, E. M., 34, 41n1
McIntosh, T., 175, 176
McLaren, P., 163, 177
McTaggart, R., 137, 138
Mediation as strategy for teachers
    and cultural diversity, 98
Mena, P., 25
Mexico and Mexican people. *See
    also* Latino/a communities in
    the United States
    bicultural and bilingual
        educational program,
        52–60

General Coordination of
    Intercultural and Bilingual
    Education (Mexico), 59n2
General Directorate of Indigenous
    Education, 47
General Directorate of Indigenous
    Education (DGEI) (Mexico),
    47, 52
Immigration and immigrant
    populations, 46–49
indigenous social identity and
    devalued solidarity, 45–60
Mixtec indigenous teachers of
    Mexico, case study, 52–60,
    59n10
Meyer, J. A., 153
Michelli, N. M., 34, 41n1
Milicic, N., 40
Mini-books created in oral history
    curriculum program, 122
Minister of Education, of Chile, 39
Ministerio de Educación de Chile,
    24, 41n1
Ministerio de Educación de España,
    82–84, 86, 87, 98
Ministry of Education
    New Zealand, 165
    Spain, 82–84, 86, 87, 98
Ministry of Home, India, 181, 182
MIS (Management Information
    System) Unit, India, 181–182
Mishra, M. K., 15, 199, 202, 205,
    206
Mixtec indigenous teachers of
    Mexico, 52–60, 199
Mohanty, C. T., 10–11
Moll, L., 107, 108, 140
Monasta, A., 180
Moniot H., 67
Monolingualism, French, 64
    comparison with plurilingual
        instruction, 72–73

Montecinos, C., 13, 25, 38, 199, 203, 205, 206
Montes de Oca, L. B., 50
Morales, M., 25–26
More, M. P., 9, 10, 204
Moreno, M., 121
Morin, E., 76
Moscovici, S., 51
Multiculturalism
  comparisons and explanations, 65–66
  French education system and, 62–77
  French ideological opposition to, 65–70
  Indian tribal community, 183
  Spain, coexistence in schools in, 93–110
Muñoz Bata, S., 95
Music activities, Indian tribal community involvement, 189, 191t
My Name is Maria Isabel/Me LLamo Maria Isabel, 122

Nahuatl, contrasted with indigenous, 52
National Council of Educational Research and Training, India, 202
National Curriculum Framework 2005 (NCF), India, 182, 202
National solidarity, imposed, 201
Nature study activities, Indian tribal community involvement, 189, 191t
NCF (National Curriculum Framework) 2005, India, 182, 202
NCLB (No Child Left Behind Act), 126, 132–133
Negative social identities, 50, 56

Negotiation as strategy for teachers and cultural diversity, 98
New Zealand, challenges to development of solidarity, 163–178
Nieto, S., 4–5, 108, 119–120, 128
No Child Left Behind Act (NCLB), 126, 132–133
Noguera, P., 133
Noticias *(Iglesia.net)*, 1

Oakes, J., 136
Odisha, India, 180–196
Odisha Primary Education Program Authority (OPEPA), 187–188
OECD (Organisation for Economic Co-operation and Development), 41n2. *See also* Program for International Student Assessment (PISA)
Ogawa, T., 143
O'Leary, C., 118
Olivos, E. M., 139, 144
OPEPA (Odisha Primary Education Program Authority), 187–188
Oral histories and curriculum, immigrant students, 114–129
Oral traditions and storytelling, Indian tribal community, 185, 188, 189, 191t, 192
Organic Education Law of 2006 (Spain), 99, 106
Organic Law of the Education System of 1990 (Spain), 99, 106
Organisation for Economic Co-operation and Development (OECD), 41n2. *See also* Program for International Student Assessment (PISA)
Orpinas, P., 39, 41n3
Ortega, P., 96

"The other" and cultural diversity, 98
Ownership schools, Spanish, 82, 83–84, 83t
Oyler, C., 5
Özerk, K., 6

Pájaro Valley Unified School District (PVUSD), California, 131–146
Parekh, B., 183
Parental involvement
  barriers to critical dialogue and participation, 142–144
  indigenous groups in New Zealand, 165
  oral histories curriculum, 114–129
  school improvement collaboration, 131–146
  social distance and, 148–160
Parents and Teachers Association (PTA), 155–156
Parés, M., 27, 39
Park, R. E., 151
Participatory democracy and parental involvement, 135–139
Passel, J. S., 151
Patall, E. A., 150
Peer-to-peer aggression
  addressing, 23–41
  school climate-related practices and, 27–37
Penetito, W., 163, 164, 165, 166, 176, 177
Perceptions and preconceived notions by teachers, 152, 192
Pérez, P. M., 7, 198
Pérez Tapias, J. A., 110
Perlich, P., 128
Petit, J., 71

Photography created in oral history curriculum program, 122
Piattelli-Palmarini, M., 70
Pickeral, T., 34, 41n1
Picower, B., 4, 204
Pini, M., 143
PISA. See Program for International Student Assessment (PISA)
Plata, O., 128
Play, Indian tribal community involvement, 186, 189, 191t
Playground interaction
  individual and institutional racism, 174–175
  and social inclusion, 35
Pluralism
  comparisons and explanations, 65–66, 201
  Spanish society and, 95
Porcher, L., 66
Portés, A., 142
"Portuguese Language and Culture" program (Spain), 88
Positive social identities, 50, 56–57
Private schools, Spanish, 82, 83t, 84
Professional development
  inclusion-oriented school, 39–40
  Te Kauhua professional development program, New Zealand, 166–167
Program for International Student Assessment (PISA)
  Chile, 24
  Spain, 89, 106
PTA (Parents and Teachers Association), 155–156
Public School Accountability Act (PSAA), California, 132–133
Pujadas, J. J., 50

Putnam, R. D., 142, 151–152
PVUSD (Pájaro Valley Unified
    School District), California,
    131–146

Quisenbery, N. L., 186

Racism. *See also* Discrimination
    and social bias; Marginalization
    and marginalized people
    immigrant students' attitudes,
        103, 104
    indigenous groups in New
        Zealand, 172–175
    and indigenous groups in New
        Zealand, 166
    Spain, multicultural coexistence
        in schools in, 93–110
Ramos, J. L., 13, 53, 59n4, 199,
    201
Reciprocity, generalized, 151–152
Redacción Lavoz, 1
Redondo, J., 25
Religious issues, 75
Representative democracy and
    parental involvement, 135
Republican model of solidarity,
    French education system,
    62–77, 200
Reuters/Tunez, 1
Reyero, D., 4
Rich, A., 115
Richards, C., 165, 170, 176–177
Richards-Schuster, K., 3, 11, 183
Rispail, M., 64
Ritchie, S. M., 4, 6, 134, 145, 152
Robinson, J. C., 150
Rodgers, J., 136
Rodríguez, J. I., 13, 27–28, 199,
    203, 205, 206
Rodriguez, N., 151

Rojas Rabiela, T., 59n4
Roth, W.-M., 4, 6, 38, 134, 145,
    152

Salt Lake City schools, Utah,
    114–129
Sánchez, J., 99
Santora, E. D., 5
Sartre, J.-P., 9, 204
Schecter, S. R., 117–118
Scheduled Caste (SC) community,
    Indian, 181
Scheduled tribes (ST), Indian, 181
Schneider, B., 38
Schneider, M., 25
School climate. *See Convivencia*
School organization issues and
    immigrant students, 104–105
School Site Council (SSC)
    (California), 133, 155–156,
    204
Schools of agreement, Spanish, 82,
    83t, 84–85
Science activities, Indian tribal
    community involvement, 189,
    191t
Secular education, French concept
    of, 62, 77n2
Segregation. *See also*
    Marginalization and
    marginalized people
    and Chile's educational system,
        23, 24
SEI (Structured English Immersion)
    program, 150
Self-awareness, self-esteem and
    self-confidence, and oral
    history curriculum program,
    124–125
Self-identification, 50, 56, 57
Semali, L. M., 183, 184

Seminario Violencia Esolar: Una Mirada desde la Investigatión y los Actores Educativos, 39, 41n6

Semprini, A., 66

Sense of belonging. *See also* Inclusion-oriented schools and promotion of social inclusion, 34, 37–39

Separation of church and state, 63

Sepúlveda, P., 25

Shannon, S. M., 143

Sheridan, C., 59n4

Singh, P. D., 181

Sistema de Medición de Calidad de la Educación (Chile), 24

Sisto, V., 25, 38

Sleeter, C. E., 1, 16, 115–116, 124, 127, 165, 184, 185, 198

Small-scale societies, solidarity in, 199

Social identity and identification, 45–60
    alter-identification, 50, 57
    definitions, 50
    and devalued solidarity, 45–60
    ethnic identity, 45–60
    ethno-political indigenous identity, 52
    French state, identification with, 62–77
    hetero-identification, 50
    indigenous groups in New Zealand, 176
    negative identities, 50, 56
    with one's own marginalized community, 6
    positive identities, 50, 56–57
    self-identification, 50, 56, 57
    as social representation, 49–51

Social inequality. *See also* Discrimination and social bias compared with cultural differences, 45–46

Social unity, solidarity as, 7–9, 13, 21–90

Socio-economic advancement opportunities, education as providing, 66–67, 69

Solidarity, 3, 56–58, 63, 81, 118–119, 179–180, 183, 198, 199, 206–207

Soriano, E., 1, 14, 96, 99, 108, 110, 203, 205

Spain
    Basic Laws on Education, 202–203
    centers of Spanish education abroad, 82–85, 83t
    emigration, 47, 79–90, 94
    immigration and immigrant students, 93–110
    intercultural education of students abroad, 79–90
    joint-ownership schools, 82, 83t, 84
    Ministerio de Educación de España, 82–84, 86, 87, 98
    multicultural coexistence in schools in, 93–110
    ownership schools, 82, 83–84, 83t
    private schools, 82, 83t, 84
    schools of agreement, 82, 83t, 84–85

Spanish Baccalaureate diploma, 87

Spanish Ministry of Education, 82–84, 86, 87, 98

Spillett, M. D., 150

Spirituality and *Te Kauhua*
    professional development
    program, 169–170
Sports, Indian tribal community
    involvement, 186, 189, 191t
Srinivas, M. N., 180
Srujan Program, 180–196
    beginnings and implementation,
        187–190
    impact of, 190–193, 194–195t
    learning outcomes, 191t
SSC (School Site Council),
    California, 133, 155–156, 204
St. Pierre, R. G., 153
Standardized testing, 126
    California Standards Test, 137
Staniszewski, D., 39
Stanton-Salazar, R. D., 142, 145
Stereotypes
    indigenous groups in New
        Zealand, 175
    perceptions and preconceived
        notions by teachers, 152, 192
Storytelling and oral traditions
    immigrant students, oral histories
        curriculum, 114–129
    Indian tribal community, 185,
        188, 189, 191t, 192
Stovall, D., 4, 204
Structured English Immersion (SEI)
    program, 150
Struggle. *See* Allies in contexts of
    struggle, solidarity as building
Student behavior
    and immigrant students'
        attitudes, 104
    and school climate in Chile,
        23–41
Student involvement, New Zealand
    reform work, 171–172

Subsede de la Universidad
    Pedagógica Nacional
    (UPN), 54
Supreme Council of European
    Schools, 88

Tan, J. E. C., 6
Tangata whenua, 165
Tapia, M. N., 6, 109
Taradutt, P., 181
Te Kauhua professional
    development program, 166–
    167
Teacher-home relationships, 118–
    121
Technical skills, oral history
    curriculum program, 122
Tejeda, C., 177
Tension, social. *See* Allies in
    contexts of struggle, solidarity
    as building; Marginalization
    and marginalized people
Thörn, H., 12
Tiakiwai, S., 165, 170, 176–177
Tobin, K., 4, 6, 134, 145, 152
Torche, F., 25
Toro, A., 23, 24
Torres, C. A., 96
Torres, M., 128
Touriñan, J. M., 98
Tranquilio, R., 59n4
Transcommunality, 207
Tribal community and school in
    India, solidarity between,
    180–196
Trillas, J., 109
Trueba, H., 108
Trust and social inclusion, 35
Turrent, J., 50
Tuuta, M., 167

UNESCO charter, right to teach
    native languages under, 69
UNICEF, 5
Unifying spaces, perceptions of,
    168–175, 176, 177
Universidad Autónoma
    Metropolitana, 50
Untouchables, Indian, 181
UPN (Subsede de la Universidad
    Pedagógica Nacional), 54
Urrieta, L., 128
U.S. Department of Education
    Office of Educational Research
    and Improvement, 153
Utah Performance Assessment
    System for Students, 116,
    128n2
Utah schools, oral history
    curriculum program, 114–129

Valdés, G., 152
Valenzuela, J., 25
Vázquez, P., 106
Vermes G., 64
Village project, Indian tribal
    community involvement, 190

Villalpando, O., 117
Villaseñor, M. C., 50
Villenas, S., 120, 121
Voucher system, Chile, 25
Vygotsky, L., 185

Wagner, A., 15, 205
Warren, M. R., 12
Watsonville, California, 131–146
Weis, T. M., 118
Wenger, E., 163, 164
Whole-school approach for
    promotion of social inclusion,
    34
Wilde, L., 3, 7, 9

Yarce, J., 12
Yosso, T. J., 117, 127
Young, I. M., 96

Zarate, G., 76
Zeledón, C., 119, 120, 124
Zibechi, R., 7, 198
Zinovyeva, N., 106
Zubero, I., 8, 199
Zulfiqar, M., 6